MARX: ECONOMIST, PHILOSOPHER, JEW

By the same author

A REAPPRAISAL OF MARXIAN ECONOMICS
KARL MARX
A TEXTBOOK OF ECONOMICS

MARX: ECONOMIST, PHILOSOPHER, JEW

Steps in the Development of a Doctrine

Murray Wolfson

First published 1982 by
THE MACMILLAN PRESS LTD
London and Basingstoke
Companies and representatives
throughout the world

ISBN 0 333 23999 7

Typeset in Great Britain by
REDWOOD BURN LIMITED
Trowbridge, Wiltshire
and printed in Hong Kong

To Marvin

With thanks for times
Of treasured talk
Since we were boys
Together

Contents

Preface

I decided to write this book in Japan. For a year I served as Fulbright lecturer on Marxian economics at various major universities where Marxists were at least well represented on, and frequently dominated, faculties in the social sciences. It was apparent that, in spite of their allegiance to Marxism, many Japanese intellectuals intuited that Marxism had become a fetter upon the progress of social reform. But the devolvement from ideology was far from complete. Despite the half-expressed and grudgingly conceded realization of the deficiencies of Marxism—certainly in the field of economic theory strictly defined—Japanese academics still searched for their guide to politics within the Marxian paradigm. The state of affairs in Japan was the canonical form of attractive "enlightened" intellectuals elsewhere. Like their European counterparts, Japanese academics interpreted and reinterpreted, reread and revised the Marxian doctrine in the light of current complexities, all the time knowing that the basic economic theory and philosophy of history were fundamentally defective.

When pressed to explain the persistence of Marxism in academe, my colleagues would seldom simply reply, as they might, "Marx was right and we simply see that fact". Rather they would cite the vertical hierarchy of the professor–disciple relationship which tends to explain the persistence of ideas and their insulation from external criticism. One prominent Marxian professor traced the pre-eminence to the influence of Germany between the wars. Marxism provided the text for rapid industrial growth, he suggested, despite its ultimate apocalyptic vision of capitalism. Another pointed to the American occupation support to academics who had opposed the militarist forces responsible for plunging Japan into the holocaust. Once entrenched in the university, they suggested, Marxism became one of the Confucian catechisms of the university-based meritocracy of Japanese society. Their suggestions have the ring of truth.

Yet Marxism is not only an innocuous academic discipline, a sieve for segregating the truly worthy from those destined for the polytechnic. Its paradigm of class struggle governs the perception of events in a single rigidly defined mould. The doctrine applied strictly leads to incongruity: I put it to a usually sensible Japanese Marxist colleague. Why in the election we had both just witnessed did not the Marxist parties offer a concrete programme of monetary, fiscal and international policies for the improvement of the conditions of their urban, labour, constituency? Why did they persist in appealing to the ultimate ideology that would only affect those already convinced? His answer was immediate, "We are not going to tell *them*"—one need not guess who "they" were—"how to save capitalism!" The irony was that it was the conservatives who read the message of labour unrest correctly. They put a programme of fiscal expansion into effect on a modest scale, and retained power despite their political vulnerability on issues of corruption as well as economic policy.

Marxism is shaken by a profound crisis. The old doctrine is seen to oscillate, owing to its very rigidity of forecast. The absence of the breakdown of capitalism beyond repair gives rise to the atrophy of revolutionary movements among the industrial proletariat. The revolutionary climax of history is put off to the indefinite future. In good conscience Japanese Marxists can join in lifetime careers in Mitsubishi advancing the "forces of production". If the pace of revolution is forced, as in the Soviet Union, the pace of revolution anticipates the collapse of the industrial states which Marx foretold; then the consequences are empty ideology, intellectual ossification and political repression.

A demand for a new revision of Marx has arisen, initially from the young, the radicals, in both the communist and capitalist nations. The new radicalism speaks in terms of "Man" as a socially cohesive creature, bound to his fellows by intrinsic ties of love and common interest. The point is to restructure society in such a way as to unleash the inherent potential of the species. The thrust of this movement is intrinsically different from the traditional reading of Marx, even though it relates to his ultimate communist society which takes from each according to his abilities and gives to each according to his needs, class conflict vanishes along with classes themselves, and the state "withers away". The operational issue is one of timing. Is it possible to create a "truly human" classless society by a purposive, conscious political act of revolution which would abolish private property? Or, does the elimination of classes depend on evolutionary development of the "forces of production" beyond conscious human control? In the long interim before communism, must love defer to class hate, and the concept of the universal essence of Man be replaced by the antithetical interests of the proletarian class and its enemy? The new generation of Marxists perceives that the "iron necessity" with which Marx held class society is to evolve, leaves precious little room for human values or individual dissent. Their demand for a more humane society has led to a reconsideration of Marx in the hopes of finding a key to effective social change without repression.

Is it possible to find in Marx's early and unpublished material a programmatic means to this end? Perhaps Marx was always really the humanist author of unpublished *Economic and Philosophic Manuscripts of 1844*? May the rest of his writing through *Capital* be reinterpreted to suit the needs of the "new left"? The truth about what Marx actually said, and the truth contained in what he said are not nearly the same. Yet the issues are intertwined. This is so not only because of the emotive force of his name, but also because Marx himself largely answered the second question in the history of his intellectual development. If we follow the evolution of his doctrine, we can see that he did change his mind, first accepting humanism, and then abandoning it. Moreover we can see why he changed his mind. Indeed, much of his polemic is devoted to refutations of his own previously held views still expounded by erstwhile associates. The new Marxism must face the discouraging fact that he passed their way once before, and tarried only a short while.

I shall argue that the basic lines of argument which Marx advanced between 1843 and 1845 actually constitute three disjoint, but internally coherent, philosophical and social systems of thought. These positions are differentiated by the solution advanced to the mind–body problem: How do human beings understand and influence the world about them? In each case the philosophical theory of knowledge and being determined Marx's method. Since these philosophical systems are mutually antithetical, it is not surprising that Marx should have put forward three mutually antagonistic systems of social thought.

Marx, I shall contend, at first advanced an empiricist philosophical position which culminated in an individualist democratic critique of Hegel in the *Critique of Hegel's "Philosophy of Right"* (1843). Less than a year later in the *Economic and Philosophic Manuscripts of 1844* he described a human essence, Man, who, as a "species being", coexisted uneasily with Nature. Despite the dualism, Marx's intent was clearly to make Man primary; the natural world as well as the social milieu is essentially "for Man" and his purposes. In the final stage, signalled by the *Theses on Feuerbach* (1845), Marx reversed the order of primacy, and attempted to explain man as a creature defined by impersonally determined material forces including his own labour. Man's conscious purposes were determined by the development of the labour process embodied in the degree of advance of the "forces of production".

To be sure, it is a commonplace of current philosophy that normative judgments, such as those Marx made about the social order, do not logically follow from any theory of knowledge. Nevertheless, the atomistic description of an individual's sense experience central to empiricism such as is found in Marx's first stage predisposes the social theorist towards individualism in economics and democracy in politics. The subsidiary propositions Marx advanced to make the leap were neither those of the utilitarian Mill nor the moral imperatives of Kant. As we shall see the connection was made by an argument for legitimacy.

The emphasis in the second stage is on Man as a collective entity. It is not surprising that we find Marx of the *Manuscripts* inveighing against the hedonistic individualism of the market, money and exchange. Market institutions included in what Hegel called civil society serve to perpetuate the alienation of individual persons from their true collective species essence. Labour which ought rationally to make the world "for Man" as collective humanity is frustrated by the individualist institution of private property.

In the final stage Marx the materialist seeks to make a positive deterministic statement about how social change comes about. He identifies the social unit as class rather than either individual men or the species, Man. He contends that the class owning the means of production extorts uncompensated labour from the non-owning class. The historically relevant issue is exploitation at the point of production rather than alienation through the market. It is not Man who must rule but the proletariat. Philosophical criticism of the irrationality of property is useless; the practical need is revolution to seize the means of production at the appropriate stage in its evolution.

The dimensions of these positions are summarized in the table below. The point of the table, and the exegesis of it in the remainder of this book, is more than taxonomy. It is a recapitulation of the reasons which drove Marx to abandon his earlier views. The method of identifying philosophical foundations is probably truest to Marx in spirit. More than most, he was aware that the foundations of his science lay in his philosophical preconceptions.

The historical Karl Marx advanced through these viewpoints in a series of intermediate steps. These reflected his personal and intellectual development against the background events of Western Europe in the first half of the last century. Not the least of these influences relates to Marx's Jewish heritage. In the process of liberation from the ghetto on the heels of the Napoleonic conquest, German Jewry went through a process of rejection of Jewishness, amendment and redefinition. Marx's father, Heinrich (originally Herschel), abandoned Judaism. At least at the conscious level, his son turned bitterly against it. Nevertheless, I shall contend that this alienated, brilliant youth constantly had to confront his Jewish heritage. The three stages of theory discussed earlier have a religious analogue. They correspond to the eighteenth-century enlightened scepticism which was the conscious religious standpoint of his father; the projection of essentially a Christian humanist view of universal love in opposition to Judaism; and, finally a return to Jewish monistic preconceptions in the mature work, which reflected the deeper Jewish ideological heritage which his father had passed on despite himself.

How far ought one push the observation of the religious parallels in Marx's writing? At the least they are signposts that permit us to see that Marx's intellectual evolution is not a seamless development, but proceeds by discrete jumps. If one can distinguish between the world outlook of an eighteenth-century sceptic, a universalist Christian, and an Old Testament Jew, then one can see the differences in the three philosophic and social positions—individualism, humanism, and historical materialism—despite the complex of overlap and cross-influences.

Inevitably, any serious social revolutionary in the early part of the last century had to consider these three alternatives in social theory. They were simply there. In like fashion, every Jew, or person of Jewish descent, had to consider the alternatives of reformation of Judaism, a turning against it, or simply retention of Jewish tradition and doctrine. These were also simply the logical possibilities. Once we are sensitive to these choices, we can see Marx's mind at work dealing with them.

As in any intellectual history, a conclusive case cannot be made for a direct causal relation between his stand *vis à vis* Judaism, and the preconceptions Marx brought to his science of society. Yet I am impelled to step beyond the signpost purpose of the religious analogue; it is hard to imagine that Marx did not absorb the unspoken and therefore incontestable preconceptions of his parents only a few years away from formal Jewish identification. Only if he were immune to his social conditioning could he have avoided the unconscious retention of the Jewish heritage along with the conscious rejection of it. We cannot crawl inside his soul, and so we observe the signposts and ponder on the persistence of culture in the face of persecution and shame.

The story of Marx's family and its turning away from Judaism to enter the half-opened door of Emancipation in Germany was repeated a century later in the American Jewish experience. Waves of Ashkenazic immigrants left the Polish ghetto for the relative freedom of the New World. Their children fought the same anguished struggles with orthodox parents as did Heinrich and Henrietta Marx.

Under both circumstances, the first generation after emancipation greeted freedom with a frenzied—even pathetic—desire to identify with the dominant culture. The past was to be blotted out as a collage of absurd folkways, superstitions, accents and attitudes that disgraced their elders. This tendency is only partially to be characterized as opportunism. Anglicizing a name, encouraging a child to pursue a career prestigious in the new milieu, and reinterpreting Judaism so as to make it virtually indistinguishable from Christianity, were all testimony to appearance of the dominant culture as the embodiment of enlightenment, reason and freedom. Where centuries of ferocious persecution had failed to dislodge identification with Judaism, emancipation initiated a powerful trend toward assimilation.

Schematization of stages in Marx's development

	Up to 1843: Marx the Individualist.	1844: Marx the Humanist.	1845 and thereafter: Marx the Materialist.
Date	Up to 1843: Marx the Individualist.	1844: Marx the Humanist.	1845 and thereafter: Marx the Materialist.
Main texts	*Critique of Hegel's "Philosophy of Right"*.	*Economic and Philosophic Manuscripts of 1844 (Paris Manuscripts); On the Jewish Question; Preface to Critique of Hegel's "Philosophy of Right"*.	*Theses on Feuerbach; German Ideology; Communist Manifesto; Grundrisse; Critique of Political Economy; Capital*
Social programme	Political transformation: Democracy. Rule by the people.	Economic transformation: Communism I. Abolition of private property, money, market mechanism, overcoming alienation of man from his essence.	Economic transformation: Communism II. Social ownership of means of production; elimination of exploitation; unleashing of the 'forces of production' until 'from each according to his abilities to each according to his work' and then 'according to his needs'.
Epistemology	Reason from concrete particular reality to general universals; induction; empiricism in a tentative way.	Reality is "for Man"; Reality is also Nature. Humanism as opposed to both materialism and idealism.	Materialism: Matter is the ultimate universal undergoing dialectical evolution. "Things in themselves" are knowable through "practice", "labour". Previous philosophers have only interpreted the world. The point is to change it.

Transformative criticism of Hegel	H: State is universal category, hence real embodiment of Idea. Active Idea (subject) determines particulars: civil society, family, individuals. (Social welfare does not consist of individual utilities, but rather the whole state.) KM: Active subject is particulars (individual men) whose collective instrument is the state (object); essence of state is democracy, collective rule by individuals.	H: Idea is the ultimate universal expressing itself in particular ways, e.g. God. KM: Man as a species-being is the Universal; Man is God. Man is in essence good.	H: Idea imposes its ultimate will on what appears as human or material reality. KM: Ideas are the reflections of material reality in the brain of men; the material (including social) world has a dialectic of its own.
Social interpretation	Rule by the people is essence of the state; irrational forms, like monarchy, bureaucracy, deny the essential nature of political state.	Labour is the human essence which is alienated from Man by work and cannot return "man to himself" because of irrational, unphilosophical private property; Man cannot realize his inherent God-like characteristics.	Man is an active, material, social animal. His activity is called labour and consists in conflict with nature; man labours in social form of production and hence stages of labour process are stages of society; human nature does not exist, but man remakes himself through social relations of production and the superstructure of ideology (culture) built upon it.
Role of workers	Part of civil society.	The universal class which has no property and therefore is able to overcome the alienation of Man through communism.	Workers driven to revolution by the "iron hand" of history working with inevitable force through development of forces of production.

Reason for Marx's change of heart	Marx sought the "universal aspect of particulars" but could not accept the uncertainty of inductive argument. Deduction not possible through examination of particulars; induction ends in Locke and Mill.	1. Two-universal problem; relation of Man and Nature. Man's essence given and undetermined. No explanation for change in human ideas, ideologies, etc. 2. Practical social change not brought about by intellectual criticism. Need for science of society.	—
Practice	—	The human attitude is theoretical criticism of religion and property. Practice is "dirty Jewish".	Practice as production: Knowing is doing.
Civil society	Individualism of men justifies humanistic "rights of Man" including alienable property.	Civil society and private property imply alienation of atomistic man through the market mechanism.	The individualism of the market and legal equality in capitalist democracy conceals the class structure of society.
Religious analogue	Scepticism.	Christianity.	Judaism.

Insofar as the movement was more than an attempt to eliminate superficial forms, anachronistic in modern times, it was bound to fail. The basic features of Jewish culture are much too deep-seated. But the tension which resulted caused the generation which followed to be characterized by widespread hostility to parents intertwined with alienation from the society with which it needed to identify. This cohort remained outside the mainstream owing to the very persistence of their own culture and the continued presence of anti-semitism. Hatred and persecution of Jews was epitomized in recent times by the Holocaust, and in Marx's experience by the rise of romantic pseudo-scientific theories of the German *Volk*.

Having accepted the premises of assimilation as a result of their upbringing, the second generation remained for a long time defenceless as Jews. Under the circumstances, it is not surprising that many Jewish young people turned instead to more universal rebellious doctrines. Marxism became one of the attracting forces to them for the same reason it arose in the mind of Marx himself. It purported to advance a programme of struggle that cut across national and religious lines as an internationalist movement. At the same time its class nature served to express the separation of these Jewish youths from the dominant circles and culture. As in the case of Marx himself, the psychological need was to vent the alienation of spirit in terms of a purportedly materialist and scientific doctrine.

These two elements are not identical. Psychologically, as a social phenomenon, Marxism surely reflected the alienation of its author and adherents from the mainstream of society; but the logical content of Marxism in maturity is a philosophical doctrine in which states of mind are purported to be derivative of material, practical circumstances and activities. These logical roots of Marxism as an attempted science are to be found in Judaism's monistic historical paradigm, which is, of course, quite distinct both from the social position of Jews in nineteenth-century Germany, and from the psychology of alienation in America many years later.

Not surprisingly, the Judaic preconceptions reappeared in the second generation after emancipation even though it did so in forms that seemed to the participants to be divorced from, and even hostile to, any sort of religious expression. In fact, as we shall see, if Marxism failed as a science, it was because its historical form was too close to the Old Testament original. Religion, Marx tells us, is a cry of pain of suffering humanity. Marxism may have failed as a science, but it has served as an outcry of the oppressed.

In coming to these conclusions I have incurred intellectual debts beyond enumeration. The theme of this book was first expressed at Waseda University (Tokyo) in the seminar of Professor Tadao Horie, as well as in a series of public lectures. I am grateful to him for advice and comment. I also wish to thank colleagues in Japan who were both encouraging and critical: Professor Hiroyasu Iida (Keio University), Makoto Itoh (Tokyo University), Shumpei Kumon (Tokyo University) and Shigeru Tanese (Hitotsubashi University). Anyone who knows the diverse views of these scholars will realize that since they disagree so completely with each other, they are not likely to agree with me either. Certainly they are not responsible for my views or errors. The United States Educational Commission in Japan (Fulbright) and its director, Mrs Caroline A. Yang, have my thanks for bringing us together. I was fortunate, also, to discuss these matters with Professor Scott Littleton of the Department of Anthropology of Occidental College in California who was in Japan at the same time.

I have been materially helped by colleagues elsewhere. Professor Kurt W. Philipp of the Department of History at Oregon State University collaborated with me in a paper, "Marx as a Jew", read to the Atlantic Economic Society. He has kindly granted me permission to include some of that material in the present work. Professor David B. King of the same department has provided information and sources on German history in more recent times.

Over the course of time I have had the help of many close friends and colleagues. In particular I should like to thank Professors Martin Bronfenbrenner (Duke University), John E. Elliott (University of Southern California), Shalom Groll (Haifa University), Ze'ev B. Orzech (Oregon State University) and Roy Rotheim (Franklin and Marshall College). This work could not have been completed without support at various stages from the American Council of Learned Societies, the Oregon State University Foundation and Graduate Research Council, as well as its College of Liberal Arts.

I should like to acknowledge the kind permission of the *History of Political Economy* and *Waseda Economic Papers* for permission to include material originally mooted in articles of mine they published.

Thanks are due, also, to Mrs Katheryn Fifarek who typed a most difficult manuscript with care and patience. Finally, I wish to thank my wife, Betty A. Wolfson, for advice and encouragement.

Corvallis, Oregon, USA   *Murray Wolfson*
1 November, 1979

The author and publishers wish to thank the following who have kindly given permission for the use of copyright material:

International Publishers Co. Inc. for extracts from *Ludwig Feuerbach and the Outcome of Classical German Philosophy* by Engels, and *Collected Works* by Karl Marx–Frederick Engels; Professor Kurt Philipp for an extract from the article 'Marx as a Jew'; Routledge & Kegan Paul Ltd for extracts from *The Philosophy of Ludwig Feuerbach* by Dr Eugene Kamenka; and Vanguard Press, Inc. for extracts from *The History of Anti-Semitism: From Voltaire to Wagner*, vol. III, by Leon Poliakov, copyright © 1977 Leon Poliakov – originally translated from the French, copyright © 1968 Calmann-Lévy.

1 Jewish Origins

What is a Jew? Can one say that Marx was Jewish, in the light of his denunciation of religion in general, and Judaism in particular? Neither of these questions can be answered without controversy. For some, Judaism consists in religious observance. According to traditional Jewish law, the *Halacha*, it is a matter of descent, traced through the maternal parent. The Nazi racial definition is, of course, only too well known. There are others. Judaism, for our purposes, is an ethnic, cultural and ideological heritage, deriving from historical and religious antecedents.

The vectors of Jewish culture are patently present in the background of our subject. There is certainly ample ground for the biographer's comment that Marx's family was "thoroughly Jewish in their origins".[1] The very name Marx is a "shortened form of Mordechai".[2] His father, Heinrich Marx, was born in 1782, the eldest son of Meier Halevi Marx who had become rabbi of Trier on the death of his father-in-law and was followed in this office by his eldest son Samuel (Karl's uncle) who died in 1827. In fact almost all the rabbis in Trier from the sixteenth century onwards were ancestors of Marx. Marx's genealogical table shows distinguished members of the rabbinate, at least as far back as the fifteenth century in Poland, Italy, Bohemia and Alsace, as well as in Karl Marx's birthplace, Trier. Karl's mother, Henrietta, was the daughter of Isaac Pressburg, rabbi of Nymegen. "She seems to have been no less steeped in the rabbinic tradition than her husband."[3] Eleanor Marx avowed that she herself was Jewish, and that in her grandmother's family "the sons had for centuries been rabbis".[4]

To suggest the relevance of the Jewish cultural heritage is much easier than enumerating the dimensions of an ancient and complex tradition. Nevertheless the features of the Jewish preconception may be briefly stated, brushing over the inconsistencies and blurred edges that are the result of millennia of history. We should see that Judaism is not Christianity; the term "Judaeo-Christian" misleads more than it reveals by its frequent abuse as a means of dissolving Judaism into the dominant Christian culture.

A core concept of the Judaic tradition is the primacy of moral issues on one hand and the belief that they can be rationally resolved on the other. Atavistically, the ethical preconception is stated in terms of the compact between Israel and God. Divine guidance and support was contingent on the collective fulfilment of the moral code made known through the infallible *Torah*.[5] Jewish literature, profane as well as sacred, reveals the continuity of preoccupation with moral questions couched in objective terms, be they legal as in the *Torah* and *Talmud*, or simply traditional. What is the law? What does it mean? How can it remain a constant and yet be applied under radically disparate circumstances? How is the ethical eternal to be resolved with the transient, pragmatic present? How can the suffering of Israel be reconciled with a good, omnipotent God?

A second leading strand in Judaism is the tension between exclusiveness and universality. In its naive form, the compact was between the Jews and God, rather than between Him and all of humanity. In biblical myth, the Hebrews were the "chosen people" who agreed to Jehovah's law in return for the power of his outstretched arm. Later sophistication softened this doctrine. The concept of a chosen people was to be interpreted as a moral injunction to the Jews to set an example for all mankind. But the original meaning never disappeared; persecution reinforced scripture as the basis for the cohesiveness of the Jewish community.

In the ultimate, Jews like Christians profess a universalist theme. God in his own time would send his Messiah. Then the world would beat its swords into ploughshares. Jews would turn from the struggle of the chosen people against the Philistines to love of all humanity. But for Jews the Messiah has not yet come as Christ. In the meantime, the practical needs are struggle for identity and survival, the reinforcement of the ethnic group by bonds ranging from common moral commitment to practical mutual support.

A third element in the Jewish tradition is the intransigent insistence on monotheism. There is *one* God. This is the first of the

Ten Commandments. The climax of the synagogue service affirms: *Sh'ma Israel! Adonai Elohenu, Adonai Echod!* "Hear, O Israel! The Lord our God, the Lord is One!" The notion of rationalist universality, the fitting together all aspects of experience into a coherent pattern, has more than religious expression. It is deeply ingrained in all aspects of Jewish life. The greatest of Jewish minds—Spinoza, Freud, Marx, Einstein—have tended to be the synthetic unifiers of diverse elements. For them the unifying principle was not religion, but science. Nevertheless, the intellectual demand they made of rational explanation is the same.

Finally, the Judaic ethic is expressed in terms of the immanent presence of God in the earthly affairs of man. His omnipotence imbues material reality with normative content. Both God's law expressed in *Torah*, and the objective circumstances in which men must strive to obey it are divinely ordained. The notion which Judaism expresses in religious form is that there is an objective ethic in the same sense that there exists an objective physical reality; the unity between positive and normative propositions is warranted since both are ordained by the divine presence. It is neither necessary nor possible to "justify the ways of God to man", to rationalize suffering and evil as perhaps a means of purging one's soul from original sin. On the contrary, it is man who must justify himself to God by righteous behaviour. The voice that spoke to Job out of the whirlwind needed no apology for the pain He induced. The injunction to obedience to the commandments of righteous behaviour was simple, absolute and unconditional. If in due course Job was rewarded for his piety, it was only because God saw fit to do so. The pain and reprieve from it both occurred on earth, in this life, not in heaven after death.[6]

The Jewish revulsion against idolatry—to the extreme of traditionally forbidding artistic works representing living creatures—stems at least as much from belief in the omnipotence of God as from His uniqueness. What galled the Hebrews was not only that the pagan religions worshipped idols as other gods, but that they made those idols with human hands. The blasphemy of idolatry was the pretension that a human product, the result of human will, could compromise the power of God and His law.

In contrast to Judaism, Christianity asserts that the Messiah has come. Jesus has made it possible to overcome original sin by

universal love. He permitted the redemption of the soul and its
salvation after death. The teaching of Jesus is that love of one's
enemy, turning the other cheek, is the prime human virtue. The
Mosaic tradition calls for righteousness, struggle and the duty of
the chosen people. The Christian ethic stressed the sacred, other-
worldly, spiritual consequences of human behaviour; while for
Judaism it has tended to be the secular, the present, this-worldly
arena in which moral conduct and its consequences progress to
their ultimate outcome.

When we first find records of the Marx family, Jews were the
outcasts of European society. Aliens in a Christian continent,
Jews were frequently confined to ghettos, and subsisted in the
occupations deemed unworthy of Christians: commerce, trade,
petty manufacture, moneylending. Ownership of land, that hon-
orific asset of feudal times, was forbidden to them. Yet even
during the darkest of the Middle Ages, the need for effective
markets in commodities and money was not absent. The market
functioned, as Marx said, "in the pores" of the manorial system.
Jews were rejected, yet accepted. Jews were indispensable, yet
inimical to a system which produced only peripherally for
exchange. Jews were hated, feared, despised, murdered and
needed.

Jews had been periodically subjected to the most ferocious persecution that Inquisition or pogrom could provide. Yet they stubbornly refused to disappear. The more they were persecuted, the
more they differed from their pursuers. The more the uncertainty
and the greater the likelihood that they would have to flee, the
more important to hold wealth in liquid-money form. In Marx's
own family history, on his father's side, the migration from
Padua of the father of Rabbi Abraham Ha-levi Minz, according
to Eleanor Marx, was due to the persecutions in Germany in the
fifteenth century. His mother's family of Hungarian Jews had
been driven to Holland by the same forces.

The tradition from which Karl Marx came combined a relatively sophisticated, legal, ethical, monotheistic world outlook,
with the involuted narrowness, insularity and parochialness of
life in the ghetto. Ghetto culture, an artifact of the Jewish
struggle for survival, became narrower and narrower as persecution and isolation compounded the narrowness of the era. The
original Talmudic commentaries were codified through the centuries into more and more strict, rigid, and irrational laws. The

process finally culminated in what is called the *Shulchan Aruch*, a "prepared table" of law which was very narrowly prescribed, utterly rigid, and completely alien to the new breath of the Enlightenment that at last swept Europe and broke the spiritual shackles of the dark ages.

This very Enlightenment and the ultimate emancipation which it produced in Europe, cast new light for Jews on their religion and social position. It also brought forth a new form of anti-semitism in "enlightened" racial and economic form. All of this is profoundly recorded in Léon Poliakov's *The History of Anti-Semitism*.[7] If we consider these circumstances, we shall understand why people like Marx's father converted from the Jewish, Herschel, to the Christian, Heinrich Marx.[8] Until the middle of the eighteenth century, the apostasy would have been unthinkable, despite the persecution.

Before then, the Jews of feudal Europe were despised by their non-liquid partners in trade, ranging from the wealthy aristocracy to the impoverished peasant. It was an age in which the "corrosive effect of the market", to use Marx's term, became increasingly important; at the same time, market and credit jobbing became even more denigrated by those who could not manage their liquidity needs in a world of estates, primogeniture and entail. This is not to say that the explanation for Jew-hatred was purely economic. One must remember that the Jews were not absolved of the charge of deicide by the Catholic Church until our century. There was a psychological basis for the hatred in the xenophobic medieval mind. Racial myths arose about their nature, although "scientific" racism came later. Even in an age of unwashed personal aroma, Jews were purported to emit a specific odour.

The Jew, Poliakov explains, was always taken to be on the "run". The "wandering Jew" bore Ahasuerus's curse for rebuking Christ. In daily life the Jew eked out a living by ingratiating himself with his Christian customers. He lived in a sweat of servile nerves, fear, and endless hurry to complete his transactions before the Christian either refused in pique or used the violence latent in their relationship. The contradictory mentality of the Christian world toward the Jews engendered an equally contradictory view of the Jews of themselves. They were what Poliakov calls a "debased" chosen people. His description of Jewish masochism anticipates what we shall have to say about the *jüdischer Selbsthass* of Heinrich and Karl Marx:

> Jewish masochism, with its numerous psychological exten-
> sions of all types, probably including a remarkable cultural
> creativity, was primarily to affect later generations of "emanci-
> pated" Jews. In the warm intimacy of the ghetto, it remained
> tempered by the mistrust in which the Christian world was
> held, by rejections of its values and indifference to its judge-
> ments. While they remained a globally oppressed community,
> and because they did so, the Jews faced their environment col-
> lectively and not individually. They looked at themselves in
> their own mirror and in the distorting mirror their detractors
> held up. Their faith in their moral superiority, culminating in
> the idea of the Chosen People, compensated for the feeling of
> insecurity that their physical weakness and vulnerability
> created. Let us repeat: a psychologically split *condition*, that is
> to say, the paradox of the debased Chosen People, was inter-
> mingled with and balanced by a tradition whereby the Chris-
> tians, significantly, were feared as wild animals much more
> than hated as men. This way, it is easier to understand how the
> Jews could endure the outrages, restrain their resentment and
> abstain fairly rigidly from any act of violence against their
> adversaries.[9]

In Germany, and to a lesser extent in other parts of Europe,
there began to develop a thin stratum of Jews who were successful in improving their social as well as economic status.[10] This development harks back to the institution of "court Jews".[11] In the
proliferation of principalities that persisted in Germany well into
the last century, the court Jew carried on the commercial,
financial and fiscal activities of the nobility he served. Thus the
despised–Chosen People were able to rise to positions of power
and wealth, by carrying on the functions which Christians could
not or would not touch. Poliakov tells how the nobility employed
the Jews' aptitude

> for covering with their Jewish label all types of unscrupulous
> transactions which went against the code of honour ... Once
> he had arrived, the court Jew escaped from the main disabil-
> ities of his class. He could choose his residence outside the
> ghetto, and carry weapons. The designation "Jew" was

replaced by "Mister" in official correspondence ... the great German nobles often honoured with their presence Jewish funerals, circumcisions, and especially weddings, sometimes celebrated in the residence of the local ruler.[12]

These Jews, of what must have been the old world to Heinrich Marx, were in a position of dependence on the power of the *ancien régime*. Jews were never in competition with the Christian bourgeoisie in the sense that Karl Marx made famous: employers of wage labour in the production process. Even their caricature remained in the image of the Rothschilds; when in positions of power they served as financial and commercial intermediaries, and later as exponents of the learned professions. Rich or poor, the Jew performed his function by standing outside—between—the established centres of power. The very existence of Jews was in opposition both to the traditional guild notions of trade on the one hand, and to the industrial bourgeois demand for both credit and political power on the other. The favours received by the court Jews seemed to isolate Jews generally from the rest of society. If it is true, as Poliakov further suggests, that "It really seems as if attentions or compliments of this sort [to the court Jews] irritated the Christian bourgeoisie more than the sight of the financial success of the Children of Israel",[13] then what can Herschel Marx, this Jewish man of the Enlightenment, have thought of them?

Clearly his feelings were mixed, just as the Enlightenment in Germany involved diverse strands. The regeneration of Germany after 1814 involved the restoration of the aristocracy in bourgeoisified form. Moreover, the earlier *Aufklärung* had taken place within aristocratic intellectual circles as well as against it. Post-Napoleonic enlightenment presupposed a Prussian nationalism including adulation of the monarch. Heinrich accepted all the trappings of Prussian nationalism at the same time as he "knew Voltaire by heart". While he considered himself as a Jew until 1817, he clearly was too bourgeoisified to identify with the majority of poverty-stricken, downtrodden Jews eking out a living in petty trade; nor could he countenance the court Jews of the bygone era who were part and parcel of the regime which enlightened Europe was striving to reject. For all his intellectual adherence to the *avant-garde* within the secure circle of his family and friends, Heinrich Marx was not beyond fawning on the great. His letters to Karl Marx in Berlin are full of urging to become friendly with this or that important person, to ingratiate himself with those in power, even at the same time as he reflected the ideals of the Enlightenment.

Much earlier, in 1815, Heinrich Marx wrote as a Jew, in an enlightened Prussia. That country had survived Napoleon and was struggling to incorporate the lessons of the French Revolution in a regenerated, bourgeois state, which was nonetheless constricted by fear of a repetition of the trauma the French had inflicted upon them. The older Marx petitioned against continuation of the discriminatory Napoleonic decrees against Jewish creditors in the Westphalian provinces turned over to Prussia by the Congress of Vienna. Yet even as he was pointing in lawyer-like fashion, to the irrationality of laws that restrict individuals by group rather than by individual criminal act, he was prepared to concede that members of his faith might require measures to make them worthy of becoming citizens of Prussia.[14] Perhaps it is not too surprising that he should have converted to Christianity one year after this piece whose main thrust was a clear, closely argued plea for equal treatment of Jews in enlightened Prussia. It is not hard to imagine that Karl was unaware of the contradiction in his father's life. Nor is it difficult to see why he once identified "servility" as the most despicable character trait, even though he carried a photograph of his father with him all his life.

The model for Heinrich Marx's response to the Enlightenment had been set by Moses Mendelssohn (1729–86). Popularized by Lessing's *Nathan der Weise*, Mendelssohn embodied in himself the counter-example to the anti-semitic view of the Jews. This hunched-back man was taken into German intellectual circles by Lessing who saw the nature of the self-fulfilling prophecy which forced Jews into the despised role of moneylender and sharp trader. Mendelssohn was a philosopher of aesthetics, whose elegant and popular style attracted a broad and admiring following. He was regarded as generous and kind by his contemporaries. The beauty of his perceived character stood out in contrast to his physical appearance, as if symbolizing the contradiction between the popular perception of the Jew and this outstanding person.

Despite Kant's refutation, Mendelssohn clung to his belief in the existence of God, accepting the ontological proof as well as

the argument from design. Mendelssohn was himself a spokesman for the new ideas, but attempted to redefine religion in a way
that would be consistent with the new ideas. This effort was the
common concern he held, of Christians and Jews. The core of
Judaism was reason, according to Mendelssohn. When challenged by the Swiss theologian, Lavater, to either refute Christianity or convert Mendelssohn declined to establish a strict
dichotomy between the two faiths, although obviously retaining
his own beliefs. In his reply, *Jerusalem oder über religiöse Macht und
Judentum*, Mendelssohn held that Judaism was, at its essence, a
belief in Law. It was the binding belief in moral principles embodied in Jewish ordinances for those who were born to it as
Jews, or those who bound themselves through moral acceptance.
Jews, Mendelssohn argued, were to interpret the notion of being
a chosen people in the moral imperative sense of a nation of
priests, rather than as a licence for exclusiveness.

Mendelssohn had argued for religious tolerance, separation of
church and state, and civil equality of Jews, and against religious
parochialism. The Enlightenment was taking place within the
ghetto walls as well as without. It cut two ways. Not only were
the Jews to be freed—as they ultimately were—from the state-
prescribed Christian religion, but they were to be freed from their
own rabbinical theocracy in civil life. In fact, Jews were entering
into the mainstream of German life. Mendelssohn's position epitomized the contradictions that the entry would pose with even
greater force after the Emancipation which followed on the
Napoleonic conquest and the Prussian Emancipation edict of
1812. In what sense were Jews still Jews, if their religion was to be
interpreted as the universalist deism of reason. How could they
be Jews when they were no longer confined to the ghetto, when
they were no longer a *Judenstaat* within the German complex of
states?

In Mendelssohn's own time effective emancipation applied to
a thin stratum of German *literati* such as might frequent the Berlin
Jewish salons where wealthy Jews played host to the intellectual
"beautiful people" of the time. Poliakov explains how "high of-
ficials and members of the Prussian nobility crowded their
receptions. The government granted them a 'general lien' which
carried with it the grant of all the rights that Christian merchants
enjoyed". He then goes on to analyse the new forces that were to
be so critical for the Marx family, as they were for others:

Thus a situation which had existed throughout history was legally recognized: a despised class makes up for its inferiority by the power of money... Association with the great led the Jews concerned to increase their violations of the Mosaic law, and some of them broke away from it completely. But even then, unless they converted, they remained Jews socially since there was no "enfranchised" society in which they could integrate. The great new fact of the Century of Enlightenment was that henceforth some Christians also not only deserted but openly challenged their religion. A social stratum, at first only a thin skin, was thus created into which Jews who had broken with Judaism could assimilate without becoming Christian, without brutally abjuring the faith of their ancestors, without acknowledging the credo and the God in whose name they were humiliated and persecuted. Moreover, their money or their talents, which they did not fail to display, enabled them to play a leading role in this society...

Now the Jews who were initiated into Western culture and who were associating with enlightened circles in Berlin hastened to adopt their ideas and opinions. They therefore tended to assess Judaism through the spectacles of the *Aufklärung*: an alienation if there ever was one, they viewed themselves through the eyes of others. They also took a violent stand against the orthodox, that is to say against the mass of Jews, whom they wanted to reform and initiate into the Enlightenment.

Traditional Jews responded with equal fervour. Poliakov continues:

To adherents of the ancestral faith, the enlightened Jews were renegades, and rabbis showered them with invective and excommunication. The Jewish *Aufklärung* or *Haskalah* which orthodox Jews (notably in Poland) called "Berlinism", became for them the worst of heresies. Moses Mendelssohn's attempts to find a point of equilibrium or a compromise between the Enlightenment and the tradition of Sinai, were soon left behind. By the force of circumstances, his emulators and descendants in their turn testified against Judaism, that is to say, ultimately against themselves.[15]

Certainly many "enlightened" Jews did turn against themselves, including Mendelssohn's own progeny as well as Heinrich and Karl Marx. At the time that Heinrich Marx converted in 1817, his brother Samuel was still the rabbi of Trier. A glimmer of Heinrich's alienation is provided us by Heinrich's comment in a letter to Karl that he got nothing from his family except the love of his mother. It is all too simple to assert that Heinrich Marx's act of conversion was a matter strictly of practical necessity, or principled enlightened progress.[16]

There is certainly ample ground for the practical necessity argument. The Napoleonic occupation had produced a short-lived emancipation of the Jews under the puppet Confederation of the Rhine as an incident in the dismantling of the apparatus of the old regime. Napoleon's act pre-empted the long-delayed emancipation act that had been under discussion for two decades in the timidly enlightened Prussian councils.[17] However, Napoleon's Decree of March 1808 imposed discriminatory commercial regulations against the Jews based on charges of usurious practice. In effect the burden of proof of innocence of fraud or usury was shifted to the Jewish creditor, rather than the complaining debtor. The decree was introduced as an "educational measure". Presumably the principle of equality was to remain, but the lifting of the disabilities was made contingent on the "improvement" of the Jews. As we have seen, the older Marx was prepared to concede that the Jews needed improvement in this respect, but argued that the law was counter-productive. In a prescient paragraph, in light of his son's later experience, he comments that attacks on the means of livelihood of the fathers by such legislation would result in a spirit of alienation, profligacy and antisocial revenge in the youth.[18]

Humiliated by their crushing defeat at the hands of Napoleon, the Prussian government repaired to Königsberg where it prepared for the regeneration of Germany as a modern enlightened country absorbing the lessons which the French had taught. Jewish emancipation in Prussia was carried out by the Law of 11 March 1812. Jews obtained most of the same rights as other Prussian citizens. They could hold all positions with the exception of officers of state in the civil service, in the law courts and in the army. However, they were permitted to act as private lawyers. This freedom to practise law did not last very long. When Frederick William III of Prussia took over the Rhineland (1815), the Rhenish Jews were again prohibited from practising law. An ordinance issued by von Schuckmann, Minister of the Interior, on 4 May 1816 was interpreted by the administration in such a way as to keep them from the bar. Without doubt it was this prohibition which was the immediate cause which compelled Heinrich Marx, who had been practising law under the French occupation and who now was in danger of losing his livelihood, to convert to the Evangelical faith. Evidently he had attempted to obtain a dispensation under the 1812 edict, and in 1816 had a favourable interview with the President of the Provincial Supreme Court, who was not only impressed with Heinrich's personal and professional capacities, but also sensitive to the economic pressures that exclusion from the desired position would bring. His urgings fell on deaf ears and Heinrich Marx was baptized within a year.

Yet there is more than the narrowly practical involved in Heinrich's conversion. It must be remembered that, to the mind of a man influenced as he was by the French Enlightenment, the Jewish ghetto mind appeared as stubborn retention of the outmoded, obscurantist, old world. Heinrich Marx exhibited a feature which Karl Marx was to accentuate, and which is expressed by the word, *Selbsthass*, self-hate. *Selbsthass* is a frequent characteristic of oppressed peoples everywhere when they first recognize the opportunities to enter the mainstream culture. Ironically, self-hatred is an artifact of liberation as the oppressed regard their own traditions as outmoded, archaic, shameful, crude, inept, disgraceful. They turn on themselves, and often embrace their oppressors by hoping to convince them that "We are really the same as you". The pathetic attempt at assimilation involves a loss of both culture and self-esteem.

For Heinrich Marx, the acceptance of Christianity had the effect of a rupture with the irrationality of the *ancien régime* as it manifested itself inside the Jewish ghetto. He tried to give Karl a Christian education and self-identification. The examination essays that Karl wrote on graduation from the *Gymnasium* are thoroughly Christian in conscious conviction. There is no mistaking either the intellectual capacity nor the adolescent sincerity. The paper on Saint John[19] is an essay on the renunciation of worldly ambitions in preference to universal love through acceptance of Christ. Christian love accomplishes what a "harsh theory of duty" in "heathen" religions cannot.

One can see Heinrich Marx's rejection of Judaism very clearly in the names of his children. The first child, Moritz David, died at the age of four. Then after Sophie (b. 1816), Karl Marx was born in 1818. His birth certificate simply reads "Carl Marx". Presumably at Karl's belated baptism before school entry, Karl Marx's parents added the middle name, *Heinrich*. What's in a name? A great deal. Deeply ingrained in the Jewish tradition is the practice of naming children only after the dead. It is unthinkable to do otherwise, since it would amount to a death-wish for the living.[20] In renaming his second son after himself, Heinrich Marx turned his back as emphatically as he could on what he regarded as archaic Judaism. This rejection is made evident by the fact that the word, "Jew", never appears in the correspondence between father and son. It is simply not mentioned. Instead we find the passing remark, previously noted, in which Heinrich expresses his alienation from his family and his feeling that they did not provide the opportunities for him that he was trying to give to Karl.

Jews have had to cope with persecution for millennia, and not all were willing to accept immolation rather than convert to the dominant religion. But Heinrich Marx was not like the Spanish Marranos, accepting Christianity in public and practising Judaism in secret. Neither do we find evidences of cynicism in either the Christian upbringing or the correspondence with his son, although Heinrich did say that he was not a "fanatic" on religious questions. Heinrich Marx was not a fanatic Christian, but he was no longer willing to be a Jew of any kind.

It is not likely that Heinrich Marx succeeded in rejecting Judaism in the cultural–ethnic sense of the term we have used. Neither is it possible, that in an age of growing German anti-semitism, he could protect himself or his son from the racist version of Jew-hatred that developed with the nationalist, romantic, concept of the *Volk*. What he did accomplish was to establish a sense of shame in his son—both for his parents' Jewishness, and for the servile aspect of his father's attempt to escape from it. Marx's mother, one must remember, accepted baptism to please her husband. But the narrower compass of her home life caused her to retain her Jewish traditions and language. Her husband, at least on the surface, was a cosmopolitan, assimilated

Jew. She was perpetually an outsider, Dutch as well as Jewish. She never learned German properly and undoubtedly was a focus of the humiliation felt by the men in her family. In the end, it was she who did more than Heinrich in withstanding the demands of her radical, profligate son. Heinrich argued with Karl that the Hegelian philosophical system which the young man had picked up as a student in Berlin was nothing but a spouting of obscurantist, learned nonsense. She was no intellectual and, somewhat immune from Heinrich's adulation of her son's brilliance, acted to preserve the family and its finances after her husband's death by refusing Karl funds and a share in his father's estate.[21]

In the Catholic Trier Gymnasium Karl was isolated from his fellow students. Although we have no explicit record of anti-semitic actions or canards, we do have biographical accounts of Marx's verbal aggressiveness towards his fellows. His capacity for expressing his hostility in the form of written jibes evidently had a long-remembered effect on his classmates.

It is in the school-leaving examinations from the Gymnasium that we can see the trace on his soul of the persistence of Jewish values as well as the conscious and sincere Christianity expressed in the essay on Saint John. In the "Reflections of a Young Man on the Choice of a Profession",[22] Marx concludes that the choice is full of pitfalls, self-deception, and narrowly conceived self-interest. In the end the "chief guide which must direct us in the choice of a profession is the welfare of mankind and our own perfection". "It should not be thought", Marx continues, "that these two interests would be in conflict, that one would have to destroy the other; on the contrary, man's nature is so constituted that he can attain his own perfection only by working for the perfection, for the good of his fellow men." Marx goes on to rank forms of personal success, and then to argue that it is not enough. "If he works only for himself, he may perhaps become a famous man of learning, a great sage, an excellent poet, but he can never be a perfect, truly great man. History calls those men the greatest who have ennobled themselves by working for the common good."[23] One could not imagine a more traditional Jewish ranking of happy men than the one which the young Marx announced. Marx does not seek to be the man of action, not an unusual self-image for a seventeen-year-old boy in a romantic era. True to his ethnic tradition, the happy man is he who has the time and means to pore over the holy writings. True virtue involves working for the common good, and learning is a means to that end; but learning is in the first instance a source of satisfaction and status to the sage himself.[24]

What is the lot of the young man who chooses wrongly? What is the worst that can happen? Failure. Self-hatred. Self-contempt. By the very stress that Karl Marx puts on the words it is clear that he is not a stranger to their meaning:

> Although we cannot work for long and seldom happily with a physical constituion which is not suited to our profession, the thought nevertheless continually arises of sacrificing our well-being to duty, of acting vigorously although we are weak. But if we have chosen a profession for which we do not possess the talent, we can never exercise it worthily, we shall soon realise with shame our own incapacity and tell ourselves that we are useless created beings, members of society who are incapable of fulfilling their vocation. Then the most natural consequence is self-contempt and what feeling is more painful and less capable of being made up for by all that the outside world has to offer. Self-contempt is a serpent that ever gnaws at one's breast, sucking the life-blood from one's heart and mixing it with the poison of misanthropy and despair.
>
> An illusion about our talents for a profession which we have closely examined is a fault which takes its revenge on us ourselves, and even if it does not meet with the censure of the outside world it gives rise to more terrible pain in our hearts than such censure could inflict.[25]

It is inconceivable that this passage is unrelated to his father's frustrations and humiliation, in a Germany which was developing its anti-semitism more and more along racist lines. Marx *looked* Jewish. At least he fitted the stereotype: stocky, swarthy, large-nosed. His wife and children would later call him the Moor. This point was made with charity by some, and with malice by most. His father was humiliated in the course of assimilation. Marx's mother in her homebound ways illustrated to the shamed Jew the features that were becoming more despised.

It is clear that the choice of profession which Marx was to make was one which he hoped would erase the shame. In the words of the psychiatrist A. Künzli,[26] Marx was searching for a "certificate of non-Jewishness". The choice of profession is one which leads as far as possible from the stereotype of the Jew. Marx decides that:

> Worth is that which most of all uplifts a man, which imparts a higher nobility to his actions and all his endeavors, which makes him invulnerable, admired by the crowd and raised above it.
>
> But worth can be assured only by a profession in which we are not servile tools, but in which we act independently in our own sphere. It can be assured only by a profession that does not demand reprehensible acts, even if reprehensible only in outward appearance, a profession which the best can follow with noble pride. A profession which assures this in the greatest degree is not always the highest, but is always the most to be preferred.[27]

In the end, Marx rejected his father's calling. The profession he chose was revolution.

2 Entering the Mainstream of European Culture

The intellectual world in which Heinrich Marx had raised his son, overlaying the unspoken Jewish substratum, was the Enlightenment in its French form. Despite his Prussian allegiance, Heinrich's model was French language, literature and science. Karl's intellectual heritage was one in which democratic freedom and the rule of reason were taken as virtually synonymous. But after the Congress of Vienna, unreason, sectarian and secular dogma, rule by the artificially resurrected privileged classes, all were the brute reality. Heinrich Marx, learned to live with the antithesis rationalized by the nationalism of a regenerated enlightened, Christian Prussian monarchy.

More savage demands surged inside his son. Possessing literary and intellectual gifts greater than the not-inconsiderable powers of his father, Karl Marx could not countenance what seemed to him to be the stupidity, the parochialism, and the opportunism he saw all around him. It is not hard to guess that in the love and hate that lie between father and son, the younger man was repelled by his father's law practice—the need to curry favour and make connections. All the same, it was to his father that Marx poured out his earliest thoughts about Hegelian philosophy and politics.

For his part, Heinrich Marx knew that only one aspect of his son's intolerance stemmed from pure reason and devotion to the cause of humanity. Involved also was an overweening pride compensating for shame, a bemusement with his own words, and a compulsion to effect a triumph of his own ideas. Perhaps misled by his own brilliance and a father's adulation, Marx exhibited an arrogance born of the belief that he alone was possessed of the absolute truth.

In letter after letter, Heinrich Marx warned his son that his reach would exceed his grasp. The price that Karl would pay, and which he would exact from his bride-to-be, Jenny, would be a terrible one measured in personal terms. The intellectual cost would be an inward turning, an isolation from the mainstream, and a hardening dogmatism that was capable of viewing opposing viewpoints only to pass judgment upon them. Heinrich Marx had more than an intimation that his son's changes in viewpoint would emerge in the form of savage polemic against his erstwhile colleagues. Marx's father seemed to have a presentiment of the unyielding Mosaic visage that his son would ultimately present to the world in the frontispiece of his books. His was not only a father's insight. We may speculate that, at some level of consciousness, it also reflected his own break with his family and its uncompromising orthodox Judaism.

The religious and social alternatives facing German Jews in that tumultuous era were in large measure a translation of the intellectual alternatives of the French Enlightenment—first into the German and then into the Jewish context. In every sphere—natural science, religion, politics, economics—the question was what was to replace faith in the Deity as the ultimate explanation of both the physical and human world. In the first instance, the issues were philosophical questions about the significance of science: (1) By what criteria should one judge the truth or falsity of propositions about man, nature, and the relation between them? (2) To what extent does the way human beings judge propositions about the natural and social world tell us something about man? (3) In the light of one's philosophy of science how ought men to behave in the practical world in which normative, ethical judgments are a prerequisite for defining the goals and constraints of action?

Their point of departure is the work of Immanuel Kant. "Kant's philosophy", Marx aptly remarked early in his journalistic career, "must be regarded as the German *theory* of the French Revolution."[1] Marx's emphasis of "*theory*", was meant in a pejorative sense; nevertheless, Kant's philosophy did constitute temporary synthesis of empiricist and rationalist philosophies which coincided with the ideology of the French Revolution. The supersession of Kantian philosophy marked the divergence of these trends. The schism formed the immediate background of Marx's thinking in philosophy paralleling the post-Napoleonic disillusion with the high hopes of the French Revolution.

Empiricism required that meaningful statements of fact be

generated from information received through the senses. To be sure, one could sensibly manipulate words or symbols in literary or mathematical tautology; but useful as these exercises might be, *a priori* reason was not capable of justifying statements of fact. In particular, thought provided no warrant for an innate belief in the existence of the Deity. Indeed Lockean empiricism took, as its point of departure, the human mind as a *tabula rasa*, devoid of any innate ideas whatsoever. Empiricism in its canonical Humean form destroyed belief in the Deity as being devoid of sense content and hence meaningless. With faith in God went the divine warrant for the authority of kings.

This did not make empiricism into a form of materialism as Marx mistakenly thought at one point when he was still formulating his mature views,[2] nor is it the "shamefaced agnostic materialism" of which Engels wrote towards the end of his life.[3] Hume considered subjective states of mind such as emotions, attitudes or feelings of pleasure or pain as simple empirical data. Empiricism carried to its conclusion effectively denied a hierarchy of facts. It was not the case that there existed a material substratum that was the true reality, and ideological "superstructure" that had to be explained ultimately in material terms.

Indeed the notion of an unobservable matter was as devoid of sensory basis as that of God. The empirical school in Humean form insisted that the only reality was the singular events observed, and that abstract ideas—even relations such as cause and effect—were creatures of the psychology of association of ideas observed in the minds of men. There was no essential material reality of which one could speak meaningfully underlying the observed phenomena. Even the self, the mind which was observed to associate ideas, could not be shown to be more than the impressions, ideas and then association. There was no room for an "I". Certainly a collective "real" self such as the "human essence" simply had no place in this system. General, abstract ideas, universal terms, such as "man", have no essential reality. They are the names of convenient classifications of observed singulars such as these. This nominalism is inherent in empiricism, and follows from the unobservability of generalizations. For the empiricist, then, knowing as such revealed nothing about the knower.

In political practice empiricism and rationalism often drew

support from each other. Their common demand for reason in government, and the insistence upon the facts without illusion, all seemed to be saying much the same thing: "*écrasez l'infâme!*". Yet they were quite different.

The absence in empiricism of an objective basis for relations and universal concepts—matter, time, space, cause and effect— was the main thrust of rationalist criticism of the Humean paradigm. To rationalism, these concepts were more than names or human conventions. In some sense they had to be "real" apart from, and prior to, experience. Belief in the reality of abstract ideas seemed essential to justify science, whose model was the triumphant Newtonian mathematics and physics. The method of deduction from axiomatic, universal truths remained both possible and necessary if reality were to be understood at all.

What of man? What is his essential characteristic? Unlike Hume, rationalist Deists were prepared to answer. Man, in a state of nature, was created by God to be reasonable and therefore good. That was his essence, Rousseau told us, although men were corrupted, perhaps by society's tendency to self-love. This humanism which occupies such a prominent position in Marx's early thought was even more deeply seated in the German *Aufklärung* than it was in the original French. To empiricism, consistently drawn, this was nonsense. Man in the abstract was a meaningless entity. At the most, the hedonistic tendency of individual men seemed to Adam Smith to be tempered by feelings of mutual sympathy. The best that could be hoped for in a science of human affairs were tentative observable uniformities in behaviour, not a defining essence from which all characteristics could be deduced.[4]

It was Kant's task to reconcile these trends in the philosophy of science, and their corollary regarding human nature. One may comprehend Kant's monumental *Critique of Pure Reason* in a simplistic nutshell, by realizing that it was against him that Marx (and Hegel) railed for insisting on a sharp distinction between "form" and "content". In the single letter we have of Marx to his father dating from student days, he speaks of his conversion to the Hegelian system and the criticism he made of his own early efforts as a first-year law student. "My mistake", Karl wrote of his attempts to rebuild legal theory *ab ovo*, "lay in the belief that matter and form must develop separately from each other, and so I obtained not a real form, but something like a desk with

drawers into which I then poured sand.'''[5]
Kant arrived at this point by arguing that there were two
classes of valid judgments: analytic and synthetic. Analytic judgments were statements about the meaning of words and symbols.
In the last analysis they were tautologies. One could not accept
one member of these identity relationships and deny the other
without self-contradiction. Synthetic judgments were matters of
fact and therefore their terms were not so connected. It is not self-
contradictory to claim the moon is made of green cheese—simply
untrue.

Clearly all analytic judgments were *a priori*, which Kant took
to mean that they were necessarily true. As factual statements,
synthetic judgments were not identities but related terms that
did not logically imply one another. Most synthetic statements
were *contingent* upon sense information to evoke a judgment of
belief. These synthetic statements were *a posteriori*, , and were
therefore not necessary propositions.

As long as he confined synthetic statements to the contingent, *a
posteriori*, Kant was at one with classical empiricism which
limited certainty to tautologies, confined factual propositions to
uncertain conclusions from sense data, and consigned the rest to
the flames. First into Hume's furnace were *a priori* abstract ideas.
As Marx might later have it, empiricism was attempting to
understand content of sensuous experience without essential
form; whereas rationalism attempted to manipulate *a priori*
forms, without sense content. Kant's "Copernican revolution"
insisted that both form and content were necessary for perception. Kant's forms of perception constituted valid *a priori* synthetic
judgments. Why do we need them? How they were possible?
These were Kant's central questions.

Do we need to make factual statements whose denial is not self-
contradictory? Obviously we do, argued Kant. Hume's failure to
realize this is what made him unable to deal objectively with relations between singular observations: persistent objects in time
and space, cause and effect, and ultimately even the existence of
the observing ego. The difficulty with Hume's associationist psychology as an explanation of causation, for instance, is that it
lacked necessity and universality. Why must each effect have a
cause sufficient to explain it? How can we carry on any science
without a universal set of interpersonal rules for causal explanation that are binding on us all? Failing this, each individual

might have his own equally valid causal science determined by his own psychological association of ideas. To say that we are all observed to have the same psychology, simply begs the question. We cannot inductively infer the universality of human forms of causal belief without believing *a priori* that the observing self exists over time, that other people are egos with minds like ourselves and that we all live in a similar world of persistent physical objects. Kant argued that scientific investigation requires an *a priori synthetic* model of the universe in which to classify our raw observation of ourselves and the objective world around us.

These forms of perception Kant said, are not logically necessary, since they are synthetic. Nevertheless they are necessary, and therefore true *a priori*. Kant could not inductively derive these truths themselves without begging the question. Rather he proved them "transcendentally", by showing them to be necessary conditions of experience.

A priori synthetic judgments, then, are the forms which anticipate experience. They are the "desk drawers", so to speak, into which the streams of sense information pouring into our mind is integrated into what we call facts. We cannot observe without these forms, yet they are not themselves sense information observed. This is what Marx meant by Kant's separation of form and content. Kant insisted on this separation on pain of self-contradiction. The range of the *a priori* synthetic judgments is the set of possible sense data, and nothing beyond. Thus Kant showed that rational proofs of the existence of God were necessarily faulty. For example the "first cause" proofs, assumes that every event has a cause, an *a priori* synthetic truth. Yet to reason from this to the unobservable first cause requires us to contradict ourselves: if every event is causal and we are here now in space and time, therefore there must have been a finite regress to a first cause; yet that event must itself have been caused, by hypothesis. So there cannot be a first cause.

The crux of the matter is really familiar to all empirical scientists. Facts simply do not speak for themselves, but must be selected from the manifold of experience by a theoretical model. What we define as a relevant fact to be observed depends on the model which we provisionally accept *a priori*. The modern scientific method emphasizes the word "provisional". Kant did not realize that while it is necessary to employ some *a priori* model, any particular model is not eternally necessary, but only a tentative theory. Indeed to be useful the model itself is subject to falsification in terms of the facts it specifies.[6] In retrospect, it is easy to see that Kant's belief that the universal necessity of his *a priori* synthetic categories derived from the apparent universality of Newtonian mechanics and mathematics. Kant took the world of solid objects and their movement to be the only possible perception of reality, unaware of the revolutionary changes in physical theory that were to take place in the next two centuries. For all that, the Kantian distinction between form and content remains at the core of inductive science as we know it. Scientists cannot *prove* an economic or physical model; they must *assume* it. But they do not *assume* the truth of experimental data that will test the model; they collect the facts that the model specifies, and then judge whether their assumptions have survived test or not.

As much as the Kantian system represented an advance, his failure to represent the *a priori* synthetic, as a tentative statement opened the floodgates to philosophical speculation which reached its epitome in Hegel.

Kant had conceded the possibility of *a priori*, universal synthetic truth. He failed to close the breach by insisting on a dichotomy between form and content: forms might be comprehended *a priori* by a transcendental deduction, their content had to be derived *a posteriori* by experience. Hegel was able to insist that the distinction between form and content was artificial and unscientific. Harking back to Platonic conceptions, he argued that all content was ultimately a system of universal terms: to say an object is "here", "red", "hard", "beautiful", "aromatic" is to express the whole content of the object as universals, *a priori* forms, rather than as a singular thing. From this "realist" position Hegel proceeded to erect a fantastic deductive edifice of speculative philosophy on the basis of the possibility Kant had originated in the *a priori* synthetic categories.

Marx was following Hegel in his letter to his father,[7] when he disparaged Kant and Fichte as idealists as contrasted with Hegel. In his student days Marx regarded Hegelian speculation as the scientific study of concrete reality: Hegel was not bemused by such useless, empty formalistic studies as mathematics; he did not stoop to physical science which was merely an empirical effort to "reason by analogy" from one observed situation to another, "always missing the essence".[8] The response of Marx's father, as he read his son's Hegelian speculation was that this was simply learned nonsense, "a meaningless torrent of words". But then a generation separated father and son.[9]

To theorists of human nature, the crucial point in the Kantian compromise was the nature of the self. What was there in the process of knowing that could reveal even the existence of an observer? Kant's answer was that the necessity for coherence of observations requires that the same observer be taken as making the synthesis of the stream of sense data. The knowing self was not observed, yet his existence is a logical precondition for perception. This was a transcendental deduction, like his other *a priori* synthetic statements. Kant emphasized that the "transcendental unity of apperception" supplied no positive information about the nature of the self, any more than the category of substance told about the nature of the "thing in itself", or the requirement for causation proved the existence of a first cause. Kant denied the possibility of a speculative "transcendental psychology". No positive human essence could be deduced from the relation between the knower and the known. Pure Reason, Kant insisted, was not an instrument capable of arriving at data about the human self or the physical world that transcended possible empirical test.

At the same time Kant retained the need for order in the universe which so profoundly appealed to the rational preconceptions inherent in Jewish as well as German traditions. The apparent reason which science had found in the universe as a consequence of the Newtonian revolution was not given the status of inherent in the material world. The *Ding an Sich* was in any event unknowable. Hence arguments for the existence of the Deity such as those which proceeded from the apparent design of the universe were doomed to failure. Nevertheless science, like all human observation, had to organize its material into rational, consistent systems. Therefore our observations were justifiably subject to rational analysis and model building. Indeed some such system of logical categories was a precondition for observation. But whether the world itself was in some transcendent sense rational was unknowable, and in any event irrelevant. Reason could proceed no further than possible observation, leaving no room in positive science for the metaphysics of the supernatural.

In this way Kant preserved the drive for intellectual and scientific order, but made it the creature of human activity. He achieved the same result that Rousseau had accomplished in the political sphere by arguing that the social order produced by government was a social contract of inherently free men. Adam Smith had done the same in the economic realm by showing that free individual self-interest led to both order and social optimization, even though neither were any part of individual intention. The rule of blind authority, whether directly divine or through the instrumentality of the divine right of kings, had been dealt blows from which it never would recover. At the same time scope had been given to the great system builders to pursue their work.

Kant did, however, advance a transcendental normative view of the self. His *Critique of Practical Reason* (1788) had an enormous religious and social influence, on Jews perhaps even more than Christians. His catchwords appear over and over again in the writings of Heinrich and Karl Marx. In this later book Kant focused on the question of human morality. There was more to practical life than knowing. Practice, Kant felt, was dominated by the moral issue: What ought I do?

Kant's supreme moral principle was the "categorical imperative" to do only such things as the individual would be willing to make into a universal law. The moral experience, required that ethical judgments be *universal*. Like the scientific categories of the *a priori* synthetic, normative practical judgments must apply to all persons or cease to be ethical judgment at all.

Kant argued that the belief in God and in one's self is a consequence of the experience of the moral imperative. Once I have the moral experience, my behaviour is regulated as if I believed in the existence of God. I am morally certain, not that it is positively proved, that God exists. The belief in a world beyond experience, denounced in the first critique, is revived in the second. Practice is the moral basis for Kant's belief in "transcendental", "noumenal" world of things-in-themselves imperceptible to the phenomenal world of sense experience and the cognitive process of knowing.[10]

The distinction between form and content which Kant defended so vigorously in the field of knowledge, now was breached. The philosophy of action, will, purpose came to dominate German philosophy, rather than science. It was possible to transcend the limits of the senses, to see the unseeable, by an appeal to practical action which Kant had first advanced as an ethical principle.

As we shall see in the next chapter, in Hegel's hands knowing and being expressed the teleological act of the objective universal will. In moral philosophy, Hegel's universal purpose replaced Kant's individual moral anguish. Politically, the universal will was construed to be the God of Protestant Prussia, and the dominance of the Prussian state over the individual. Kant himself had used his normative–practical ethic quite differently to justify individual freedom and political equality. Since for Kant the very act of making the moral judgment implied a willingness to make it a universal law, each person must be allowed to make the judgment if any of them did. Hence each individual was the moral equivalent of any other. The welfare of human beings was seen as the "end" of moral and political institutions. Individuals were never justifiably to be regarded as "means" to some other, Hegelian, holistic purpose such as the interest of the state. Moreover, since rational law was the moral imperative to which each individual was subject, special privilege was, by its nature, immoral. The statutes of the old regime might be enacted by monarch or legislature, but they were not the law of reason.

This is the democratic Kant that Marx's father knew, and which made him sceptical of the Hegelian "new immoralists" with whom his son was involved in Berlin. Hegel held that Kant had made each individual the "slave" of his own moral imperative, and pure thought the prisoner of finite individual egoistic desires. For Hegel, individual liberty was not freedom, but slavery. It is no wonder that Heinrich Marx reacted negatively to the "distorted ideas" Karl was repeating.

Kant's moral theism had opened the way for an ethical interpretation of religion. Many Jews seized on this to reinterpret their relation to Judaism. How they did it depended on the individual. Heinrich Marx turned his back on Jewish religion, at least in part, for its apparent obsolescence. It seemed to Jews who identified themselves with the new Kantian viewpoint that the original moral texture of the *Torah* and *Talmud* had been rendered into a sclerotic codified law, which was the subject of endless rabbinical debate over the *minutiae* of sectarianism. From our vantage point, we can see that these features were artifacts of the unyielding Jewish struggle for existence and identity in a hostile, intolerant, Christian world. The *minutiae* over which rabbinical scholars fought doctrinal battles were no less important to them, in historical context, than the younger Marx's ferocious contentions against his ideological opponents.

Shortly after his abortive petition on behalf of the Jews, Heinrich Marx turned to the Protestant Evangelical Church in the predominantly Catholic city of Trier. Like Heine, who was later to be Karl Marx's friend in Paris, Heinrich Marx accepted baptism to enter into the "mainstream of European culture". To be sure he also made the move to secure his practice of the legal profession. Yet it would be unfair to regard the conversion of either man purely as opportunism. Protestant notions of the unmediated relation between the individual and God seemed consistent with their own view of themselves as cosmopolitan, modern, moral persons. Pursuit of one's own worldly self-interest was seen as consistent with the general social advance toward Kantian freedom and universal understanding among men.

Heinrich Marx expressed himself in this vein in a letter to his son asking that he pursue potentially useful contacts with an influential person. Heinrich comments on the moral virtues of friendship, and then continues:

> That you will continue to be good morally, I really do not doubt. But a great support for morality is pure faith in God. You know that I am anything but a fanatic. But this faith is a real requirement of man sooner or later, and there are moments in life when even the atheist is involuntarily drawn to worship the Almighty ... for what Newton, Locke and Leibniz believed, everyone ... can submit to.

Then, reacting to his son's romantic poetry, Heinrich writes as a man of good sense:

> Apropos! I have read your poem word by word. I frankly confess, dear Karl, that I do not understand it, neither its true meaning nor its tendency. In ordinary life it is an undisputed proposition that with the fulfillment of one's most ardent wishes the value of what one wished is very much diminished and often disappears altogether. That is surely not what you wanted to say. That would be worth consideration at most as a moral principle, because guided by this idea one avoids immoral enjoyments and even puts off what is permissible, in order by the postponement to retain the desire or even secure a heightened enjoyment. Kant felicitously says something of this

sort in his anthropology.

Do you want to find happiness only in abstract idealizing (somewhat analogous to fanciful reverie)? In short, give me the key, I admit that this is beyond me.[11]

Heinrich Marx was a small-town liberal. He argued for the emancipation of the Jews, and his liberal expressions in the local Casino incurred the ire of the authorities at one point. Yet he was not a radical. His abandonment of Judaism was not atheism, but the acceptance of the liberal view of the Enlightenment which in his case took the form of Jewish self-contempt. In fact his failure to even mention Jewish themes to his son is significant. It is reasonable to see in this behaviour an identification of Jewishness with ghetto exclusiveness, cabbalistic superstition, false Messiahs, poverty, and what Karl Marx was to call Jewish "queer ways". The negative side of Heinrich Marx's enlightened attitude was its place as a precursor to the Jewish *Selbsthass* which Karl Marx was to display in his writings *On the Jewish Question* in 1844.

Success was to elude Heinrich. Liberation came too late for him to fulfil the potential he felt in himself. His hopes transferred to Karl:

I should like to see in you what perhaps I could have become, if I had come into the world with equally favourable prospects. You can fulfil or destroy my best hopes. It is perhaps unfair and unwise to build one's best hopes on someone and so perhaps undermine one's own tranquility. But who else than nature is to blame if men who are otherwise not so weak are nevertheless weak fathers?[12]

But having cut the ties to tradition and opened the way to contempt for the practical Jewish struggle for survival which underlay all the anachronisms of Jewish life, is it any wonder that Karl should turn away from his father? For all his fine talk, Heinrich was involved in Jewish means of survival—in business, in contracts, and in currying favour with those in authority.

In effect Heinrich's conversion left Karl emotionally defenceless against the barbs of anti-semitism from friends and enemies. Schoolboys in his youth cast the usual slurs, as did such erstwhile associates as Ruge. But even Jenny, his beloved wife, never seems to have mentioned his Jewishness, but carried on at length how she loved her "black" Moor. Marx resented his father for being weak, and despised his mother for failing to assimilate her Jewishness in the face of the intellectual airs of the men of her family.[13] Yet Marx never could simply rebut the anti-Jewish, sneer by simply replying that he did in fact come from honourable rabbinical antecedents. In feeding his son's ego, Heinrich had exposed him to all the demands of an exaggerated self-image by teaching him that he was above the mundane and beyond the reach of the authority of tradition; yet at the same time had disarmed him against the alienation that was still the lot of the Jew.

In the final analysis Heinrich Marx had practical matters to discuss with his son: career, money, prospective marriage, various aspects of legal practice and the cultivating of the circle of contacts that are a lawyer's routine. Karl moved from romantic poetry in Bonn to Hegelian obscurities in Berlin. He demanded funds from his parents. He involved his father and sister in maintaining the liaison with Jenny behind the back of Baron Westphalen next door. (Evidently despite having taken an interest in the bright young man, the baron's literary humanism did not easily extend to permitting his daughter to marry the swarthy converted Jewish boy next door.[14]) Given his situation and upbringing, it was inevitable that Karl would identify his father with the old, the opportunistic and, though we have no record of his saying so, with the Jewish.

As he reaped the fruit of his permissiveness, Heinrich realized that his hopes were doomed. In one of his last letters he wrote bitterly to his son.[15] He reminded Karl of his duties to his family and to Jenny, and denounced the Hegelian metaphysics which Karl expressed in his occasional letters. The old man forced himself to write sternly:

All these obligations together form such a closely woven bond that it alone should suffice to exorcise all evil spirits, dispel all errors, compensate for all defects and develop new and better instinct. It should suffice to turn an uncivilized stripling into an orderly human being, a negating genius into a genuine thinker, a wild ringleader of wild young fellows into a man fit for society, one who retains sufficient pride not to twist and turn like an eel, but has enough practical intelligence and tact to feel that it is only through intercourse with moral-minded people that he can learn the art of showing himself to the world in his most pleasant and advantageous aspect, of winning respect love and prestige as quickly as possible, and of making practical use of the talents which mother nature has in fact lavishly bestowed upon him.

That in short was the *problem*. How has it been solved?

God's grief!!! Disorderliness, musty excursions into all departments of knowledge, musty brooding under a gloomy oil-lamp; running wild in a scholar's dressing-gown and with unkempt hair instead of running wild over a glass of beer; unsociable withdrawal with neglect of all decorum and even of all consideration for the father. The art of association with the world restricted to a dirty work room, in the classic disorder of which perhaps the love letters of a Jenny and the well-meant exhortations of a father, written perhaps with tears, are used for pipe spills, which at any rate would be better than if they were to fall into the hands of third persons owing to even more irresponsible disorder. And it is here, in this workshop of senseless and inexpedient erudition, that the fruits are to ripen which will refresh you and your beloved, and the harvest to be garnered which will serve to fulfil your sacred obligations?

The father struggles to sustain the tone of reproach he set for himself in the letter. He almost retreats, but then returns to his theme:

> I am of course, very deeply affected in spite of my resolution. I am almost overwhelmed by the feeling that I am hurting you, and already my weakness once again brings to come over me, but in order to help myself, quite literally, I take the real pills prescribed for me and swallow it all down, for I will be hard for once and give vent to all my complaints. I will not become softhearted, for I feel that I have been too indulgent, given too little utterance to my grievances, and thus to a certain extent have become your accomplice.

Heinrich Marx then makes clear that he means more than Karl's failure to write regularly, to pursue business connections, and to behave with some financial responsibility. He clearly does not accept the torrent of Hegelian verbiage having, finally, received a letter in which Karl explains his plans to reform the entire corpus of legal thought, as well as a diary:

On several occasions we were without a letter for months, and the last time was when you knew Edward was ill, mother suffering and I myself not well, and moreover cholera was raging in Berlin; and as if that did not even call for an apology your next letter contained not a single word about it, but merely some badly written lines and an extract from the diary entitled *The Visit*, which I would quite frankly prefer to throw out rather than accept, a crazy botch-work which merely testifies how you squander your talents and spend your nights giving birth to monsters; that you follow in the footsteps of the new immoralists who twist their words until they themselves do not hear them; who christen a flood of words a product of genius because it is devoid of ideas or contains only distorted ideas.

A year later Heinrich is close to the end. The next letter shows the toll that illness has taken of the father's precise and forceful prose. We do not know what Karl's reply was to the previous letter except that Heinrich comments at the end that "Your last proposal concerning me has great difficulties. What rights can I bring to bear? What support have I?" The old man knows that he has lost in his battle for his son. "It is only because I am tired that I lay down my arms...", he says, "But always believe and never doubt, that you have the innermost place in my heart and that you are one of the most powerful levers in my life".[16]

Clearly the father is dying. Henrietta writes in a postscript, "Good father is very weak ... I am resigned to my situation and calm". And then, reflective of her character, and her position in a family dominated by two such verbally brilliant men, she says,

Write to me, dear Carl, about what has been the matter with you and whether you are quite well again. I am the one most dissatisfied that you are not to come during Easter: I let feeling go before reason, and I regret, dear Carl, that you are too reasonable. You must not take my letter as the measure of my profound love; there are times when one feels much and can say little. So good-by dear Carl, write soon to your good father, and that will certainly help towards his speedy recovery,
     Your ever loving mother,
     Henrietta Marx

Heinrich appended another brief note a few days later[17].

Dear Karl,
I send you a few words of greeting, I cannot do much yet.
  Your father,
  Marx

Death came to Heinrich Marx that year. Karl was too involved in Berlin to attend the funeral.

Other German Jews searched for a preservation of their Jewish identity through reinterpretation of Judaism along Kantian ethical lines. They attempted to avoid the *Selbsthass* which served to poison the relationship between generations in families such as that of Karl Marx. Inevitably failure to come to reconciliation with their heritage would lead to estrangement from both modern and traditional Jewish values. As we have seen, Moses Mendelssohn attempted to read Judaism in Deist terms, as a religion of reason and ethics, blurring the distinction between that faith and Christianity, while pressing Jews to abandon the archaic, self-isolating elements of their ghetto culture.

Leopold Zunz began the scientific study of Jewish history culminating in the publication of the monumental *Gottesdienstliche Vorträge der Juden*. "In order to know which of the new is to be adopted", he wrote, "we must betake ourselves to the study of the people, both in its political and moral sense." It was Zunz who, in 1819, brought together young Jews in a society for the scientific study of Judaism. Included in that number was Heinrich Heine, Marx's friend in Paris, and Eduard Gans, Marx's teacher in Berlin and famous for his edition of Hegel's *Philosophy of Right*.

Out of this ferment German Jewish intellectuals rang all the changes of possible positions. Heine rejected Judaism, but remained a cynical, alienated, though lyrical poet, who, it is said, died with *Sh'ma Israel* on his lips. Gans, who gave Marx the highest marks in Berlin, endured Hegel's anti-semitic lectures, and finally adopted Christianity. The ethical and historical work of Zunz inspired the evolution of Reform Judaism under Abraham Geiger. This doctrine abandoned most of the ritual of the orthodox. Based on the later prophets it reinterpreted Isaiah's notion of Jews as a "chosen people" as an injunction to set a moral example.

As Karl Marx entered into the revolutionary democratic

movement centering on the University of Berlin, he brought with him the alternatives facing the Jews of his time. (1) He could follow his father, and for reasons of intellectual fashion and personal advancement, simply adopt the norm. He could, in public, have been properly but not fanatically, Christian and in private remained an eighteenth-century sceptic. (2) He could adopt Christianity with fervour, and reject Judaism with equal fervour and fanaticism. (3) He could return to the Judaic tradition. We shall see, in what follows, that he did all three—albeit in a philosophic and atheistic guise.

3 Towards a Philosophy of Freedom

After a tumultuous episode at the University of Bonn, filled with at least the usual number of student scrapes, the young Karl Marx transferred in 1836 to the University of Berlin. His father's blessing and financial support went with him. Heinrich's goals, if not Karl's, was for the young man to study jurisprudence and make a career in the law. Heinrich hoped that his son would achieve that status of respectability, acceptance and relative affluence for which the older man had sacrificed much in his own life.

In the new University of Berlin, the young Marx encountered the turbulence of philosophical and legal ideas churned up by the opposing currents in German life in the wake of the final defeat of the French. Marx was drawn to the debate over the philosophy of law which served as a surrogate for the conflict between the newly restored aristocracy and the bourgeois intellectual adherents to the ideals of the French revolution. The "historical school of law", expounded by one of Marx's teachers, von Savigny, sought legal legitimacy in precedent and custom. Justice was to be defined in an historically relative sense, rather than in absolute terms. To the *avant-garde* this was an apology for every irrationality and brutality of the *ancien régime*. For them, justice was to be found in the rule of reason, rather than the dead hand of past infamies. Marx identified with this radical democratic expression of the spirit of the Enlightenment upon which he had been nurtured. His later appeal to history for legal legitimacy reflected the forced marriage of reason and history which he ultimately took over from Hegel.

For the democratic radicals, however, the fact remained that it was the west wind that had brought the revolutionary implementation of reason to Germany. It arrived as the trumpeting of Napoleon's legions and the crushing of the German national spirit. Reason had come to Germany by means of the force of alien empire. The very nationalist emotion to which the French Revolution had given impetus, was channeled by Metternich's Reaction into the restoration of the patchwork of miniature states dominated by Prussia, which the world called Germany. Even as it expelled the French, Prussia sought the regeneration and modernization of economically and socially backward Germany. This was exemplified in the establishment of the new University of Berlin, which aimed at attracting the new great minds of the time. Yet at the same time, the timid Prussian monarchy reacted with police repression to any intimation of Jacobinism among the intellectual youth. Germany was, as Marx said so many times, incapable of rousing itself to the practical task of throwing off the "muddled" institutions of political fragmentation and social backwardness.[1] For all the brilliant ratiocination of Kantian philosophy, Germany's flabby bourgeoisie palpably lacked the will to act.

These cross currents were fixed, as much as they could be in print, by Hegel's philosophy of Being and its application to the theory of law and the state. Only such an intellect could, even in the fantasy world of speculative philosophy, bring apparent order to a nation rent by irreconcilable forces. In embracing contradiction, Hegel did more than philosophize about the dialectic. He expressed the very spirit of his times as he attempted to marry reason to history, freedom to reaction and the cool analyses of the philosophy of science to the romantic idealisms of the primacy of the Will. Hegel's dialectic of the contradiction was expounded with an overawing erudition. Yet the contradiction remained. This same man who welcomed the armies of Napoleon at Jena, and planted a liberty tree in the name of freedom, was able to rationalize the absurdities of the Prussian monarchy, the repression of dissent, and the nascent ideology of the superiority and destiny of the German *Volk*. It was this poison which was to ferment with anti-semitism and ultimately erupt spewing death in the Holocaust which enveloped Germans as well as Jews.[2]

The formal philosophical kernel of the romantic revision of the scientific spirit of the eighteenth century was Hegel's insistence that it was impossible to maintain the Kantian distinction between necessary forms of perception and contingent sensuous content.[3] "Sense certainty", Hegel agreed with Kant, did indeed require a system of *a priori* synthetic universal categories.[4] But

Kant's formulation was at best incomplete: if these formal categories are truly both synthetic *a priori* and universal, why is their scope limited to a few aspects of perception such as time and space? By what warrant do they arbitrarily relegate the rest of experience to a residual mass of brute, sensuous, contingent, *a posteriori*, singular facts? If any *a priori* synthetic categories are to be admitted, then all synthetic information had equal claim to derive from the same metaphysical source.

The Hegelian critique went further. The Understanding, his rubric for Kant and positive science, offered no rational justification for the necessity of the *a priori* categories themselves—except as apparently necessary preconditions for meaningful perception. Kant himself remained agnostic in principle as to whether the *a priori* synthetic forms were merely a psychological necessity to human observation, or were ontological principles of ultimate reality. Hegel wanted to leave no room for the first alternative. In this latter case, as necessary principles, the forms of perception themselves should be rationally demonstrable from some larger, more encompassing principle which would ensure their coherence and consistency. Yet in Kant's hands, the categories remained finite, contingent forms, devoid of intrinsic content. Hegel saw the need to merge form and content in order to preserve the possibility of a rational, necessary universe. The Kantian distinction perpetuated the finiteness of reason. It placed most factual information beyond the reach of necessary demonstration, and made the categories of themselves contingent facts of perception. Hegel's rationalism demanded that they be necessary features of reality.

The romantic urge to enlarge the boundaries of Will and Spirit served as the unifying principle. Hegel's *Phenomenology of Mind* held that it was necessary to abandon the distinction between the world of spirit and the unperceived world of things in themselves. Reality was constituted of the universal, the spiritual, the unifying process of Reason.' Modern nineteenth-century science, Hegel claimed, was rooted in uncovering the work of Reason, in which the spirit of universal evolutionary necessity would be uncovered as the hidden process at work behind the apparent static, contingent particular. For Hegel, categories were not models into which empirical data was to be stuffed, but rather represented aspects of the idea stuff of which reality was being made.

Hegel's philosophy that followed this motif was a speculative fantasy which purported to expound the emanation of reality from the ultimate universal, Absolute Idea, and the subsuming of finite forms back into it. Reason consisted first in comprehending how objective were contingent singular facts of apparent experience, conjunctures of the universals in their essential aspect, and then in relating these defining essences to the most general Absolute Idea. To the extent that the teleology of this movement of reason was understood, to the extent that the progressive "notion" of *a priori* forms encompassed the contingent, to that extent the alien object was taken over into spirit. The progress of Consciousness was the overcoming of the estrangement of the spirit from an alien, limiting, brutally contingent, irrational world which limited spiritual progress toward ultimate realization. As Marx was to point out, in this speculative philosophy invincible reason served as a wish-fulfilling proxy for the frustrated longings of the German nation and the German bourgeois man, unable to achieve in reality the destiny that they felt was their inherent nature.[5]

Earlier systems of universal consistency had foundered, not so much on the unity of the universe as on its particularity. How was one to derive less inclusive, particular forms from such all inclusive universals such as Plato's "Good", Spinoza's "Substance" or Hegel's "Idea"? Kant had argued that such deductions were bound to end in self-contradiction. Hegel's new dialectical logic, however, did not shrink from such antinomies of pure reason. He purported to subsume contradiction into a higher level of rationality which would subsume the mere Understanding into Reason. Reason constituted the determinate self-movement of universal concepts.

Hegel agreed that the simple *thesis* statement of a universal term was a mere empty form. Turning this truth to philosophical advantage, he claimed that the thesis contradicted itself; it alienated itself from itself in the *antithesis* of the thesis. The interaction between the thesis and its own self-estrangement gives rise to a new, more concrete universal term, the *synthesis*. The process of alienation and supersession starts over again, until all the states of human knowledge are generated by the process of active, teleological, reason working through "concrete negation". For example, Hegel considered the most general thesis statement to be Being—everything exists. But this gives no information, therefore contradicting itself. Being becomes not-Being. The synthesis of the two is Becoming, the "negation of the negation". In turn, Becoming suggests continua and hence quantity, which was then identified with time, space and the physics of mechanical bodies. These quantitative elements, in turn suggest qualitative differences and so on and on, until Hegel purportedly generated all knowledge as moments of the process of Reason.[6]

There is both sense and nonsense in all this. To say anything about singular events does indeed require the use of universal terms as Hegel pointed out in *The Phenomenology of Mind*. One cannot point to an object and say it is "here" without assuming some sort of spatial framework, denying that the object is "there". But the fact that we need universal concepts to say anything about objects, does not raise our conceptions to a degree of reality above the limits which Kant had stated: the conceptual framework of space is our theory about the contingent singular data we observe. Saying something about objects is not at all the same as converting objects into the words we use. Universal names does not imply the existence of universal entities. Confounding the two is the essence of magic words and totem worship. It is the hubris of idolatry which imagines that words and symbols which the Young Hegelians showed ultimately derived from human mental activity, can dominate the objective world, making a God of man. It is for this reason that, despite his spiritual monism, Hegel is fundamentally antithetical to Judaism. We shall see, in the remainder of this book, how Marx was first attracted to and then repelled by Hegel's conception of the power of the will.

Hegel's logic is clearly absurd when he produces an empty category (even though it is given the all-inclusive name, Being) and then claims that it contradicts itself because it is empty. In any case a category cannot contradict itself; unlike a proposition it cannot be true or false. The failure of a category to refer to specific objects or sub-categories of object merely means that it is the name of a set which is void. For example, the term "red" is not subject to contradiction, but the proposition, "This apple is red", certainly can be contradicted by the statement, "No, this apple is green". "Being" as a universal term cannot be contradicted any more than the word "red".

If by contradiction of a category Hegel meant the complement of a set (the elements in the universe of discourse not included in the set), then the question becomes what is meant by the complement of the empty set, Being? The complement of an empty set is the universal set. So if Being is empty, not-Being is everything. If Being is everything, then not-Being is nothing. Either way there is no logical means of extracting more information from these classes than the dichotomy, everything and nothing, from which the discussion started. No information is to be gained from the juxtaposition of these terms.

Despite the pretentious nonsense of the dialectic which tells us nothing of the content of science, it must be conceded that Hegel was telling us a great deal about the process through which science develops as a body of human thought. It is true that the development of science has followed a movement towards greater generalization on one hand, and its application to particular experimental cases on the other. The particular serves as a test of the general, and contradiction compels a revised scientific paradigm. The Hegelian system, then, is of interest as an account of the sociology or psychology of the scientist, rather than the content of science itself. Indeed, it is the psychological conditioning of the reader which impels us to follow Hegel and insert Becoming when confronted with the terms Being and not-Being. We know something about time and space and put it in the picture as a synthesis, even though it is not a logical consequence of thesis and antithesis. All this is to say that contrary tendencies towards generalization and particularization are at work in the sociology of science, but Hegel's identification of Idea with reality attempted to give ontological status to his description of the mental process of acquiring knowledge. Hegel blurred the distinction between the knowledge we have and the way we get new knowledge. He identified knowing and being, even though they are logically distinct.

In his time, conventional religious opinion saw in Hegel a restatement of the Spinozist heresy which they took as only a step away from atheism. To the Hegelian school itself the statement of the primacy of all-embracing universal spirit was understood as an *avant-garde*, modern restatement of Christianity. As a Protestant believer, Hegel insisted that the Christian vision of God was the true expression of the universal Idea which embodied and superseded the individual and finite soul. Christianity was to be contrasted with Judaism which was characterized, he said, by the narrow vision of a finite, egoistic people. The Jews purported to have made a compact with God as a chosen people. Judaism separated individuals from God, who remained an other, alien Being rather than an entity with which men were united through the mediation of Christ. Hegel had turned his back on the rational Deism and materialism of the previous century. He philosophized about a world in which both freedom from the unreason of the old regime, and natural science as opposed to religious belief had apparently failed. It seemed all-too-clear that the teaching of the *savants* had not achieved the self-fulfilment of the spirit, either in individual or nationalist terms. Indeed the very individualism spawned by the modern era generated systems of political constitutions, ethical dicta and economic equilibria which restricted the spirit even more effectively in their impersonal working than the lordship and bondage of the previous age. Newtonian physics in natural science and French conceptions of the rational social contract had removed capricious intervention—both divine and human—from the material and social universe. But these expressions of the Understanding only confined the Will in seemingly more solid walls of natural, and therefore immutable, constraints. Freedom from unreason, was not yet freedom to express the potential that Hegel's romanticism believed was inherent in the spirit.

In Germany, it seemed to Hegel, that Kantian philosophy was the *reductio ad absurdum* of the eighteenth-century euphoria. Spirit as described by Kant was the prisoner of what the sense could detect. There was no purposive teleology in the Kantian categories. Spirit was confined by the categories limiting pure reason. It was a prisoner of Aristotelian disjunctive logic, geometry, mathematics and the precise causal relations that made up the Newtonian mechanical world machine.

In the social sphere of practical human action, Hegel held that Kant had made spirit the slave of morality. Purpose, action, passion, the deed—all these hallmarks of romanticism—were denied to the limited spirit of individual men; they must obey the categorical imperative which served to inhibit their actions from within. Kant's stricture never to use individuals as a means served as a barrier to the working of the national will embodied in the state. The spiritual wholes of nation, religion, philosophy, aesthetics and law could not express their active propensities in a system limited by individual perceptions and desires. Hence they were not free!

Freedom for Hegel meant the "infinite". Freedom was the unbounded. It was not to be found in the constrained, finite, world of the Understanding in science; nor was it a society ruled by individual utilitarian considerations (civil society). In the physical world described by science infinity escapes us. Hegel turned to the world of Idea. He identified the spiritual activity of knowing with overcoming the dualism between the knower and the world he knows; by progressively taking the world into spirit, through knowledge, the activity of spirit transcended all boundaries. Idea was the active process of coalescence of the knower and the known. Idea was therefore universal. It was infinite and hence free.

If one understood this process of spiritual development one was free. This was the conservative side of Hegel which Marx and the radical Young Hegelians did not fail to notice. Freedom was not achieved by overt political and social deeds, but by spiritual actions in knowledge, religion, aesthetics and, ultimately, Hegel's philosophy.

Hegel's own early works cast these ideas in overt religious terms. The dominance of the general is put in terms of submission of individual desires to Jesus's teaching of universal love:

> The Sermon does not teach reverence for the laws; on the contrary it exhibits that which fulfills the law but annuls it as law and so is something higher than obedience to law and makes law superfluous ... Jesus makes a general demand on his hearers to surrender their rights, to lift themselves above the whole sphere of justice or injustice by love, for in love there vanish not only rights but also the feeling of inequality and hatred of enemies which this feeling's imperative demand for equality implies.[7]

The whole, the universal, has a movement, a purpose, a will of its own. Freedom is not a state of individual liberty at all, but consisted in seeing that what appear as individual acts, desires, wishes, are merely expressions of the workings of Idea. Engels liked to quote Hegel to the effect that "Freedom consists in the recognition of necessity". The individual is free when he is identified with, part of, the self-working development of the whole. Individuals can never be free, but must remain finite.

As a student of Hegel's immediate successors at Berlin, Marx originally could make nothing of the Hegelian morass. But after the initial negative reaction he embraced the doctrine with fervour. He wrote to his father that "he had read fragments of Hegel's philosophy", during his first term at Berlin. "The grotesque craggy melody ... did not appeal to me."[8] Then he tells of his ultimate conversion. In this long letter Marx reports his intensive programme of reading in law and philosophy, in translation and literary experiments:

> Busy with these various observations, during my first term I spent many a sleepless night, fought many a battle, and endured much internal and external excitement. Yet at the end I emerged not much enriched, moreover I had neglected nature, art and the world and shut the door on my friends. The above observations seem to have been made by my body. I was advised by a doctor to go to the country, and so it was that for the first time I traversed the whole length of the city to the gate and went to Stralow. I had no inkling that I would mature there from an anemic weakling into a man of robust bodily strength.

After this crisis, strikingly reminiscent of Mill's romantic revulsion against the confines of the cold, unfeeling logic of eighteenth-century science, the constraints of the Understanding were shed. Marx continued:

> A curtain had fallen, my holy of holies was rent asunder, and new gods had to be installed. From the idealism which, by the way I am compared and nourished with the idealism of Kant and Fichte, I had arrived at the point of seeking the idea in reality itself. If previously the gods had dwelt above the earth, now they became its center.

Marx found new friends who shared the modern Hegelian view:

> While I was ill I got to know Hegel from beginning to end, together with most of his disciples ... I came across a Doctor's club ... I became ever more firmly bound to the modern world philosophy from which I had thought to escape, but all rich chords were silenced and I was seized with a veritable fury of irony ... I could not rest until I had acquired modernity and

the outlook of contemporary science through a few bad pro-
ductions such as *The Visit*, etc.[9]

This last is the "botch-work" to which Heinrich alluded so dis-
paragingly in his letter discussed in the previous chapter. Marx
tried to explain his new world view of the unity of form and
content to which his father was to respond with forthright com-
tempt. His previous work, Karl explained, consisted of
"metaphysical propositions". "At the end of the section on
material private law, I saw the falsity of the whole thing, the
basic plan of which borders on that of Kant."[10] The issues went
much deeper than those of legal theory. Marx struggled to make
clear to his father how Hegel had rendered Kant obsolete in criticizing his own efforts:

Here above all, the same opposition between what is and what
ought to be, which is characteristic of idealism stood out as a
serious defect and was the source of the hopelessly incorrect
division of the subject matter. First of all came what I was
pleased to call the metaphysics of law, i.e. basic principles,
reflections, definitions of concepts divorced from all actual law
and every actual form of law as occurs in Fichte, only in my
case it was more modern and shallower. From the outset an
obstacle to grasping the truth here was the unscientific form of
mathematical dogmatism, in which the author argues hither
and thither, going round and round the subject dealt with,
without the latter taking shape as something living and developing in a many-sided way. A triangle gives the mathema-
tician scope for construction and proof, it remains a mere
abstract conception in space and does not develop into anything further ... On the other hand, in the concrete expression
of a living world of ideas, as exemplified by law, the state,
nature and philosophy as a whole, the object itself must be
studied in its development; arbitrary divisions must not be
introduced, the rational character of the object itself must
develop as something imbued with contradictions in itself and
find its unity in itself.[11]

Marx was fascinated by Hegel's demonstration of the necessary connection between what seemed to be unrelated, singular
events. Hegelian reason was the concrete, realistic, scientific

mode of reasoning. The Kantian forms were idealistic empty boxes. After describing his earlier formulation of legal theory, Marx identifies his mistake:

> I had further divided this part into the theory of formal law and the theory of material law, the first being the pure form of the system in its sequence and interconnections, its subdivisions and scope, whereas, the second on the other hand was intended to describe the content, showing how the form becomes embodied in the content ... I understood by form the necessary architectonics of conceptual formulations, and by matter the necessary quality of these formulations. The mistake lay in my belief that matter and form can and must develop separately from each other, and so I obtained not a real form, but something like a desk with drawers into which I then poured sand.

The Hegelian "notion" or concept overcame the division:

> The concept is indeed the mediating link between form and content. In a philosophical treatment of law, therefore, the one must arise in the other; indeed, the form should only be the continuation of content. Thus I arrived at a division of the material such as could be devised by its author for at most an easy and shallow classification, but in which the spirit and truth of law disappeared.

The young man had exhausted himself with his efforts to explain:

> Please, dear father, excuse my illegible handwriting and bad style; it is almost 4 o'clock, the candle has burnt itself out and my eyes are dim; a real unrest has taken possession of me, I shall not be able to calm the turbulent spectres until I am with you who are dear to me.[12]

Hegel's philosophy had struck a deep emotional movement in the soul of this romantic young man. Hidden mystical meaning lay behind the phenomenal world of experience. To grasp the dialectic was to comprehend the working of the transcendental universal spirit in the mundane. Had Hegel touched on a cabbalistic chord which resonated in Marx's ancient heritage? One can only speculate on such matters. The fact remains that the mysticism of the Cabbala, emerging from the ancient despair of the Jews, was discussed with no little sympathy by Hegel in spite of his antipathy toward Judaism of a more rational kind. He commented in his *Lectures on the History of Philosophy*:

> The Cabbalistic philosophy and the Gnostic theistic theology both occupied themselves with the same concepts which Philo also had. To them also the First is the abstract, the unknown, the nameless; the Second is the unveiling, the concrete, which goes forth into emanation. But there is also to be found in some degree the return to unity, especially among Christian philosophers, with Philo, Wisdom, the teacher, the high priest was that which the contemplation of God leads back the Third from the First.

To be sure Hegel characterized the Cabbala as a "medley of astronomy, magic medicine and prophecy". Yet his affinity for it is evident in comparison to his view of the Judaism of *Torah* and *Talmud* that remained the orthodoxy of the Jewish community, despite the pull of cabbalistic mysticism in the Diaspora:

> In earlier times there is no representation among the Jews of God as being in His essence Light, of an opposite to God, Darkness and Evil, which is in strife with the light; there is nothing of good and evil angels, of the Fall of the wicked, of their condemnation, of their being in Hell, of a future day of judgement for the good and the evil, of the corruption of the flesh. It was not until this time that the Jews began to carry their thoughts beyond their reality; only now does a world of spirit, or at least of spirits, begin to open itself up before them; before this these Jews cared only for themselves, being sunk in the filth and self-conceit of their present existence, and in the maintenance of their nation and tribes.

Hegel's Pythagorean comments make clear his affinity and this "dark and mysterious philosophy" which reproduces the world from emanations and delimitations of the universal principle:

> Further particulars of the Cabbala are these. One is expressed as the principle of all things, as it is likewise the first source of

all numbers. As unity itself is not one number among the rest, so it is with God, the basis of all things, the *En-Soph*. The emanation therewith connected is the effect whose boundary it is.[13]

Later in such works as *The Holy Family* (1845) Marx was to turn at least nominally against any doctrine which ascribed mystery to the reality of experience. He directed particular venom against the early efforts of Eugène Sue who was later to write of the Cabbala in *The Wandering Jew*. Yet in Marx's earliest writings, in such demonic poems as "The Fiddler", the main theme is the mystical struggle between light and darkness.[14] More important, in what Marx claimed to be the science of society of his maturity, there remains the Hegelian hidden meaning, which is discoverable in the triads of dialectical thought. Certainly Marx was not aware of a resonance between his dialectic and Jewish mysticism. And, after all, we can only point to the resonance rather than show a causal connection. Nonetheless, it is certainly easy to see how Marx may well have been attracted to Hegel for this strain in his philosophy, and it is equally easy to understand why Heinrich Marx would regard such thinking as mystical nonsense.

4 Individualism and Freedom

The Hegelian treatment of freedom was expressive of the contrary tendencies of his time: on the one hand the desire for individual self-expression, and on the other the holistic urge to identify self-fulfilment with the destiny of the state. In a period when Prussian nationalism was intertwined with regeneration and freedom from French domination, it was possible to believe that, however much the state might repress individual liberty, the power of the state and the advance of freedom were identical. Yet when the holistic and individual interests collide, no amount of dialectic can cover over the opposition. In *The Philosophy of Right*, Hegel was to insist in the final analysis on the primary authority of the state.

Berlin radicals, the Young Hegelians, attempted to oppose the limitation of individual expression, while at the same time remaining within the Hegelian philosophical system. Their shafts were first aimed at organized religion, and thus indirectly at the Christian German state and its monarch. With increasing stridency the Young Hegelians were to argue that religion rationalized the authority of the state by minimizing the possibilities of human freedom. Religion saw human beings as sinful, imperfect creatures requiring direction in their temporal and spiritual lives. Finding room for freedom from religion and for the individual, while still writing as an Hegelian, was the unspoken theme of Marx's doctoral dissertation. It was to be followed in 1843 by the *Critique of Hegel's "Philosophy of Right"* which dealt with the same issue, in overt polemic against the philosopher and his political outlook.

Marx's dissertation dealt with the relation between individual freedom and universal necessity as it was expressed in the philosophical differences between Democritus and Epicurus in classical Greek philosophy. The thesis was written for what seems to have been the diploma mill at the University of Jena. The degree was granted in April 1844 within a week of its receipt and without public examination. Marx's association in Berlin with the radical theologian, Bruno Bauer, made it unlikely that he would—or could—satisfy the authorities in that university.

The dissertation, *Difference between the Democritean and Epicurean Philosophy of Nature*,[1] is best understood when counterposed against the portions of Hegel's *Lectures on the History of Philosphy*, which deal with the same comparisons. Marx is writing as an Hegelian. He tells us in the foreword that *"Hegel* has on the whole correctly defined the general aspects of the above-mentioned systems"[2] But Marx pushes much further in finding in Epicurus the seeds of individualism, freeing men from the fear of the gods. He cites Hume as the justification for coming to conclusions contrary to revealed religion.[3]

To be sure Marx finds Epicurus to be inadequate: he could not supersede the contradiction between the singular and universal which Hegel had propounded. But Marx's conclusion was not Hegel's judgment that Epicurus was a mere empiricist, a creature of the Understanding. Rather Epicurus had made a great contribution in pushing Greek philosophy as far as it could go in developing individualism, indeed to the point of contradiction. This was his great achievement as opposed to the unfreedom of the materialist determinism of Democritus. The dissertation then, is the first step in the process of Marx's retreat from Hegel toward empiricism and individualism.

Democritus and Epicurus are likely candidates for a comparative study of the meaning of science because they both advanced their natural philosophy in atomistic terms. Consequently, their differences reflected philosophical outlook rather than controversies in physics. Democritus, the great pre-Socratic theorist, espoused a materialist conception of the universe. It consisted, he said, of atoms and the void. The motion of the atoms, their arrangement and rearrangement, was subject to rational, deterministic physical laws of motion. The materialism of the atomic theory constituted Democritus' ontological ground for the logical method in the physical sciences. Coherent demonstrations about the universe were available through the science of physics, mathematics and logic; and certainty was available to the human mind as it analysed the world of experience.

Democritus was quick to concede that the atoms themselves

were unobservable. Marx cites his remark that, "In reality we know nothing, for the truth lies at the deep bottom of the well".[4] Nonetheless, the contradiction Marx describes in the atomism of Democritus is only at the surface. Democritus' atomism was really a device to validate the use of sense information in models which could be manipulated by mathematics. In fact, Democritus devoted his life to scientific research, both empirical and mathematical. "We see Democritus", Marx remarks, "wandering through half the world in order to acquire experiences, knowledge, and observations."[5]

Inevitably Democritus had to deal with the problem of perception: how do our senses tell us about the world of reality, when the material world of atoms is itself unobservable? Democritus' explanation is that our senses are affected by material *eidola*, streaming from the surfaces of natural bodies into our souls through the sense organs. Democritus does not, and cannot tell us about the atoms themselves. He uses them, as Marx says as a "material substrate" to describe the physics–physiology of perception. Do our senses deceive us? Not really. They do not tell us about atoms, to be sure, but they respond to them in a regular way. In this sense, what we detect is really there, even though Democritus is hard put to say that our mental images are copies of reality. As Marx says, there remains the "antinomy" between matter and idea—the Kantian term is appropriate in light of the similar function performed by the Democritean atoms and Kant's "noumenal" world of the *Ding an sich*. Like Kant, Marx says, Democritus has turned the "sensuous world into subjective semblance"[6] of an objective world; he does not comprehend the Hegelian idea stuff which "really" exists and which can be comprehended by spirit.

In light of Marx's later views, it is striking to see how vigorously he criticizes Democritus, not for his lapses from materialism, but for his adherence to it. In fact, like Democritus, the later Marx of the *Thesis on Feuerbach* relies on the interaction of material man with nature to solve the perception problem. For the mature Marx as well as Democritus, perceiving is described as the facts of how we form ideas and perceptions rather than a justification for their correctness. But at this stage Marx was still a Hegelian and attempted to overcome the antinomy by making reality subjective spirit. Following Hegel, he asserted that the atoms could not simply be described as spiritless objects. Marx argued that atoms as singular objects were not really divorced from their universal forms, which were necessarily matters of mind or spirit. The very location of the atoms in the void, their relation to one another in the permutations which the habit of the senses construes to be natural objects, implies that reality consists of more than atoms. Space was the universal term, correlative with location, which was necessary to speak of the individual atoms at all. The void implied a universal and hence ideal continuum.

Marx sided with Epicurus against the deterministic physics of Democritus. He realized that such a deterministic system must contain a set of static elements as its core assumption; any explanation that is more than a mere record of events must be stated in terms of parameters which at least provisionally hold constant. This is so even if the parameters define the highest degree of rates of change of physical or social systems. Democritus expressed his version of the Millian "law of the uniformity of nature" in terms of the immutability of the atoms. Contrary to Epicurus, he denied chance events. The Democritean non-stochastic world could be run backwards in time without doing violence to physical laws, given appropriate changes in sign to the measures of space and time. There was no forward drive, no purpose, no true individuality in the atoms of physical bodies, nor was there free will in the atoms that are human souls.

The commentaries of both Hegel and Marx on Epicurus start from his forthright phenomenalism, 'All senses are heralds of the true". Hegel showed that for Epicurus sensation *is* reality, so the atomic substructure has no significance whatsoever in the logic of his position. Hegel and Marx quote Epicurus' *Canon* to this effect: "Nor is there anything which can refute sensations, neither like can refute like, because of their equal validity, nor can unlike refute unlike, because they do not pass judgement on the same thing".[7]

Hegel took this point in his lectures to identify Epicurus with the empiricist method of natural science and damn him accordingly.[8] Epicurus, he said, is neither better nor worse than the experimental scientist who collects his observations, classifies them into categories according to their similarity with previous experience, assigns names to these classes and then takes the leap and "reasons by analogy" to unseen objects and causal relations. The proof of the superficiality of the inductive method, according to Hegel, was the fact that even alternative and mutually exclusive observations might be retained by Epicurus and his descendants as long as they did not conflict with observation. To retain opposing theories in the absence of critical test was, to Hegel, the equivalent of abandoning rational explanation altogether.

The distinctive aspect of the Epicurean philosophy that involved both Hegel and Marx was the role assigned to chance events. The issues raised are still appropriate today and may be expressed in modern terms: Does an explanation based on a series of random events deny the objective rationality of the scientific method? Does it imply that there are no regularities in nature? Is a stochastic model so completely the antithesis of deterministic explanation as to remove the explanation from the realm of science and transfer it to the outcome of free will?

Stochastic processes are, of course, a commonplace in today's science. Complex systems often make it a practicable impossibility to make a completely—or even reasonably—enumerated deterministic model of the forces at work. This is so even if the physical laws governing each of the components are known. Recourse must then be had to statistical methods such as statistical mechanics in physics and econometrics in economics. Clearly the outcome of an analysis in which only some of the events and forces are specified cannot be any more determinate than the information given. It remains impossible to predict events with certainty. Therefore, since every situation ultimately is so complex in its ramifications, a degree of uncertainty is inevitable in even the most finely tuned measurement or carefully specified model.

Nevertheless, it is possible to make a useful hypothesis about the nature of the collective forces which are not specified. The explanation in the statistical sense suggests a set of probabilities that might be appropriate to encompass the unexplained variation. The "normal curve of error" is such an explanatory function, and predictions may be made in terms of it, specifying the probabilities of given outcomes. Unlike the deterministic models, there is no way in which a stochastic explanation can explain why a chain of events had to occur as it did, even given a set of initial conditions. The ultimate outcomes depend on which of the intermediate events occurred in the chain.[9] Despite these differences, Hegel was right to point to the essential similarity between stochastic and non-stochastic empirical explanations. Each model specifies a universal statement in the shape of a functional form—in the stochastic case a probability statement, in the deterministic case one in which the random terms are suppressed and their consideration postponed until measurement is undertaken. In both stochastic and non-stochastic cases an explanation of observed events ultimately is chained back to a set of contingent, factual initial conditions as the unexplained starting point. In the former case, the irrationality of brute fact is more apparent, but it is involved in both forms of scientific explanation. These unexplained particulars are the hallmark of empirical science, and it was this that Hegel could not abide.

Epicurus was obviously treading the very thin line between constructing a model based on a chain of stochastic processes, which is compatible with the process of Understanding, and a description which could be taken to deny the objective rationality of science and to rely on a teleology based on individual will. Hegel pushed him in the former direction, while Marx opted for the latter. Their choice reflected their different emphasis on the role of the individual.

Hegel's account is that the atoms of Epicurus were in random motion, adhering and arranging themselves in patterns which caused sensory experiences in the soul. Epicurus was following Democritus insisting that the "atoms do not change".

Similar sensory images are the reflection of similar arrangements of the atoms, and hence exhibit the uniformity of nature which justifies induction. Singular events of sense experience may be classified and dealt with in a rational, consistent manner, leading to the peace of mind (*atraxy*) of the observer. Sense experience was not capricious, even though the objects described by the senses were nothing but the collection of images in the mind. Even while observation was subject to generalization, Epicurus reasoned that since the atoms were in random motion, the particular course of events was only describable by a chain of probabilities. There were no necessary connections between singular events; there was no essential nature inherent in each physical object or human being which foretold their fate. Events moved on in an irreversible series of experiences over time. There were uniformities of nature in the world of sense yet the course of events could not be foretold with certainty.

Epicurus advanced no doctrine of inherent essences. Individual objects were compilations of atoms as they appeared to the mind, not necessary criteria in themselves. "All these", said Hegel, "are empty words, and a crystal, for instance is not a certain arrangement of parts which gives the figures."[10] Hegel held the view that there is an organic unity to objects that defines an essence. Moreover these essential features form an objective, dialectically rational, evolving process. The dialectic is inherent in the universal essential aspect of singular items. In Epicurus, Hegel railed, events are "merely an accident brought about by their chance-directed motion".[11]

Epicurean atomism, Hegel noted, made it impossible for him to comprehend the infinite, to see God as the Absolute Idea. Nevertheless, he held that Epicurus was right to deny an operational role to the Greek gods.[12] Superstition consisted in assigning the explanation of "finite" events to the gods with the resulting terror of them. Phenomenalism served to free men from fear of the supernatural. Moreover, since Epicurean phenomenalism identified the self with sensation, and since there was no sensation after death, there should be no fear of death based on terror of an after-life.[13] Thus Hegel conceded that Epicurus' description of constant atomic flux served as a useful, though one-sided, counterbalance to what he contended was Aristotle's effort to deduce the finite from static *a priori* notions of essential causes. Taking these two one-sided views together only showed that a rational universe is to be understood in Hegel's own non-Aristotelian dialectical logic of the unfolding of the Idea.

As Marx covered the same set of questions as Hegel, he struggled to retain significance for free individual activity. Exploiting the element of chance in Epicurus' system interpreted as pure indeterminacy, Marx built on Epicurus' alleged "contempt for the positive sciences". He emphasized Epicurus' disdain of empirical research and even his reported denial of the disjunctive judgment.[14] Marx praised Epicurus for his escape from the science of the Understanding, while Hegel damned him for his adherence to it. Where Hegel saw in chance Epicurus' tendency to avoid the "notion", Marx saw it as struggling for room for the individuality of the human being—the atom of the soul. To be sure, Marx must conclude with Hegel that it is impossible to maintain the pure individuality of the atom, but Epicurus is to be praised over Democritus in stressing this element, and showing the contradiction with the universal. Marx even defended Epicurus' notion of the "swerve" of the moving ("declining") atoms as a result of their own pure individuality. Long regarded as a laughing stock, Epicurus permitted his atoms a "small" self-caused swerve from their prior path to avoid determinacy in his system. "The declination", Marx says, "represents the real soul of the atom, the concept of abstract individuality."[15]

Marx pursues the theme of freedom as opposed to necessity in its various dimensions—the role of time, repulsion of the atoms, the irregular path of meteors—and instead of finding conventional science in Epicurus, Marx concludes that he had expressed the contradiction between universals and singulars. This is his great accomplishment, Marx argues:

> For Democritus the atom means only *Stoicheion*, a material substrate. The distinction between the atom as *arche* and *stoicheion* as a principle and foundation, belongs to Epicurus... The contradiction between existence and essence, between matter and form, which is inherent in the concept of the atom, emerges in the individual atom itself once it is endowed with qualities. Through the quality the atom is alienated from its concept, but at the same time is perfected in its construction. It is from repulsion and the ensuing conglomerates of the qualified atoms that the world of appearance now emerges.[16]

Marx and Hegel also differ in their reading of the hedonism which is a natural consequence of Epicurean phenomenalism. In Hegel the stress is on the primacy of universal considerations in the determination of what Epicurus sees as the human aversion to pain and search for pleasure. Even within the finite individual soul, there is a need to construct some means by which each particular sort of pleasure or pain can be compared. The system of aggregation and comparison cannot itself be an individual matter, according to Hegel's reading of Epicurus. He comments how despite himself, Epicurus expected that training and reason would lead to preferences for "higher" pleasures rather than debauchery. Hegel concludes that Epicurus' abstemiousness in practice made him a Stoic, returning to the realm of moral reason.[17]

For Marx, matters are quite different. From the beginning the point of Epicurean philosophy was not knowledge for its own sake, but the satisfaction of the philosopher. Epicurean practice places a great subjective worth in reducing the negative elements, the pain, which results from fear of death and terror of the gods.[18] The purpose of reason is to contribute to the peace of mind, the *atraxy*, of the egoistic philosopher. Marx says:

His method of explaining aims only at the *atraxy of self-consciousness, not at knowledge of nature in and for itself*...
[Democritus] who considers the sensuous world as subjective semblance applies himself to empirical natural science and to positive knowledge, and represents the unrest of observation, experimenting, learning everywhere, ranging over the wide, wide world. The other [Epicurus], who considers the phenomenal world to be real, scorns empiricism; embodied in him are the serenity of thought satisfied in itself, the self-sufficiency that draws its knowledge *ex principio interno.*[19]

It is important to take notice of Marx's respect for hedonism as a form of individualism, especially in the light of his later denunciation of Bentham as the "leather tongued oracle of the bourgeoisie" in *Capital*. As he worked as a radical journalist this trend was to become stronger. Marx was being driven toward the bourgeoisie and to what he later would call the "bourgeois democratic" position. Marx's favourable comments on Bentham, his inclusion of Bentham as one of the radicals, continued up to the point when Marx himself became a materialist, communist theorist.

Degree in hand, Marx was faced with earning a living. Although his father had died in 1838, Marx was unable to claim his portion of the estate owing to his mother's objection. A university career was by now out of the question as a result of Marx's association with Bruno Bauer and the other radical Young Hegelians such as Moses Hess and Arnold Ruge. It was to this group that Marx turned to pursue a radical journalistic career. He arranged to contribute to Arnold Ruge's *Deutsche Jahrbücher* published in Dresden and the *Anekdota zur neuesten deutschen Philosophie und Publicistik* which Ruge published in Switzerland to avoid the censorship.

There were more radical plans afoot. In the summer of 1841 Marx returned to Bonn after a brief stay in Trier. He joined Bruno Bauer who had, for a time, managed to obtain a chair at the University of Bonn. There was some talk of the two of them involving Ludwig Feuerbach in their journalistic efforts. Feuerbach had by then made a name for himself as a religious critic. His *Essence of Christianity* (1841) capped the historical debunking of religion by showing God to be a projection of human virtues rather than a supreme being. The tone of this group may be seen from a letter to Arnold Ruge by one of the old Doctor's Club:[20]

> Dr. Marx, Dr. Bauer and L. Feuerbach are getting together to make up a theological–philosophical journal and when so, may all the angels gather around old God the Father and may he have mercy on himself, for these three are certain to throw him out of his heaven and chase with a legal suit to boot. Marx, for one, calls the Christian religion one of the most immoral, and he is, by the way, albeit a most despairing revolutionary, one of the cleverest heads I know.

In fact, Feuerbach kept his distance both from politics and from Marx[21] and the plan for a journal fell through, although Feuerbach did contribute to the *Anekdota*.

Following Bauer's dismissal from the University of Bonn for atheism, Marx reportedly collaborated anonymously with him in the writing of *The Trumpet of the Last Judgement on Hegel the Atheist and Antichrist*. McLellan describes this work as a parody of what an "arch pietist attack on Hegel" might be, showing that "he was really an atheist revolutionary".[22] As he moved to Cologne, in 1842, Marx began to slip away from the Young Hegelian fixation with religion as the sole dimension of radical attack on reaction. He started to write political articles regularly for the *Rheinische Zeitung* and eventually was its editor until it was suppressed in 1843.

The *Rheinische Zeitung*, and the articles that Marx wrote for the *Anekdota*, were more dangerous to the Prussian establishment than the more shocking atheism of the Young Hegelians. In his journalistic writings Marx was attacking the political institutions themselves as well as their religious rationale. Marx's new practicality is seen in his letter to Ruge. Referring to Feuerbach's *Preliminary Theses on the Reform of Philosophy* which appeared in the *Anekdota* in 1842, Marx wrote:

> Feuerbach's aphorisms seem to me incorrect only in one respect, that he refers too much to nature and too little to politics. That, however, is the only alliance by which present-day philosophy can become truth.[23]

The actual political goal of the philosophical sound and fury in

Berlin was to establish democratic political institutions and an unencumbered capitalist market economy. It was this feature of the left press that won the support of such wealthy lawyers as Georg Jung, and the various liberal Cologne businessmen on the board of the *Rheinische Zeitung*. There were, of course, editorial disputes that led Marx to have some uncharitable things to say about the courage and consistency of the German bourgeoisie. Yet despite the trauma of the militant atheism that the Young Hegelians caused to the proprieties of the older generation, their function was not to destroy the whole social fabric, and certainly not the institutions of the ascending bourgeoisie. Rather, it was to neutralize religious belief as a legitimization of the ambivalent Prussian state, just as French materialism and English scepticism had undermined the divine right of kings. As he gained greater political perspective himself, Marx was to point out that prolonged preoccupation with religion reflected the petty scale of German capitalist development, and the consequent pusillanimous character of the German petty bourgeois.[24]

Marx's brief career as a radical journalist for the *Rheinische Zeitung*, was an exercise in radical, bourgeois, democratic polemic. In the drumfire of articles appearing in that journal and in the *Anekdota zur neuesten deutschen Philosophie und Publicistik*, Marx hammered away at the ambivalent position of the Prussian authorities caught between their desire to produce a renewed enlightened monarchy on the one hand and their desperate fear of revolutionary democracy on the other.

Merely to list the demands that Marx advanced in these brilliant lawyer–like articles is to characterize his position: freedom of the press and abolition of censorship; freedom of conscience and an end to laws against expressions of thought; legal equality of all persons before the law and the abolition of feudal privilege in property rights; freedom of trade and an end to protective tariffs as restrictive of the development of trade and industry; open, public proceedings of legislative and executive branches of government; separation of church and state. These are no mere "tactical", immediate, demands that pave the way for a more profound social revolution as they appear in *The Communist Manifesto* in 1847. On the contrary, Marx is suspicious of communism at this stage, and at most advocates free discussion of alternative economic systems. Rather, he is advocating a capitalist democratic programme, entirely in keeping with the composition of the board of directors of the *Rheinische Zeitung*.

These are demands of eighteenth-century democracy such as Heinrich Marx might well have advanced in the Kantian spirit. Law is properly derived from reason, not the dead hand of precedent and custom. Rational and universal law was the methodology of Heinrich Marx's *Eingabe* against the Napoleonic discrimination against Jews, just as it was the basis for Karl Marx's strictures against Savigny's teaching in Berlin.[25] To accept the rule of custom is to agree to the feudal rights and irrationality of the *ancien régime*. Marx explains this view in another context:

> The customary rights of the aristocracy conflict by their content with form of universal law. They cannot be given the form of law because they are formations of lawlessness. The fact that their content is contrary to the form of law—universality and necessity—proves that they are *customary wrongs* and cannot be asserted in opposition to the law, but as such opposition they must be abolished and even punished if the occasion arises, for no one's action ceases to be wrongful because it is his custom... Customary right as a *separate domain* alongside legal right is therefore rational only where it exists *alongside* and in addition to law, where custom is the *anticipation* of a legal right.[26]

In this widely misinterpreted piece, Marx is defending the rights of peasants to collect fallen wood on enclosed forest lands. He does not justify his position out of opposition to private property, at least in the bourgeois sense of the term, nor because it is the peasants' customary right to make use of fallen wood; rather, he argues, perhaps somewhat tenuously, that the very nature of fallen wood makes it a common property resource, and hence there is no natural or universal law which makes it rationally the property of the forest owner:

> The gatherer of fallen wood only carries out a sentence already pronounced by the very nature of the property, for the owner possesses only the tree, but the tree no longer possesses the branches that have fallen from it.[27]

and:

There exist objects of property which, by their very nature, can never acquire the character of predetermined private property.[28]

The notion of rational law as identical with universal law is applied in a most telling fashion against repression and special privilege. In the "Comments on the Latest Prussian Censorship Instruction"[29] in the *Anekdota*, and in "Debates on Freedom of the Press"[30] in the *Rheinische Zeitung*, Marx turns the arguments for censorship against the censor. No doubt, he concedes, somebody must decide what is worthy of being put into print. This, however, is the task of an editor not a censor. In what way, Marx asks, is the judgment of the censor superior to the editor? Does he have a monopoly on wisdom granted by his policy or bureaucratic status? Is he an authority on all fields of knowledge, superior to the specialized journalist? If not, and if the same laws that apply to individual citizens also apply to the authorities, then the censor himself must be censored. Granted the major premise of the universality of law, Marx neatly reduces the notion of censorship to an infinite regress.

Marx is not opposed to a law of the press. If there were objective laws defining overt acts rather than intellectual tendencies, meaningful legal standards could be enforced by the courts. But the censorship instruction which required the censor to judge the intent of the work, was vague and not applicable in the same way to each idea. Its very vagueness, its requirement that an ad hoc judgment of intent be made by the police, made it contrary to law in Marx's sense. The new censorship instruction of the regenerated Prussia was touted as a liberalization of previous decrees. But in fact, Marx said, it has:

fallen victim to the *most frightful terrorism*, and is subjected to the *jurisdiction of suspicion*. Laws against *tendency*, laws giving no objective standards, are laws of terrorism... Laws which made their main criterion not actions as such, but the *frame of mind* of the doer, are nothing but *positive sanctions for lawlessness*... Only insofar as I *manifest* myself externally, do I enter the sphere of the legislator. Apart from *my actions*, I have no existence for the law, am no object for it... The law against a frame of mind is not a *law of the state* promulgated for its *citizens*, but the *law of one party against another party.* The law which punishes tendency abolishes the equality of the citizens before the law. It is a law which divides, not one which unites, and all laws which divide are reactionary. It is not a law, but a *privilege* . . . The *moral state* assumes its members to have the *frame of mind of the state*, even if they act in *opposition to an organ of the state*, against the *government*. But in a society in which *one* organ imagines itself the sole, exclusive possessor of state reason and state morality, in a government which opposes the people in principle and hence regards its *anti-state frame* of mind as the general, normal frame of mind . . . The very laws issued *by the government are the opposite of what they make into law.*[31]

In these essays Marx employs the same logical structure to justify his other demands ranging from free trade to freedom of religion. The whole essay leans heavily on the rights of the individual. There is no class structure of society, no dictatorship of the proletariat, no objective truth knowable by proletarians but incomprehensible to their class enemy. All this is yet to come.

Even while these articles in the *Rheinische Zeitung* constitute a ringing, cogent defence of individual freedom, they were filled with Hegelian verbiage as much as they expressed Kantian democratic concepts. Given his intellect, it as inevitable that Marx would attempt to escape from Hegel. For all its emphasis on impermanence and evolution the dialectic had its conservative side which Marx did not fail to notice. After all, through the myriad of interweaving events, the moments of the universal, a rational element was at work. It was therefore not an accident that Hegel's legal theory, *Philosophy of Right*, should come to essentially conservative conclusions. In the end it defended the Prussian attempt at a liberal monarchy as well as its feudal hangovers.

In Hegel's hands, the process of the Idea, the Notion, was not designed as either a predictive or a prescriptive device. Like any evolutionary theory—biological or otherwise—it could only be applied *ex post*. This was the sense behind Hegel's famous remark in the "Preface" to the *Philosophy of Right* to the effect that the "owl of Minerva" spread her wings only after "the shades of dusk have fallen". Hegel's remark was a sound warning about the limits of dialectical logic. The task of the speculative philosopher,

Hegel had argued, was not to advocate change but to rationalize it after it had taken place.[32] To Marx's revolutionary impatience, Hegel was simply rationalizing the present.

Marx's attempt to break with the Hegelian doctrine was the manuscript, *Critique of Hegel's "Philosophy of Right"*.[33] It was written in the Kreuznach home of his mother-in-law during the first half of 1843, just before his marriage to Jenny in June. The work was never published. By the time Marx wrote the introduction, he had moved to the humanist position, superseding the original manuscript.

The "Introduction"[34] was published in Paris in the *Deutsch-französische Jahrbücher* in 1844. In it, Marx speaks of the proletariat as the agent of total human emancipation through the elimination of private property. The *Critique* itself takes a narrower political tack within the system of private property and individual self-interest known in the Hegelian tradition as "civil society". Marx advances on two fronts in the *Critique*. (1) He argues from whthin the Hegelian system to show that the undemocratic Prussian state is irrational on Hegel's own standards. (2) He offers an empiricist critique of the Hegelian method. Marx's dual approach has given rise to some misunderstanding by commentators who mistake the internal critique of Hegel's conclusions for the whole argument. Thus they miss the individualist philosophy and politics that Marx was advancing as well.[35]

Part of the difficulty is that in this writing Marx was directly influenced by Ludwig Feuerbach's *Essence of Christianity* (1841) and *Preliminary Theses on the Reform of Philosophy* (1842).[36] His language is frequently Feuerbachian as well as Hegelian. Feuerbach was an inconsistent, confused thinker as well as a creative one. On the one hand as an iconoclastic student of Hegel, he was capable of writing as a dogmatic empiricist in the introduction to *The Essence of Christianity*. There he insisted on sense information as the sole source of knowledge, and in later works even went to extremes of crude (*"Mann ist was er isst"*) materialism. At the same time as he was pretending to empiricism, Feuerbach posited the existence of a non-observable human "species essence" whose essence was universal love. He depicted man in this fashion in the face of the facts of exploitation, inquisition and hate.

So there were two sides to Feuerbach. One led away from Hegel haltingly and crudely to empiricism; the other led back to the philosophy of essences that had its origins in Plato and its dynamic expression in Hegel. It was this first theme that Marx emphasized—with lapses—in his 1843 *Critique* of Hegel;[37] the second dominated the *Economic and Philosophic Manuscripts of 1844* where Feuerbach's influence is most usually recognized.[38]

In view of what has just been said and the raw state of the manuscript it is not always easy to see that Marx has really broken with the dialectic. Marx follows Feuerbach in insisting that the subject of a meaningful proposition is a singular term, and the predicate is the universal. Marx might say, "I observe that this apple is red", while Hegel might say, "Redness and fruitness have alienated themselves and congealed in the moment of what finite senses myopically call this apple". Following Feuerbach, Marx says that Hegel inverted the subject–predicate form of the sentence and made the subject the universal and the predicate the singular.

By extension of philosophy, Hegel moved from the primacy of the universal to assert the dominance of the state over the individual. Marx imagined that by insisting on the primacy of singular observations he had restored the real relationships and demonstrated the political primacy of the individual over the state. Marx argued for the social priorities of individualist considerations as a social fact, rather than a value judgment, and defended this ontological statement of being from the epistemology of knowing. Marx believed that a criticism of Hegel's speculative philosophy yielded the truth of the "essentially" democratic, individualistic nature of the state to be contrasted with the irrational Prussian regime.[39]

These issues all turn on the relation of what Hegel called "civil society" *vis-à-vis* the state. Civil society was the collection of individuals seeking their own egoistic welfare, maximizing their utility if we may lapse into economists' jargon. Civil society certainly included the competitive market. But Hegel obviously meant much more. He included in civil society non-market relationships of people scrabbling for themselves, each in conflict with others. In harmony with the German cameralist tradition, Hegel did not see the order of the hidden hand of competition in the economic sphere. There had to be a larger conscious purpose—even if only at the abstract level of philosophical reason—to provide the order in individual interactions. In practice this meant that individual interests were to be subordinate to the authority of the Prussian state.

In the *Critique of Hegel's "Philosophy of Right"* Marx's main concern as he settles accounts with Hegel for the first time, is to complete the democratic revolution in Germany. Marx properly points out that Hegel's *The Philosophy of Right* is "only a parenthesis to Hegel's *Logic*" in which speculative reason was alleged to be the source of scientific knowledge.[40] With uncharacteristic clarity, Hegel had said as much in his "Preface". There he proclaimed his intention to probe deeper into knowledge than the empiricial "half-philosophy that locates knowledge in an 'approximation to truth'"; at the same time he planned to resist the temptation to describe the "state as it ought to be". The task of Hegelian science—speculative reason—was to understand the concept of the state from which its actuality may be deduced:

> The great thing is to apprehend in the show of the temporal and transient the substance which is immanent and the eternal which is present. For since rationality (which is synonymous with the idea) enters upon external existence simultaneously with its actualization, it emerges with an infinite wealth of forms, shapes and appearance. Around its heart it throws a motley covering ... which the concept has first to penetrate before it can find the inward pulse and feel it still beating in the outward appearance.[41]

"The abstract actuality or the substantiality of the state", Hegel asserted, "consists in the fact that its end is the universal interest as such and the conservation therein of particular interests since the universal interest is the substance of these."[42] The state was not a globule of political legitimacy pushed in different directions by opposing interests.[43] It was an active purposive entity: "The state, therefore, knows what it wills and knows it in its universality, i.e., as something thought ... it acts with precise knowledge of existing conditions and circumstances...".[44]

Marx read the turgid presentation of what obviously was Prussia as an attempt, after the fact, to justify the regime and its feudal hangovers. But to say that Hegel simply apologized for the Prussian regime of his day as somehow real and rational is to underestimate both Hegel's thesis and Marx's critique. For, as Marx and the Young Hegelians had pointed out, there is a revolutionary potential in the Hegelian dialectic: its stress on the evol-

ution and impermanence of particular finite forms. Only the
process of the dialectic of Idea was absolute, while each of its
moments was transitory. Consequently Marx could fault Hegel
as an Hegelian for painting Prussia as the rational philosophical
order. In a "transformative criticism" he claimed that Hegel
actually exposed the unreason of the Prussian regime by holding
up the ideal of the state as universal interest and making it possible to show how the actual departs from the ideal. But the Hegelian doctrine of the state is more profound: It holds that the state
is the more general "universal" category than family or individual, and hence is logically prior to them. The state is the
"reality" which supersedes individual interests and desires of
"civil society". Society's welfare is that of the state and its holistic
will, rather than some summary index of individual utilities.

Marx is certainly right to argue that Hegel's identification
of the will of the state with the person of the monarch as in
Prussia contradicts its notion as a "universal will". It should,
he says, more properly be the elected legislature as the universal will which should confront individual "civil society". But
he makes a much more significant point when he attacks the
Hegelian notion of the higher legitimacy of the state over the
people. In this he is attacking Prussian*ism* and Hegel's philosophical defence of it.

Marx also contends against the Hegelian system of logic and
uses this criticism to argue for political democracy. Following
Kant and Feuerbach, Marx argued that Hegel could not justly
claim to have deduced anything at all about the nature of the
state by speculative reason. It is true, that Marx's later materialism amounts, in fact, to a return to Hegelian efforts to deduce
matters of fact *a priori*, substituting the apparently hard-headed
word "matter" for the fuzzier expression "Idea".[45] However, in
the *Critique* Marx did not regard himself as a materialist, if by
that is meant that empirically observed events are the workings
of some universal substance, material rather than spiritual.
Indeed he remarked, in a related context, that this position is
equivalent to the very speculative reason he was attacking:
"Each extreme is its other extreme. Abstract spiritualism is
abstract materialism; abstract materialism is the abstract spiritualism of matter."[46] In the *Critique* Marx was attacking the Platonic "realist" logical structure of Hegelian dialectics, its
attempt to deduce information about the objects of experience

from universal forms. In so doing, Marx was stating in a confused way the same fundamental nominalist propositions which were stated contemporaneously with more clarity in John Stuart Mill's *System of Logic*:[47] Information about reality proceeds from observations of factual particulars. Universals are shorthand names of classes of particulars, so that knowledge can only expand by reasoning "from particulars to particulars". Certainty was not available through this method. Such absolute truth that might appear to be available *a priori* to reason, deals only with essentially tautological transformations of the meaning of names, words or symbols, not with the reality to which these names sometimes are taken to refer.

To see this in Marx's words rather than Mill's, we turn to the place where Marx agreed with Hegel that the state is understood best as being similar to a living organism, rather than by appealing to the eighteenth-century mechanical analogy:

> When Hegel says, "this organism (namely the state, or the constitution of the state) is the development of the Idea to its differences, etc." he tells us absolutely nothing about the specific idea of the political constitution. The same thing can be said with equal truth about the animal organism as about the political organism. By what means then is the animal organism distinguished from the political? No difference results from this general determination; and an explanation which does not give the *differentia specifica* is no explanation. The sole interest here is that of recovering the Idea simply, the logical Idea in each element, be it that of the state or of nature; and the real subjects, as in this case the political constitution, become their mere names. Consequently there is only the appearance of a real understanding, while in fact these determinate things are not understood in their specific essence.[48]

Marx makes a similar point two pages later emphasizing the impossibility of deducing matters of fact:

> Hegel has advanced not a single step beyond the universal concept of the Idea or at most of organism in general (for strictly speaking it is a question only of this specific idea). Why then is he entitled to conclude that "this organism is the constitution of the state"? Why not "this organism of the solar

system"? The reason is that he later defined the various members of the state as the various powers. Now the statement that "various members of the state are the various powers" is an empirical truth and cannot be presented as a philosophical discovery.[49]

The problem which Marx faced was, what can be put in place of the Hegelian fantasy? John Stuart Mill had argued from the uncertainty inherent in induction to the utility of political freedom. Writing in a different world, but in exactly the same year as Marx's critique of Hegel, Mill's *A system of Logic* threw down the gauntlet to rationalism, and denied all *a priori* knowledge. Only through the inductive mode of reasoning, which expressed experience in a systematic way, was it possible to have any knowledge of the physical or social universe. For utilitarian reasons, society required freedom of the individual from coercion of thought. Mill's justification for individual freedoms derived from the uncertainty that must remain in any inductive argument. Even though Mill based induction on the general "uniformity of nature", induction of particular scientific laws had to be tentative and open to falsification. Mill argued that our very belief in scientific statements depended on freedom of criticism to subject them to constant test and potential falsification. Mill identified the cause of tyranny, religious persecution, and the like, in the deductive pretence at *a priori* truth. All these horrors followed from the infallibility assumed of the possessor of absolute knowledge. Mill went further. The majority—the people—could represent as terrible a tyranny as the old oligarchy.[50]

Marx's solution in the *Critique* was quite different, arguing for democratic forms from legitimacy rather than utility. Marx wanted to reverse Hegel's logical priority of the universal concept embodied in the state over the individual: transposing Hegel's active, purposive, teleological universals, Marx wanted to make the individual the active agent. Like Epicurean atoms they were to express their own will and capacity to "swerve" from their determinate paths. People were to be the active subjects, and the state their product:

> Hegel conceives of society, family, the artificial person in general, not as the realization of the actual empirical person, but as the *real* person which, however, had the moment of

personality in it only abstractly. Whence also comes his notion that it is not actual persons who come to be a state but the state which must first come to be the actual person. Instead of the state being brought forth, therefore, as the ultimate reality of the person, as the social reality of man, a single empirical man, an empirical person [Marx refers here to the monarch. M.W.] is brought forth as the ultimate actuality of the state. This inversion of subject into object and object into subject is a consequence of Hegel's wanting to write the biography of the abstract Substance, of the Idea, with human activity, etc., having consequently to appear as the activity and the result of something other than man; it is a consequence of Hegel's wanting to allow the essence of man to act for itself as an imaginary individual instead of acting in its actual, human existence, and it necessarily has as its result that an empirical existent is taken in an uncritical manner to be the real truth of the Idea, because it is not a question of bringing the truth to empirical existence, and thereupon the obvious is developed as a real moment of the Idea,[51]

No doubt Marx wanted to achieve social knowledge by direct inspection of reality, taken to be particular, individual human beings. But he also wanted to leap from this definition of the domain of his factual inquiry to a rational justification for democratic political institutions. Two intermediate steps were required: Marx would first have to inductively arrive at general propositions about the nature of human beings; he would secondly have to show that the democratic form of government was the optimal one for the features he had identified. In the *Critique* these two steps are elided. Marx thought that by understanding the "essential" nature of the relation of men to states he could show that democracy was the "essence" of a "true" state. Democracy would be made "actual" by philosophical criticism and political action. In criticizing Hegel, he says that "the universal appears everywhere as a determinate particular thing, while the individual nowhere arrives at his true universality",[52] as the essence of the democratic political state.

There is little explicit economics in the *Critique*, but what there is, is fully consistent with the view that legitimacy flows from the individual in "civil society" to state. The form of Marx's statement is his rebuttal of Hegel's defence of primogeniture. Marx specifically did not assault all private property; rather his argument was aimed against the *in*alienable ownership of landed property.[53] Hegel had viewed the property of the aristocratic "agricultural class" as the highest form of private property since it was immune to the pressures of the market and the money nexus. Entail and primogeniture were a mainstay of the Prussian order, dominated by Junker aristocrats against the growing power of the bourgeoisie. Marx summarizes his understanding, notably *not* attacking the "business class":

> Its [the agricultural class's] capital is independent of the uncertainty of business, the quest for profit, and any sort of fluctuation in possessions. From this aspect it is opposed by the business class as the one which is dependent on needs and concentrated on their satisfaction.
>
> This capital is independent of favor, whether from the executive or the mob.
>
> Finally, it is even fortified against its own willfulness, because those members of this class who are called to political life are not entitled, as other citizens are, either to dispose of their entire property at will, or to the assurance that it will pass to their children, whom they love equally, in similarly equal division.[54]

Only in the humanist stage in his intellectual development, does Marx attack private property in the ordinary bourgeois sense of the word for its *alienability*, its capacity to *separate* the individual from the social fabric. In the *Critique* Marx's complaint is not that there is not too much individualism in Germany, but too little. Civil society is not decried. Rather the difficulty is that the individual in civil society is artifically subordinated to Hegel's Prussian state, and the landed power that is its essence. Property of this feudal type, is "independent property", independent of the needs of the rest of society and even of the will of the property owner.

Not one to defend the profit motive, it is also clear that in the *Critique* Marx is not ready to attack it:

> Over against the crude stupidity of independent private property, the uncertainty of business is elegaic, the quest for profit solemn (dramatic), fluctuations in possessions a serious *fatum*

(tragic), dependence on the state's capital ethical. In short in all of the qualities the human heart pulses throughout the property, which is the dependence of man on man.[55]

True, this is an uneasy and shamefaced defence, couched in ironic metaphor; but there it is nonetheless. More important than the wording is the fact that the defence must be there as a direct consequence of Marx's line of argument.

The temptation is overwhelming in the light of Marx's later views to take ambiguous quotations aimed at feudal property forms and construe them as assults on alienable property as a form of special privilege.[56] For instance Marx says:

Where we find primogeniture in classical form, in the Germanic nations, we find also the constitution of private property. Private property is the general category, the general political bond. Even the general functions appear as the private property now of a corporation, now of an estate.

The different subdivisions of trade and industry are the private property of different corporations. Court dignities, jurisdiction, etc., are the private property of particular estates. The various provinces are the private property of individual princes, etc. The spirit is the private property of the clergy. My dutiful activity is the private property of another, as my rights are again a particular private property. Sovereignty, here nationality, is the private property of the emperor.

It has often been said that in the Middle Ages every form of right, of freedom, of social existence, appears as privilege, as an exception to the rule. In this context the empirical fact that all these privileges appeared in the form of private property could not be overlooked. What is the general cause of this coincidence? Private property is the specific mode of existence of privilege, of rights as exceptions.[57]

One might take the last sentence out of context and view it as a characterization of property in its bourgeois form as well. It is much more plausible in the light of what we have said in this chapter to regard such expressions in the same way as Proudhon's much more explicit "property is theft" turns out to be an attack on feudal privilege rather than bourgeois private property. Marx is at pains to defend "freedom, social existence" which appear as privileges under feudal system, but are rights under bourgeois civil society. He is not denouncing civil society for its freedoms, but showing how in previous societies these appeared as exceptions and the special property of a few.

Although his name is not mentioned, Marx wrestles with Proudhon's problem of how to create a truly democratic society and at this stage comes to related but less extreme conclusions. Individual liberty in its most complete form might oppose even the most responsive of representative governments, but in economic affairs it required individual interest, private property, and exchange. To be sure Proudhon was obsessed with economic equality, but despite his arresting epigram, neither he nor Marx at this point saw it as arising out of the elimination of property or the market. We can see this Proudhon-like strain of thought in the following juxtaposition Marx makes of the alternatives for a democratic state and the institutions of civil society:

Either: Separation of political state and civil society takes place, in which case *all* cannot *individually* share in the legislative power. The political state is a phenomenon *separated* from civil society. On the one hand, civil society would abandon itself if all were legislators; on the other, the political state, which confronts civil society, can bear it only in a form appropriate to the *scale* of the political state through *delegates* that is the *expression* of their separation and of their merely dualistic unity.

Or, conversely: Civil society is *actual* political society. In this case, it is nonsense to raise a demand which has arisen only from the notion of the political state as a phenomenon separated from civil society, which has arisen only from the *theological* notion of the political state. In this situation the significance of the *legislative power* as a *representative* power completely disappears. The legislative power is representation here in the sense in which *every* function is representative—in the sense in which, e.g., the shoemaker, insofar as he satisfies a social need, is my representative, in which every particular social activity as a species-activity merely represents the species, i.e., an attribute of my own nature, and in which every person is the representative of every other. He is here representative not because of

something else which he represents but because of what he *is*
and *does.*[58]

If Marx is opposed to civil society, exhange and the division of
labour—if he sees in it an alienation, dehumanization of man—it
certainly does not appear in the foregoing. Rather, this passage is
reflective of what he later would call Proudhon's "petty bourgeois" anarchism; Marx contemplates a situation where "civil
society is actual political society" without the mediation of a
state.

Once again Marx makes the charge that Hegel has inverted
the relationship which ought to flow from particular to general,
from individual ownership of alienable property to a democratic
state consistent with civil society. Hegel made landed property
own man in the aristocratic state: the laws of land tenure pre-
scribe human action; men are artificially separated from each
other by the arbitrary restrictions placed on the market nexus.
Later, in the second period of his work, Marx was to speak of the
alienation due to property relations in seemingly similar terms;
but there the alienation is of men from the bonds of species love
that tie them to Man, rather than to other individuals; moreover,
the property relations that Marx decried in the second stage in
the *Paris Manuscripts*, are precisely the ones upon which he relies
in the *Critique* to bring men together in civil society based upon
self-love rather than love of species. The Marx of the *Critique* did
not share Hegel's terror of the anarchy he saw inherent in the
market response to individual desire. Although he had only a
general notion of its coordinative role, the logic of Marx's position in the *Critique* drove him toward the sort of society that was
based on individual self-interest rather than a collective or statist
regime.

Despite his insights, Marx's philosophy and hence his social
theory is less than adequate. He used the nominalist germ of
empiricist criticism against Hegel, but could not use the empirical method constructively himself. Had he done so, he would
have realized that in inverted form or not, he, as much as Hegel,
was attempting to deduce facts from *a priori* principles; he would
have had to realize that he was attempting to deduce normative
judgments about political systems and their legitimacy from
positive statements about the source of human knowledge.
Perhaps with the same diffidence as Mill, Marx would have con-

tinued to accept the morality of civil society even though it was not pleasant to see people so intent on "getting on". Marx too would have been as much concerned with safeguarding the dissident individual even in democratic societies, rather than searching for the ultimate rationality of rule by the people.

A year after the *Critique*, Marx turned to the transcendental trend in Feuerbach which treated Man as an abstract universal. He was thus led to the position of the 1844 *Paris Manuscripts*. Marx's acceptance of the humanist Christian aspect of Ludwig Feuerbach was accompanied by expression of antipathy to Jews, expressed in ever more vituperative anti-semitic language. But in early 1843 this had not yet occurred. He had not yet moved to Jenny's mother's house in Kreuznach in May and married in June. He still operated within his earlier, individualistic framework. Marx wrote to Ruge that he had "fallen head over heels in love" with Jenny and tells of his struggles with both his own Jewish family and her Christian relatives:

> I can assure you, without the slightest romanticism, that I am head over heels in love, and indeed in the most serious way. I have been engaged for more than seven years, and for my sake my fiancée has fought the most valiant battles, which almost undermined her health, partly against her pietistic aristocratic relatives, for whom "the Lord in heaven" and the "lord in Berlin" are equally objects of religious cult, and partly against my own family, in which some priests and other enemies of mine have ensconced themselves.[59]

Yet Marx is still willing to make an effort on behalf of the Jewish community, even though he explains it in terms of his opposition to the Christian state:

> I have just been visited by the chief of the Jewish community here who has asked me for a petition for the Jews to the Provincial Assembly, and I am willing to do it. However much I dislike the Jewish faith, Bauer's view seems to me too abstract. The thing is to make as many breaches as possible in the Christian state and to smuggle in as much as we can of what is rational. At least, it must be attempted—and the embitterment grows with every petition that is rejected with protestations.[60]

Of course Marx never abandoned his advocacy of the civil emancipation of the Jews, even in his most anti-semitic diatribes. But
the interesting thing is that in 1843 he still responded to the
Jewish community, albeit shamefacedly.

5 *Humanismus* and *jüdischer Selbsthass:* Love of Man and Hate of Self

The Kreuznach period in Marx's life is named for the interval from May to October 1843 which he spent in the home of his mother-in-law. It was in Kreuznach that he composed the *Critique of Hegel's "Philosophy of Right"*, largely before his marriage to Jenny Westphalen in June, and where he drafted *On the Jewish Question* on the honeymoon and after his return with his bride. This is the period in which Marx makes the transition from the individualist empiricism that characterized his reading of Feuerbach, reflected in the *Critique of Hegel's "Philosophy of Right"*, to the internalization of the humanistic aspect of Feuerbach which was to find its fullest expression a year later in Paris in the *Economic and Philosophic Manuscripts of 1844*. This is also the period in which the latent "Jewish self-hate" erupts in pustulant form as Marx accepted Feuerbach's slander of the Jews, but raised it to a higher pitch.[1]

Marx was now married to his Christian childhood sweetheart. His mother did not attend the wedding of her eldest son, having given written permission for the marriage. Never was she to be close to Karl again, although there was an outpouring of warmth towards Jenny when she returned to Trier with the first grandchild.[2] Ostensibly Marx now was accepted in the inner core of the Westphalen family, despite the opposition of the more distant relatives to this radical of Jewish origins. Yet it is unlikely that it was possible to forget those origins, in the intimacy of his own family, indeed even in the love of Jenny. To the German eye, newly enamoured of "scientific" racial concept, Karl Marx looked as Jewish as did his father Heinrich. An inkling of the degree to which this permeated his life may be gained from the remark of his daughter, Eleanor, who herself harked back to her Jewish origin. She noted that Karl Marx always carried a picture of his father:

The face seemed very beautiful to me. The eyes and the forehead were like those of his son, but the lower part of his face around the mouth and chin were more tender. The whole was of a markedly Jewish type, though handsomely Jewish.[3]

Similar remarks by his friends and associates abound. Poliakov mentions a few in his book on anti-semitism such as the physical description of Dr Lafargue which found its way into Franz Mehring's orthodox, adulatory biography:

In fact he was very powerful, his height exceeded the average, the shoulders were broad, the breast well developed, the limbs well proportioned, although the trunk [literally, "spine" M.W.] was somewhat too long in relation to the legs, as one finds frequently in the Jewish race.[4]

Jenny loved Karl. She agreed with every word he said. She asked him to suggest good books for her, only not too difficult. She sat on his committees and interminable meetings. Eventually she endured his extramarital affair and illegitimate child. But he was for her the swarthy, the alien, the Moor—the man who excited her. In the tender letter written in the spring before their marriage she says in ending: "Parting is painful. It pains the heart. Good-bye, my one and only beloved, black sweet, little hubby... Ah! you knavish face...".[5]

The same theme occurs again and again. From friend and enemy—erstwhile friend and erstwhile enemy—Karl Marx is told that he is a dark-skinned, thickset, Jew. Thus, after Marx's collaboration with Ruge in the *Deutsch-französische Jahrbücher* collapsed in the spring of 1844, his one-time friend wrote to his mother that Marx was "a most extraordinary fellow and an insolent Jew". "Marx", says Ruge in a letter to Julius Froebel, "professes communism, but he is the true believer in egoism".[6] "Egoism", as we shall see is the catchword for the hateful Jewish mercantile spirit as opposed to Christian humanism. And yet,

Marx's repression of his Jewishness is so great that he never mentions his origins. Never! What did he endure? Whom did he really mean when many years later he called Lassalle a "Mr Itzig" and a "nigger"? Why did he feel compelled to say of Lassalle: "the shape of his head and his hair show that he is descended from the Negroes who joined Moses' flock at the time of the exodus from Egypt"?[7]

Karl and Jenny Marx returned from their honeymoon to Kreuznach where Karl set to work earning his living as a journalist. The *Rheinische Zeitung* had been suppressed earlier in the year for its radical views, so Marx and Ruge planned to publish the *Deutsch-französische Jahrbücher* in Paris. Marx himself left for Paris with Jenny in the autumn of 1843. Marx's efforts for the single issue of that journal were two essays. *On the Jewish Question*, which had been drafted before his departure, shows his conversion to Feuerbach's humanism on one hand, and his violent statement of revulsion against Jewishness on the other. His conversion to communism and reliance on the proletariat for humanization of man is expressed in the "Introduction" to the *Critique of Hegel's "Philosophy of Right"*—where the philosophic and religious foundations for the 1844 *Manuscripts* are put in place.

Ludwig Feuerbach's humanist religious philosophy and his inversion of Hegelian philosophy came as a revelation to Marx. It offered him a fundamental critique of the religious foundations of the old regime. Moreover the communist conclusions that Marx drew from Feuerbach, served to rationalize the growing consensus among the frustrated young radicals that formal political liberty and legal equality meant neither fraternity nor effective rule by the people.

Marx's communist humanism served another function: it offered a release from civil society and thus from Jewish self-contempt. Civil society eliminated the special claims of the aristocracy from the corrosive forces of the market. Yet civil society was based on alienable private property, commerce, trade, profits. Like it or not, in the *Critique* he had come back full circle not only to his father's ideas in philosophy but also to his father's life. Heinrich Marx was a man of civil society. His lawyer's trade was part of the commercial and property transactions arising from the Rhine valley wine trade. To accept civil society was also to accept what Marx saw as the practical reality of Jewish life. To flee from his background, Marx had to find shelter in a doctrine opposed to economic individualism.

Forty-five years later, Engels recalled the impact of Feuerbach's work:

> Then came Feuerbach's *Essence of Christianity*. With one blow it
> pulverized the contradiction, in that without circumlocutions
> it placed materialism on the throne again. Nature exists in-
> dependently of all philosophy. It is the foundation upon which
> we human beings ourselves products of nature have grown up.
> Nothing exists outside nature and man, [Note the dualism for
> later reference. M.W.] and the higher beings our religious fan-
> tasies have created are only the fantastic reflection of our own
> essence.
>
> The spell was broken. The "system" was exploded and cast
> aside. And the contradiction, shown to exist only in our im-
> agination, was dissolved. One must himself have experienced
> the liberating effect of this book to get an idea of it. Enthusiasm
> was general; we all became at once Feuerbachians.[8]

"Feuerbach", Marx said in the *Paris Manuscripts*, "is the only
person who had made real discoveries in this field." Feuerbach's
"vanquishing of the old philosophy" was an achievement accomplished with "unassuming simplicity".[9] So complete and sudden
was this revolution in Marx's thought that his "Introduction" to
A Contribution to the Critique of Hegel's "Philosophy of Right"
published in the *Deutsch-französische Jahrbücher* in 1844, is incompatible with the *Critique* itself. The "Introduction", the *Paris
Manuscripts*, *On the Jewish Question* and *On James Mill* are the defining works of this second, humanistic period of assimilation and
extension of Feuerbach.[10]

Feuerbach's thesis was that Idea, expressed either in terms of
religious belief in God, or Hegel's philosophy of Spirit, was a
human activity which reflected the nature of Man rather than the
superhuman entities it purported to describe. The Hegelian
notion of a disembodied Spirit, Feuerbach argued, was absurd on
its face. It was not abstract Reason that went through the processes of alienation and supersession of estrangement. Human
thought alienated itself from itself, projecting its own character
on to another alien being, never realizing that the Deity was
made in the human image by human beings themselves. Instead
of worshipping God, or Hegel's Absolute Idea, it was Man who

should be worshipped. If God was purportedly all-good, wise, universally loving, all-powerful, it was because these described the nature of Man in his essence.

Man is a "species being" (*Gattungswesen*) according to Feuerbach, in that his essence (*Wesen*) is given by the attribute of universal love for, and identification with, his own species. However, this attribute of universal love is taken as an attribute of God. God is an alienation of the essence of Man from himself. Through religion, man sees himself as a poor, depraved, brutish creature, needful of guidance, discipline by pastor and monarch, if he ever is to achieve salvation for his sins. Overcoming religion, or at least returning it to the worship of Man, would open the door to the realization of human species love which is humanity in its essence. Politically, Feuerbach remarked, humanism amounts to republicanism; as we shall see Marx was to make it into communism.

As we observed previously, there are both empirical and metaphysical aspects to Feuerbach's position. The notion that religion is a human product is certainly in keeping with empirically based cultural anthropology. Indeed, Feuerbach's *Essence of Christianity* may be viewed as a precursor of the anthropological view that religion is a projection of human hopes, wishes and fears. Insofar as a society's god is an idealized projection of itself, one can certainly learn a great deal about a culture through study of its religious mythology.

Feuerbach's metaphysical aspect appears when he departs from viewing the attributes associated with God as a reflection of a social belief system, and translates them into the innate features of the human species essence. It is this leap which fails to take into account that idealized ethical systems and practical activities often do not match; Marx was to point to the latter as shaping human beings when he was ready to rupture with Feuerbach. Which is the true human essence? Is it Man who is good, loving, kind, selfless? Or is it Man who is egoistical, nasty and brutish? Feuerbach and Marx in the stage we are now traversing, viewed the former as the essential man and regarded his practical life as a distortion of his essence.

The whole notion of an essential character of Man ignores the fact that human cultures have evolved markedly different men, and correspondingly different gods. Thus, in identifying God with the Protestant Christian vision of him as a means of discovering the nature of Man, Feuerbach and Marx reveal their ethnocentric bias as well as their metaphysical philosophy. Feuerbach views German Protestant Christianity as the ultimate outcome of the evolution of religious thought. Christianity, he says, reveals the human essence as clearly as any religion can. All that is required is the final *coup de grâce* to be administered by himself, to reveal the pure human essence hidden in Christian theistic concepts of universal love. Love is

> the tie, the principle of mediation between the perfect and the imperfect, the sinless and the sinful, the universal and the individual, the law and the heart, the divine and the human. Love is God himself and outside it there is no God. Love makes man God and God man ... love is the true unity of God and man, of spirit and nature.[11]

Kamenka quotes the key passage from Feuerbach in which he proclaims his Protestant ethnocentrism:

> The God who is man, the human God—i.e., Christ—he alone is the God of Protestantism. Protestantism is no longer interested in the question that concerns Catholicism, the question what is God in himself. Protestantism therefore no longer has a speculative or contemplative tendency like that of Catholicism; it is no longer theology but essentially only Christology, i.e., religious anthropology.

Kamenka goes on to comment that:

> It is with the God of the Christians, and especially with God as Luther saw him, that Feuerbach is concerned in the *Essence of Christianity*. The God of Christianity, Feuerbach argues, is essentially but universally man—man stripped of his individual limitations, man as a species-being, man as an expression of the essentially human.[12]

And what of Jews and Judaism? "The Israelitish religion", Feuerbach tells us, "is the religion of the most narrow hearted egoism."[13] The origin of Jewish egoism, Feuerbach makes clear, is not the Jews' religion; rather the origin of the religion is Jewish egoism. Judaism is a predecessor of Christianity and Feuerbach is aware of the transitional books of the Old Testament in the development of Christian viewpoints out of the Jewish tradition.[14] Stubbornly the Jews refused to be elevated. As Bauer puts it, they refused to be historical. The persistence of Judaism in the face of the persecution and the Diaspora—not to speak of revelation— only underlines Feuerbach's application of his main thesis: the religion of the Jews is a projection of their essential nature. Judaism is egoistical, narrow-hearted, gluttonous, because this is the nature of Jews:

> Man first unconsciously and involuntarily creates God in his own image and after this God consciously and voluntarily creates man in his own image. This is especially confirmed by the development of the Israelitish religion. Hence the position of the theological one-sidedness, that the revelation of God holds an even pace with the development of the human race. Naturally; for the revelation of God is nothing else than the revelation, the self-unfolding of human nature. The supernaturalistic egoism of the Jews did not proceed from the Creator, but conversely, the latter from the former; in the creation the Israelite justified his egoism at the bar of his reason.[15]

Feuerbach's commentary on the Jewish religion is therefore more than a critique of a theology; it is a vilification of the Jewish people itself. In his chapter on "The Significance of the Creation in Judaism"[16] Feuerbach argues that Genesis makes Nature the "vassal" of Man's "selfish interest, of his practical egoism". Man is to conquer Nature, which the Old Testament myth rationalizes as having been created for Man. Man is not a part of Nature, nor is he to passively behold it as a thing of beauty. Nature is to be a hostage to the human will.[17] Feuerbach sees a totemic worship of Nature in the idolatry of the gentiles, and views the Jewish recoil from graven images at God's command as utilitarianism, egoism rather than a revulsion at the blasphemous hubris of man. *A fortiori*, Jewish egoism is exemplified by the concept of an exclusive divine compact with Israel, which sets them above other nations.

Feuerbach is perfectly clear that his account is of an atavistic, tribal myth. But in his inability to see the myth in an historical and culturally relativistic way, he uses Genesis to characterize the Jews of nineteenth-century Germany; their essential, inherent, egoistic Jewish nature persisted over millennia says Feuerbach. In these passages Feuerbach is not debating the virtue or failings of the Jewish religion, but is giving vent to the anti-semitic prejudices which pullulated in the German humanism of his time. Jews are inherently greedy, gluttonous, egoistic, intolerant, selfish people, as opposed to the humanistic Hellenistic culture which was the model for the affected, romantic elite of the last century:[18]

The Greeks looked at Nature with the theoretic sense; they heard heavenly music in the harmonious course of the stars; they saw Nature rise from the foam of the all-producing ocean as Venus Anadyomene. The Israelites, on the contrary, opened to Nature only the gastric sense; their taste for Nature lay only in the palate; their consciousness of God in eating manna. The Greek addicted himself to polite studies, to the fine arts, to philosophy; the Israelite did not rise above the alimentary view of theology. "At even ye shall eat flesh, and in the morning ye shall be filled with bread; and ye shall know that I am the Lord your God." "And Jacob vowed a vow, saying, If God will be with me, and will keep me in this way that I go, and will give me bread to eat and raiment to put on, so that I come again to my father's house in peace, then shall the Lord be my God." Eating is the most solemn act of the initiation of the Jewish religion. In eating, the Israelite celebrates and renews the act of creation; in eating, man declares Nature to be an insignificant object. When the seventy elders ascended the mountain with Moses, "they saw God; and when they had seen God, they ate and drank." Thus with them what the sight of the Supreme Being heightened was the appetite for food.

The Jews have maintained their peculiarity to this day. Their principle, their God, is the most practical principle in the world,—namely, egoism; and moreover egoism in the form of religion. Egoism is the God who will not let his servants come to shame. Egoism is essentially monotheistic, for it has only one, only self, as its end. Egoism strengthens cohesion, concentrates man on himself, gives him a consistent principle of life; but it makes him theoretically narrow, because indifferent to all which does not relate to the well-being of self. Hence science, like art, arises only out of polytheism, for polytheism is the frank, open, unenvying sense of all that is beautiful and good without distinction, the sense of the world, of the universe.

This passage has a darker side than Feuerbach's lack of comprehension of the concern for food in Jacob's subsistence pastoral economy. Poliakov's work on anti-semitism explores the relation between the sterotypic association of Jews with gluttony, and the tales of cannibalism and child-eating that fill the anti-semitic horror stories.[19] It appears that Feuerbach was a close friend of one George Friedrich Daumer, whose book *Die Geheimnisse des christlichen Alterthums* explained that:

Easter was "the solemn festival when the Semites sacrificed children". But the Hebrews purified their cult in the most distant time, and introduced offerings of animals. However, "a sect which did not cease to perpetuate the old cannibalistic horrors" continued to exist in their midst. Jesus was the leader of this clandestine sect.[20]

Poliakov continues:

Needless to say, although Daumer distinguished between the enlightened Jews, whose prototype was Judas, and cannibal Jews, whose prototype was Jesus, he found followers who hastened to set lucubration back on its feet. There was in the first place, his pupil Friedrich Wilhelm Ghillany... At Daumer's instigation, it seems, he left his post as pastor and also set out to expose the Jews' cannibalism... In his opinion, evidence of this "molochism" was provided not only by the ritual murder of Jesus ... the ritual murders the Jews did not cease to commit ... in the Germany of his day.[21]

Completing the ring, Poliakov calls attention to Feuerbach's citation of T. Eisenmenger's *Unmasked Judaism (Entdecktes Judenthum)* in *The Essence of Christianity*[22] with the comment that Daumer had regarded Eisenmenger as one of his major sources. Feuerbach paraded himself as very scientific, indeed materialistic; but the irrational anti-semitic stain seeps out of the pages of his lofty philosophy just as it did in Hegel before him and in Marx afterwards. While staying in Kreuznach with his new bride in the fall of

1843, Marx drafted two lengthy review essays which have come to be called *On the Jewish Question*. These articles, thoroughly in the spirit of Feuerbach, consist of critical discussions of Bruno Bauer's *Die Judenfrage* and *Die Fähigkeit der heutigen Juden und Christen frei zu werden*. Marx and Jenny took the manuscripts with them to exile in Paris, where they were published in the *Deutsch-französische Jahrbücher* in 1844. *On the Jewish Question* constitutes the transition from the *Critique of Hegel's "Philosophy of Right"* to the *Economic and Philosophic Manuscripts* in more than a chronological sense. It makes clear why Marx could not rest content with the economic aspects of civil society: the pursuit of self-interest was identified with Jewishness—egoism. Marx applied his *jüdischer Selbsthass* to a market oriented society, heaping all the anti-semitic adjectives of abuse on an economic order run by the hand of competition. Marx takes it without question that market relations are venal, disgusting, degrading, and therefore Jewish.

Although he did not protest, Marx may have understood Jew-baiting by the authorities and by the mob as a feature of German reaction; but he nevertheless accepted their premises. He was in favour of civil emancipation of the Jews. But Marx went on to propose to emancipate the Jews from themselves. He wanted to eradicate Jewishness in practical as well as religious aspects. Marx was repelled by his forebears, and the most he could say in their defence is that Christian Germany is a vast hypocrisy, no better than the Jewry it despises.

The first of Marx's essays opens with a *précis* of Bauer's position: emancipation is impossible as long as the "state is Christian and the Jew is Jewish, the one is as incapable of granting emancipation as the other is of receiving it". For recognition of their rights to exist as Jews, "in wanting to be emancipated from the Christian state, the Jew is demanding that the Christian state should give up its *religious* prejudice. Does he, the Jew give up *his* religious prejudice?" On the contrary, says Bauer, since the Jew does not identify with the Christian state: "The Jew ... can behave towards the state only in a Jewish way, that is by treating it as something alien to him ... by putting his trust in a future which has nothing in common with the future of mankind in general, and by seeing himself as a member of the Jewish people, and the Jewish people as the chosen people". Bauer concludes that emancipation is only possible when Jews cease to be Jews and Christians cease to be Christians. As Marx says, Bauer "analyzes the *religious* opposition between Judaism and Christianity", and asks: How is *religious* opposition made impossible? Bauer's answer is: "By abolishing *religion*".

Marx denounces Bauer's tacit acceptance of a Germany where the state "recognizes Christianity as its basis". The political state and religious practice are logically separable: Marx points to the separation of church and state in the United States as a prime example. Neither Christianity nor Judaism needs to be abolished as religions for democratic political emancipation to be achieved. "It is possible", Marx says, "for the *state* to have emancipated itself from religion, even if the *overwhelming majority* is still religious."[23] Religion is simply a private matter of civil society.

So far, so good. Marx's defence of the separation of church and state, and its corollary of the emancipation of Jews from legal disabilities, is consistent with the democratic individualism he espoused in the *Critique of Hegel's "Philosophy of Right"*: The rational state such as the United States of North America "asserts its universality" as the sovereign power over individuals considered as equal citizens in civil society rather than as members of groups differentiated by religion or "birth, social rank, education, occupation". The state "proclaims, without regard to these distinctions, that every member of the nation is an equal participant in national sovereignty".[24]

Now Marx asks the question which was conspicuously missing in the *Critique of Hegel's "Philosophy of Right"*: Is political equality enough? No. Political freedom "is not the final form" of "real practical emancipation". In practice, man is not freed from religion by the separation of church and state, as in America. On the contrary, in America religion is practised more fervently, Marx says, because of—not in spite of—the religious freedom provided. Instead of achieving his essence as a species being, Man is still alienated from humanity:

> Man emancipates himself *politically* from religion by banishing it from the sphere of public law to that of private law. Religion is no longer the spirit of the state, in which man behaves— although in a limited way, in a particular form, and in a particular sphere—as a species-being in community with other men. Religion has become the spirit of *civil society*, of the sphere of egoism, of *bellum omnium contra omnes*. It is no longer the essence of *community*, but the essence of *difference*. It has become

the expression of man's *separation* from his *community*, from himself and from other *men*—as it was originally... But one should be under no illusion about the limits of political emancipation. The division of the human being into a *public man* and a *private man*, the *displacement of* religion from the state into civil society, this is not a stage of political emancipation, but its *completion*; this emancipation therefore neither abolishes the *real* religiousness of man, nor strives to do so.

Civil society maintains the alienation of man, from his species. The democratic state in civil society makes a pretence at being man's species life but this is:

> *opposed* to his material life. All the preconditions of this egoistic life continue to exist in *civil society outside* the sphere of the state, but as qualities of civil society. Where the political state has attained its true development, man—not only in thought, in consciousness, but in *reality*, in *life*—leads a two fold life, a heavenly and an earthly life: life in the *political community* in which he considers himself a *communal being*, and life in civil society, in which he acts as a *private individual*, regards other men as a means, degrades himself into a means, and becomes the plaything of alien powers.[25]

This is as it had to be, Marx believes. The actual political state in civil society is inevitably consistent with its individualism and egoism. After all, Hegel was right to see that the secular, democratic state and the economic and social hedonism of civil society mutually imply one another. Marx comments that the result is a society of new distinctions and divisions:

> The state proclaims ... that every member of the nation is an *equal* participant in national sovereignty... Nevertheless, the state allows private property, education, occupation to *act* in *their* way... Far from abolishing these *real* distinctions, the state only exists on the presupposition of their existence.[26]

Marx then goes on to remark that the attempt to identify the state with religion by Hegel in his *Philosophy of Right* was designed to preserve the universality of the state in the face of economic realities. Nevertheless, the economic rule of civil society is just as egoistic as Hegel said it was. Marx is driven to find a way to organize society, both in its practical and political aspect, according to some collective, universal, principle that will supersede the hedonism of civil society and the state it organizes. This is not to be rule either by Hegel's God or his Idea, but rule by Man as a species being. Marx wants rule by Man, but not rule by men.

Ultimately, Hegel, Feuerbach and Marx are grappling with the contradictory nature of the Kantian ethic they inherited: the categorical imperative is an individualistic and universal morality; it depends on the common moral experience of every person. Yet, as much as it served as a criticism of the privileged power of the old aristocracy, its injunction never to use others as means is at variance with the individualistic calculations of capitalist society. How is the rule never to use others as means to be reconciled with division of labour when men literally have to use others? Marx could not accept Adam Smith's solution that the social welfare of civil society is maximized by the hidden hand of competition which directs the individual to an end which is socially moral despite his egoistic intention. At this stage, Marx's presupposition was that morality consisted precisely in the intentions of the participants. The alternative which Marx hoped to achieve through the abolition of private property was nothing less than labour *for* the social good, freely cooperating men, the elimination of the market, and perhaps the elimination of division of labour, although this last is never quite unequivocal.

Economists might shake their heads sadly at this point, and ask how a society based on good intentions would be different from Smith's competitive model in terms of the allocation of resources and the satisfactions provided to its members. The point is that Marx was not concerned with the operationalism of his results, but with their effect on man in the ethical sense in which he regards himself as a human being among others of his species. If he does not identify his *purpose* with those of mankind, he is not human in the Feuerbachian sense that species-love be the essence of humanity, visible through its projection in religion.

What religion? For Marx as much as Feuerbach, the presupposed outcome of human religion is Christianity:

> The state which is still theological, which still officially professes Christianity as its creed, which still does not dare to proclaim itself *as a state*, has, in its *reality* as a state, not yet

succeeded in expressing the *human* basis—of which Christianity is the high-flown expression—in a *secular, human* form. The so-called Christian state is simply nothing more than a *non-state*, since it is not Christianity as a religion, but only the *human background* of the Christian religion which can find its expression in actual human creations.[27]

Marx concludes that the actual state and civil society upon which it is based is a vast hypocrisy. In practice civil society is Jewish, at variance with the human–Christian virtues it preaches. Despite this atheism, Marx wanted to apply the Christian doctrine of universal love to the world of labour, and achieve the Kingdom of God on earth.

The perfectly democratic state embodied in the French Rights of Man remains inhuman since it is based on civil society, on protection of individuals from the actions of others, on the separation of man from his species:

> Political emancipation is the reduction of man, on the one hand, to a member of civil society, to an *egoistic, independent* individual, and, on the other to a *citizen*, juridical person.
>
> Only when the real, individual man re-absorbs in himself the abstract citizen, and as an individual human being has become a *species-being* in his everyday life, in his particular work, and in his particular situation, only when man has recognized and organized his *"forces propres"* as *social* forces, and consequently no longer separates social power from himself in the shape of political power, only then will human emancipation have been accomplished.[28]

But what of the Jew who is not Christian, either in religious profession or in worldly practice? Marx is for granting political emancipation. That seems to go without saying. But what is the "human" significance of Jews and Jewishness? This is the subject of the second of the two articles on Bauer.

According to Marx, Bauer contended that the Jew must emancipate himself: first by relinquishing his separateness from the rest of society by rejecting his Jewish religion; and then, together with Christians, by renouncing religion altogether. In contrast to Bauer, Marx held that the political aspect of emancipation was compatible with Jewish religious identity. Civil rights in civil

society left all religion a private affair. Human emancipation is
another matter. For Marx Judaism is incompatible with human
emancipation. Marx explains what he understands as Judaism:

> Let us consider the actual, worldly Jew, not the *Sabbath Jew*, as
> Bauer does, but the *everyday Jew*.
>   Let us not look for the secret of the Jew in his religion, but let
> us look for the secret of his religion in the real Jew.
>   What is the secular basis of Judaism? *Practical* need, *self-
> interest*.
>   What is the worldly religion of the Jew? *Huckstering*. What is
> his worldly God? *Money*.
>   Very well then! Emancipation from *huckstering* and *money*,
> consequently from practical, real Judaism, would be the self-
> emancipation of our time.[29]

What can Marx mean by this outburst? Is it that all Jews are
hucksters? Or that all hucksters are Jews? He denies both of these
propositions in a way which is central to his argument. It is certainly possible for a Jew—or at least a person of Jewish descent—
not to be a huckster.

> An organization of society which would abolish the precon-
> ditions for huckstering, and therefore the possibility of huck-
> stering would make the Jew impossible. His religious
> consciousness would be dissipated like a thin haze in the real,
> vital air of society.

In fact, it is not necessary to wait for the transformation of society
for the individual Jew to free himself from Jewishness. Marx has
to leave an escape route for himself as we can see by continuing
the previous passage:

> On the other hand, if the Jew recognizes that this *practical*
> nature of his is futile and works to abolish it, he extricates
> himself from his previous development and works for *human
> emancipation* as such and turns against the *supreme practical*
> expression of human self-estrangement.[30]

At the same time it is not the case that all hucksters are Jews,
according to Marx. Far from it. Indeed the whole point of the

exercise is to show that in practice, civil society is the source of hucksterism. Official Christian society is a vast hypocrisy: it preaches universal love, but practises the hucksterism which Marx calls Judaism. Thus, after projecting the stereotype of the Jew as the financial power, the moneylenders manipulating states behind the scenes (ignoring the poverty-stricken and oppressed Jews dispersed throughout all Europe), Marx concludes that Christians and Jews are equally guilty!

We recognize in Judaism, therefore, a general *anti-social* element of the *present time*, an element which through historical development—to which in this harmful respect the Jews have zealously contributed—has been brought to its present high level, at which it must necessarily begin to disintegrate.

In the final analysis, the *emancipation of the Jews* is the emancipation of mankind from *Judaism*.

The Jew has emancipated himself in a Jewish manner, not only because he has acquired financial power, but also because, through him and also apart from him, money has become a world power and the practical Jewish spirit has become the practical spirit of the Christian nations. The Jews have emancipated themselves insofar as the Christians have become Jews.[31]

What are we to make of this argument? Jewish people have participated in "zealously" civil society. But so has the rest of European society which has contributed to the power of money "apart from" the Jews. Huckstering and egoism is by no means confined to the Jews as a people according to Marx's presentation. Is the issue a religious one? Certainly not, for Marx's whole point against Bauer is that this is not so; one must look to practical aspects of civil society to understand the nature of Judaism, and the means to the emancipation of Jews. "The Jew"', Marx tells us, "is perpetually created by civil society from its own entrails. What, in itself, was the basis of the Jewish religion? Practical need, egoism."[32]

Why does Marx identify civil society with Judaism, if it really is the case that it is a feature of Christian as well as Jewish practice? The answer is too obvious: "Jew" is a dirty word—as in the term "dirty Jew" which appears even later in the *Theses on Feuerbach*.[33] Marx would not see the social, useful, human, coordinative role of the competitive market mechanism embodied in civil society, because the motivation of each individual was self-interest. Marx does not claim that civil society is disfunctional, as he was to argue in his mature economic analysis of the breakdown of capitalism. Rather, he makes a moral judgment that self-interest is evil, regardless of its operational outcome. Marx is driven to that position by his identification of self-interest with "Jew" and with the shame that the word evoked. Following Feuerbach, Marx had accepted the Christian ethic as the norm, even though he sees it honoured in the breach rather than in the observance. Marx bases his moral judgment on the purity of intent rather than on the effect of the act itself. Jewish concerns with a this-worldly ethic governed by law appear to Marx as despicable.

Marx makes all this painfully clear in a passage which previews the later argument of the *Manuscripts* in content, and exposes its otherwise unexplained assumption that there is something inherently degrading about exchange of commodities and labour. Continuing on from the passage just cited Marx exclaims:

> The monotheism of the Jew, therefore, is in reality the polytheism of the many needs, a polytheism which makes even the lavatory an object of divine law. *Practical need, egoism*, is the principle of *civil society*, and as such appears in a pure form as soon as civil society has fully given birth to the political state. The god of *practical need and self-interest* is *money*.
>
> Money is the jealous god of Israel, in the face of which no other god may exist. Money degrades all the gods of man—and turns them into commodities. Money is the universal self-established *value* of all things. It has therefore robbed the whole world—both the world of men and nature—of its specific value. Money is the estranged essence of man's work and man's existence, and this alien essence dominates him, and he worships it.
>
> The god of the Jews has become secularized and has become the god of the world. The bill of exchange is the real god of the Jew. His god is only an illusory bill of exchange.
>
> The view of nature attained under the dominion of private property and money is a real contempt for and practical debasement of nature; in the Jewish religion nature exists, it is

true, but it exists only in imagination...

Contempt for theory, art, history, and for man as an end in himself, which is contained in an abstract form in the Jewish religion, is the *real, conscious* standpoint, the virtue of the man of money. The species-relation itself, the relation between man and woman, etc., becomes an object of trade! The woman is bought and sold.

The *chimerical* nationality of the Jew is the nationality of the merchant, of the man of money in general.[34]

Christianity, Marx tells us, has only in a "semblance overcome real Judaism", but is unable to implement its ideals because Christianity is an alienation from Man, and worships God instead of Man as a collective species. As such it cannot achieve its ideals. Christianity actually constitutes a diversion of universal love into heaven, leaving the real world open to the world of dirty-Jewish civil society where private property alienates man from himself:

Judaism reaches its highest point with the perfection of civil society but it is only in the Christian world that civil society attains perfection. Only under the dominance of Christianity, which makes all national, natural, moral and theoretical conditions extrinsic to man, could civil society separate itself completely from the life of the state, sever all the species-ties of man, put egoism and selfish need in the place of these species-ties, and dissolve the human world into a world of atomistic individuals who are inimically opposed to one another.[35]

The human defeat of Judaism, Marx argues, is the task of atheism and communism. Christianity has failed:

Christianity sprang from Judaism. It has merged again in Judaism.

From the outset, the Christian was the theorising Jew, the Jew is therefore the practical Christian, and the practical Christian has become a Jew again.

Christianity had only in semblance overcome real judaism. It was too *noble-minded*, too spiritualistic to eliminate the crudity of practical need in any other way than the elevation to the skies.

Christianity is the sublime thought of Judaism, Judaism is the common practical application of Christianity, but this application could only become general after Christianity as a developed religion had completed *theoretically* the estrangement of man from himself and from nature.

Only then could Judaism achieve universal dominance and make alienated man and alienated nature into *alienable*, vendible objects subjected to the slavery of egoistic need and to trading.[36]

In the end, Marx concludes, whatever the political aspect of emancipation, "The *social* emancipation of the Jew is the *emancipation of society from Judaism*".[37]

His catharsis of self-hate accomplished, Marx the humanist set about preparing the *Critique of Hegel's "Philosophy of Right"* for publication. The "Introduction"[38] to the *Critique* was drafted at the end of 1843 and the first of 1844 as Karl and Jenny left Germany. It is easy to see why Marx was able to publish the "Introduction" in that single issue of the *Deutsch-französische Jahrbücher* in Paris in 1844, but allowed the main manuscript to languish, unprinted and unknown. In fact the "Introduction" is incompatible with the views drafted before his marriage in the spring of 1843 in Kreuznach. Marx no longer feels that a politically democratic state can incorporate the needs of human beings as long as that state is based on civil society. The institution of private property in civil society perpetuates the alienation of Man from society. Alienation, Marx now feels, is the central social problem.

The increasingly radical position to which Marx moves in the "Introduction" reflects his frustration with the timidity of the German intellectuals, and their inability to mobilize the nation to effective revolutionary activity. In exile, driven by the need to find a popular base, Marx comes to identify the proletariat as the vector of human emancipation. Rationalizing this political need, takes him toward the identification of the human essence with labour. In different ways the identification of humanity with the proletariat was to be the keystone to the *Economic and Philosophic Manuscripts* and everything written later. The position of *On the Jewish Question* is a denunciation of human alienation through the money nexus. The "Introduction" is the first focus of that critique in terms of the exchange of labour directly as wages, and indirectly, through commodities produced by labour and sold on the market.

"For Germany", Marx's opening sentence asserts, "the *criticism of religion* is in the main complete." But this is not enough. Repeating the theme of *On the Jewish Question* Marx asserts in a famous passage that the issue is not essentially a theological one:

> Religious distress is at the same time the *expression* of real distress and also the protest against real distress. Religion is the sigh of the oppressed creature, the heart of a heartless world, just as it is the spirit of spiritless conditions. It is the opium of the people.[39]

To be sure, the atheistic movement was necessary and useful:

> To abolish religion as the *illusory* happiness of the people is to demand their real happiness. The demand to give up illusions about the existing state of affairs is the *demand to give up a state of affairs which needs illusions* ... the criticism of heaven turns into the criticism of the earth, *the criticism of religion* into the *criticism of law* and the *criticism of theology* into the *criticism of politics*.[40]

The abolition of private property, Marx declaims is the ultimate outcome of the movement that started as a religious debate:

> The criticism of religion ends with the teaching that *man is the highest being for man*, hence with the *categorical imperative to overthrow all relations* in which man is a debased, enslaved, forsaken despicable being.[41]

None of this had appeared in the body of the *Critique*. Marx explains away the discrepancy by arguing that the *Critique* dealt with the issues of Germany, which had yet to achieve political emancipation. Hence its criticism of law and politics "deals immediately not with the original, but with a copy, the German *philosophy* of state and of law, for no other reason than that it deals with *Germany*". German conditions are only a preface, Marx says, to the struggle for human emancipation evident in modern France.

In what way does Marx see Germany as different from France? Why is the concern of German theorists and revolutionaries different from that of the French? There are two answers provided in the "Introduction": one is an intimation of the developmental theory of history which Marx was to expand in later years. The other is a francophile explanation of national differences. Marx's contempt for Germany is expressed as a conviction that the German bourgeoisie is simply incapable of performing the revolutionary role of the French capitalist class.

The developmental explanation is only an intimation of the materialist conception of history that was to come. The emphasis is not yet on the march of forces of production, on problems posed and solved. Germany, Marx simply says, is behind France: "If I negate the German state of affairs in 1843, then according to the French computation of time, I am hardly in the year 1789, and still less in the focus of the present".[42]

As a consequence, the programmatic position taken in the body of the *Critique of Hegel's "Philosophy of Right"* is still appropriate for German conditions, Marx says. The decision not to publish the *Critique* supports our contention that the philosophical basis of Marx's thought had moved on from the individualist defence of civil society in general to a humanist attack on it:

> *War* on German conditions! By all means! They are *below the level of history, beneath any criticism* ... however, once modern politico-social reality itself is subjected to criticism, once criticism rises to truly human problems, it finds itself outside the German status quo... For instance, Germany is still struggling with issues of tariff protection of monopolies, while in France and England the issue is *political economy* or the *rule of society over wealth*... This is an adequate example of the *German* form of modern problems, an example of how our history, like a clumsy recruit, still has to do extra drill in matters that are old and hackneyed in history.[43]

The national difference explanation is laced through with contempt for Germany, even while Marx considers himself a German and speaks of his countrymen in the first person plural. This self-contempt was to fester and merge with its anti-Jewish expression in such works as *The German Ideology* a year or so later. The German bourgeoisie, unlike its French counterpart, is too weak and too irresolute to carry out the achievement of the political revolution which would then place the human reorganization of society on its agenda. Marx is so convinced of the impotence of the German bourgeoisie, that he is impelled to abandon the developmental approach, and argue that the only way Germany will advance is omitting a stage of bourgeois rule. "Can Germany", Marx asks, "attain a practice *à l'hauteur des principles*, i.e., a *revolution* which will raise it not only to the *official level* of the modern nations, but to the *height of humanity* which will be the near future of those nations?"[44] If not, all is lost for Germany.

Marx contrasts France and Germany, and explains the conditions for a class to successfully lead a revolution in the name of the whole population:

> In France it is enough for somebody to be something for him to want to be everything... In France partial emancipation is the basis of universal emancipation; in Germany universal emancipation is the *conditio sine qua non* of any partial emancipation... In France every class is *politically idealistic*... The role of *emancipator* therefore passes in dramatic motion to the various classes of the French nation one after the other until it finally comes to the class which implements social freedom... In Germany, on the contrary, where practical life is as spiritless as spiritual life is unpractical, no class in civil society has any need or capacity for general emancipation until it is forced by its *immediate* condition, by *material* necessity, by its *very chains*.[45]

France which is taken as the canonical form of social revolution advances by positing political questions which follow from one another in a logical sense, while Germany, alas, is forced along by the material necessity of its immediate condition. Marx is not yet a materialist.

The French bourgeoisie, Marx explains, are capable of revolution, while the Germans are constitutionally incapable of the act.

> It is not the *radical* revolution, not the general human emancipation which is a utopian dream for Germany, but rather the partial, the *merely* political revolution, the revolution which leaves the pillars of the house standing. On what is a partial, a merely political revolution based? On the fact that a *part of civil society* emancipates itself and attains general domination; on

the fact that a definite class, proceeding from its particular situation, undertakes the general emancipation of society. This class emancipates the whole of society but only provided the whole of society is in the same situation as this class, e.g., possesses money and education.

No class of civil society can play this role without arousing a moment of enthusiasm in itself and in the masses, a moment in which it fraternises and merges with society in general, becomes confused with it and is perceived and acknowledged as its *general representative*; a moment in which it is truly the social head and the social heart. Only in the name of the general rights of society can a particular class lay claim to general domination. For the storming of this emancipatory position, and hence for the political exploitation of all spheres of society in the interests of its own sphere, revolutionary energy and intellectual self-confidence alone are not sufficient. For a *revolution of a nation* and the *emancipation of a particular class* of civil society to coincide, for *one* estate to be acknowledged as the estate of the whole society, all the defects of society must conversely be concentrated in another class, a particular estate must be the general stumbling block, the incorporation of the general imitation, a particular social sphere must be looked upon as the *notorious crime* of the whole of society, so that liberation from that sphere appears as general self-liberation. For one estate to be *par excellence* the estate of liberation, another estate must conversely be the obvious estate of oppression. The negative general significance of the French nobility and the French clergy determined the positive general significance of the immediately adjacent and opposed class of the *bourgeoisie*.

But no particular class in Germany has the consistency, the severity, the courage of ruthlessness that could mark it out as the negative representative of society. No more has any estate the breadth of soul that identifies itself, even for a moment, with the soul of the nation, the genius that inspires material might to political violence, or that revolutionary audacity which flings at the adversary the defiant words: *I am nothing* and I should be everything. The main stem of German morals and honesty, of the classes as well as of individuals, is rather that *modest* egoism which asserts its limitedness and allows it to be asserted against itself.[46]

The sycophant German burgher is too like Heinrich Marx. But there is hope for Germany apart from the bourgeoisie. Germany has developed the philosophical basis of communism. "We are *philosophical* contemporaries of the present without being its *historical* contemporaries . . . What in advanced nations is a *practical* break with modern political conditions, is in Germany, where even those conditions do not yet exist, at first a critical break with the philosophical reflection of those conditions."[47] Philosophy can evidently play a role in history; later Marx will have no truck with it.

More important for Marx, the industrial development of Germany signals the growth of the proletariat, which presents "the positive possibility of a German emancipation". This is a different sort of developmental idea from the civil society (capitalism) to communism evolution along French lines. For Marx it is a thought of desperation. German civil society does not give rise to a revolutionary class, and so revolution must initiate outside civil society. Revolution will be found, Marx said,

in the formation of a class with radical chains. A class of civil society which is not a class of civil society, an estate which is the dissolution of all estates, a sphere which has a universal character by its universal suffering and claims no particular right because no *particular wrong* but *wrong generally* is perpetrated against it: which can no longer invoke a historical but only a *human* title; which does not stand in any one-sided antithesis to the consequences but in an all-round antithesis to the premises of the German state; a sphere, finally, which cannot emancipate itself from all other spheres of society, and thereby emancipating all other spheres of society, which, in a word is the *complete loss* of man and hence can win itself only through the *complete rewinning of man*. This dissolution of society as a particular estate is the *proletariat* . . .

The proletariat is coming into being in Germany only as a result of the rising *industrial* development . . .

By proclaiming the *dissolution of the hitherto existing world order* the proletariat merely states the *secret of its own existence*, for it is in fact the dissolution of that world order. By demanding the *negation of private property*, the proletariat merely raises to the rank of a *principle of society* what society has made the principle of the *proletariat*.[48]

The "Introduction" purports to be an analysis of the political likelihood of the democratic change in Germany outlined in the *Critique* itself. Its answer is that the chances are not great. Subsequent events have borne out the estimate. But the relation between the "Introduction" and the body of the *Critique* shows that in the meantime Marx's *goals* and philosophical rationalization have changed. Political democracy would be a "partial victory" anyway. He is now a communist, based on the extension of Feuerbach's humanist philosophy. As is made clear in his discussion of France, political democracy is not responsive to the dehumanization of man in general and labour in particular that he sees all around him in Paris. Indeed, he relies on communist revolution in France to trigger off a similar revolution in Germany. "When all inner requisites are fulfilled, *the day of German resurrection*", he concludes, "will be proclaimed by the *ringing call* of the Gallic cock".[49] Marx concludes that "The only *practical* possible liberation of Germany, is the ultimate revolution which proclaims man to be the highest being for man. The *emancipation of the German* is the *emancipation of the human being*". Responding to the call from France, emancipation will come in the German way skipping the intermediate stage: "The head of this emancipation is *philosophy*, its *heart* is the *proletariat*".[50]

One cannot help being struck with Marx's solution to the Jewish question and his answer to the German question. For Jews to be emancipated as human beings, they must cease to be Jews. The highest achievement to which they can aspire and still maintain their identity is civil emancipation within German civil society. Germans are different. For all their backwardness and servility, they are capable of becoming human. This is because they are a nation of philosophers who can respond to the Gallic call and lead the proletarian masses to Nirvana. Herschel Marx, the Jew, must be eliminated; Heinrich Marx, the German, can become human despite his weakness.

Before we leave the "Introduction", it is well to emphasize that it is not yet an historical materialist document. There is no suggestion of either an inevitable process of history of class struggles, nor any economic mechanism of the breakdown of capitalism through crises, stagnation or the like. Even the hints at "increasing misery" of the proletariat are here only faint anticipations, based on the growing size of the industrial proletariat rather than intensity of exploitation. Nonetheless Marx has more than an intimation of developmental processes. These are variously expressed as the development of the philosophical "head" of the revolution which springs alternatively from German philosophy or the French rationalist political man, and the "heart", the rise of the proletariat. There is no clear suggestion that the economic development is prior to the ideological; indeed the whole point of the rationale for a German revolution is that the ideology has already been established by the philosophers prior to industrialization.

It is nevertheless tempting to read the "Introduction" as if it were an expression of his mature thought. In particular the loose and aphoristic use of words has permitted a blurring of materialism by later Marxists in a fashion consistent with any programme which seems pragmatically appropriate. Indeed this mode of expression reflects the pragmatic political need which prompted Marx to turn to the German proletariat. When the "stages of history" doctrine becomes too confining, and materialism inadequate to explain events the "Introduction" is frequently cited to justify the view that philosophy or propaganda can bring about social change independently of the advance in the "forces of production":

> The weapon of criticism cannot, of course, replace criticism by weapons, material force must be overthrown by material force; but theory also becomes a material force as soon as it has gripped the masses.[51]

For Marx the point at this stage in his thought is that Germany can make revolution, even though it is a whole epoch behind France socially. The German bourgeoisie is hardly developed, it has yet to go through a period of industrialization; the working class is correspondingly minute and dispersed, and yet he believes that the proletariat is capable of transforming German society:

> As philosophy finds its *material* weapons in the proletariat, so the proletariat finds its *spiritual* weapons in philosophy. And once the lightning of thought has squarely struck this ingenuous soil of the people the emancipation of the *Germans* into *human beings* will take place.[52]

Marx in his maturity was as capable as his followers of hedging on the materialist conception of history and the doctrine of inevitable stages. But it obviously caused him more than a little embarrassment to admit the influence of ideological superstructure in overwhelming the power of the material base in the "forces of production". Thus in *Capital*[53] Marx writes of the "iron necessity" of Germany passing through the stages of capitalism he was describing in British canonical form. *"De la fabula narratur!"* he tells his compatriots. Yet he wrote a famous letter in 1881 to the Russian revolutionary Vera Sassoulitch in which—after struggling with several drafts—he limits the "historical inevitability" process to western Europe. Marx tells her that the Russian "rural commune" might be the "mainspring of Russia's social regeneration", but that the "analysis given in *Capital* assigns no reasons for or against the vitality of the rural community" as a Russian precursor of communism.[54]

In the "Introduction", it is not fair to say that Marx was fudging on a doctrine held. The point is that the doctrine was not as yet developed, and though at this point Marx's appeal to the German proletariat was a grasping at straws, Marx would not long remain in this position. Once having suggested the possibility of labour as the mainspring of the revolution, he proceeded to rationalize his hopes in an extension of Feuerbach's criticism of religion to a critique of alienated labour in the *Economic and Philosophic Manuscripts* and related documents.

En passant Marx must divest himself of associates such as Ruge who had remained in the radical democratic camp of civil society. This break, which was responsible for the demise of the *Deutsch-französische Jahrbücher*, is recorded in a two-part article in *Vorwärts* "Critical Marginal Notes on the Article 'The King of Prussia and Social Reform' by a Prussian".[55] Ruge is the "Prussian" who is drenched with those vials of vitriol which Marx reserved for former associates, proxies for views he once held himself.

Moving in the direction of a class view of society, Marx writes: "Let us *distinguish*—which the 'Prussian' neglects to do—the different categories in the expression 'German Society': the Government, the bourgeoisie, the press and, finally, the workers themselves. These are the *different* masses with which we are concerned here. The 'Prussian' lumps all these masses together..."[56] More concretely than before, Marx is concerned with the struggles of the Silesian weavers which prompted the original Ruge article. He relates the poverty of workers in Germany and France to the "pauperism" in England. Indeed he cites the "cynical and scientific economists", Ricardo, McCulloch and Malthus as evidence of the general perpetuation of pauperism. The problem of poverty is a "universal state of distress" of workers.

Marx makes clear that he now believes political democracy cannot be an end in itself, but only a partial step toward social revolution:

> The mightier the state, and the *more political* therefore a country is, the less it is inclined to grasp the *general* principle of *social* maladies and to seek their basis in the *principle of the state*, hence in the *present structure of society*, the active, conscious, and official expression of which is the state. The *political* mind is a political mind precisely because it thinks *within* the framework of politics. The keener and more lively it is, the *more incapable* it is of understanding social ills. The classic period of political intellect is the *French Revolution*. Far from seeing the source of social shortcomings in the principle of the state, the heroes of the French Revolution instead saw in social defects the source of political evils. Thus, *Robespierre* saw in great poverty and great wealth only an obstacle to *pure democracy*. Therefore he wished to establish a universal Spartan frugality.[57]

The state and private property in civil society are the cause of poverty *because* private property is concerned with the private interests of individuals as opposed to the public interest. "The existence of the state and the existence of slavery are inseparable".[58] The very existence of the proletariat, Marx thought, entails poverty. The proletariat are the new slaves, the creatures of civil society and private property. The only way out is to abolish private property and all its consequences: civil society— the state—the proletariat.

It seemed self-evident to Marx that because workers did not own material wealth they were poor. There was nothing that political action could do about that. To Ruge's suggestion that education at the public expense would help eliminate poverty Marx replied:

Why does the King of Prussia not at once issue a decree for the education of all uncared-for children? Does the "Prussian" know what the King would have to decree? Nothing less than the *abolition of the proletariat*. In order to educate children they have to be *fed* and freed from *wage-labour*. The feeding and education of uncared-for children, i.e., the feeding and education of the *entire rising generation* of the proletariat, would be the abolition of the proletariat and pauperism.[59]

This remark is, of course, a juvenile gaffe. But it reveals the essential extremism of his position, and exposes its absurdity. Over the years the specific criticisms Marx made of capitalism have been subject to amelioration and correction. These never can satisfy the extremist who must bring down the whole system. For Marx there are two disjoint domains for human action, the political and social, and two equally separated ranges of problems which they can treat. Political action, by its acceptance of the state inevitably accepts individual interest, the proletariat, poverty, the market and the dehumanization of man. Social action involves the revolutionary dismantling of the whole apparatus and the creation of the community of many in a propertyless society. To do as Ruge suggests, to use the political instruments of the democratic state to attack social problems, seems to Marx to be logically—even grammatically—absurd:

Let the "Prussian" allow us to make a comment of a *stylistic* nature. His antithesis is defective. In the first half it says: "When *distress* produces *understanding*", but in the second it says: "when *political understanding* discovers the roots *of social distress*". The *simple* understanding of the first half of the antithesis becomes the *political* understanding in the second half, just as the *simple* distress of the first half of the antithesis becomes *social* distress in the second half. Why does our stylistic artist endow the two halves of his antithesis so unequally? I do not think that he realised why he did it. I will explain to him his correct *instinct* here. If the "Prussian" had written "when *social* distress produces *political* understanding, and *political understanding* discovers the roots of *social* distress", no unbiased reader could have failed to see the *nonsense* of this antithesis. Everyone would at once have asked himself; why does the anonymous author not couple social understanding with social distress, and political understanding with political distress, as the simplest logic requires?[60]

There is, of course, no logical reason for the dichotomy between social and political factors. Marx's rage at civil society, his identification of Jewish humiliation with it, made it impossible for him to see the democratic process as a means of eliminating social ills.

Where is Marx now? His previous critique of Hegel is unsatisfactory. At best it is parochially German. The philosophy of empiricism led to civil society instead of away from it. His understanding of economics is woefully inadequate, yet he is now convinced that the ills of society are bound up in its essential economic relations. Marx must now try to sort out the nature of capitalist society and the significance of wage labour. His attempt is first made in Paris in terms of the philosophical preconceptions imported from Feuerbach's humanism.

6   A First Course in Economics

Paris! To the mother of revolution came the radicals, the seers, the dreamers of social transformation to expound their ideas and to act out their fantasies. Here Marx met Heinrich Heine through the good offices of the "red rabbi", Moses Hess. Marx spent time in the company of them and Proudhon, and even hobnobbed in the salons of the *avant-garde* wealthy intellectuals. Germany was a less developed country compared to this glittering metropolis and country it dominated. Economically still preindustrial and politically disunified, even the German claim to fame in philosophy was seen by Marx as testimony to the incapacity of its timid bourgeoisie.[1] In contrast, a century of radical thought had taken French politically aware society past the need to debate philosophy as a proxy for revolution. It seemed to Marx that French communism had superseded philosophy and was in the business of designing new societies, applying various versions of a science of social mechanics to remake human institutions.

Marx had come to Paris to meet Arnold Ruge with a sheaf of manuscripts for the *Deutsch-französische Jahrbücher*. Unable to win Feuerbach's active participation in the journal, Marx brought Feuerbach with him in spirit. In this Paris episode, Marx needed to follow Feuerbach through to his logical conclusions in the *Economic and Philosophic Manuscripts*. With the catharsis complete, Marx could reject humanism only a few months later.

August 1844 saw the publication of the only edition of the *Deutsch-französische Jahrbücher* which contained Marx's *On the Jewish Question* as well as the "Introduction" to *A Contribution to the Critique of Hegel's "Philosophy of Right"*. For all their contentiousness, these pieces asked more questions than they answered: in economic theory, Marx had damned the market nexus as egoism—and capped it with the epithet "Jew". Nevertheless he failed to generate a reasoned economic argument why the egoistic motivations of the market should not be the vehicle for social cooperation. Young Hegelians might simply wave philosophical arms in Germany, but that could not do in sophisticated France. Marx identified the proletariat as the instrument that would complete the revolution that the German bourgeoisie was too timid to initiate. Yet he knew nothing of the economic relations which defined this group upon which he had pinned his hopes.

In philosophy itself, Marx had advanced no further than Feuerbach's break with Hegelianism. According to the Feuerbach's *Preliminary Theses for the Reform of Philosophy*, it was a further alienation of Man. Hegel's abstract Spirit, like God, was alienated human thought now in the guise of idealist philosophy. Philosophy was equivalent to the religious anthropomorphism analysed in the *Essence of Christianity*.

Marx had done battle with Hegel under Feuerbach's banner once before in the *Critique of Hegel's "Philosophy of Right"*. There he read Feuerbach's aphorism: "The true relation of thought to being is only this, being is the subject, thought the predicate. Thought is a product of being, not being of thought,"[2] to mean that being consisted of singular objects about which human beings make generalizations of a universal nature. Now it was necessary to settle accounts with Hegel once again.

The opportunity presented itself after Marx and Ruge fell out in acrimonious squabble. As a result financial support for their journal was withdrawn, so that the publication did not survive its first number. Marx turned his pen to the columns of *Vorwärts*, another *emigré* journal. Relieved of editorial responsibilities, he had time for reflection and study of the economics of an exchange economy.

Marx's introduction to economics came in the form of Frederick Engels's contribution to the short-lived *Deutsch-französische Jahrbücher*. The *Umrisse*, "Outlines of a Critique of Political economy"[3] was a critical review of the current state of political economy. Marx was deeply impressed by this work. He wrote a summary of it as part of his preparation for the *Economic and Philosophic Manuscripts* as well as the related essay, "Comments on James Mill". This was the beginning of the collaboration of the two men that lasted a lifetime.

The *Umrisse* reveals the primitive level of their economic knowledge at the time. Engels frequently simply did not understand what he read of the classical economists and contradicted himself from line to line. The charitable editors of the Marx–Engels Institute concede that it shows "some signs of immaturity".

Marx himself recalls this stage in the "Author's Preface" to the *Critique of Political Economy* (1859): "As far back as in 1842–43, as editor of the *Rheinische Zeitung*, I found myself embarrassed at first when I had to take part in discussions concerning the so-called material interests". He tells of his concern with the law of the thefts of wood, and continues:

> Finally, the debates on free trade and protection, gave me the first impulse to take up the study of economic questions. At the same time a weak, quasi-philosophic echo of French socialism and communism made itself heard in the *Rheinische Zeitung* in those days when the good intentions "to go ahead" greatly outweighed knowledge of facts. I declared myself against such botching, but had to admit at once in a controversy with the *Allgemeine Augsburge Zeitung* that my previous studies did not allow me to hazard an independent judgement as to the merits of the French schools. When, therefore, the publishers of the *Rheinische Zeitung* conceived the illusion that by a less aggressive policy the paper could be saved from the death sentence, pronounced upon it, I was glad to grasp that opportunity to retire to my study room from public life.[4]

Retrospectively, Marx claimed that beginning in his Paris studies, he had always been struggling toward a materialist view of history:

> The first work undertaken for the solution of the question that troubled me was a critical revision of Hegel's Philosophy of Law; the introduction to that work appeared in the *Deutsch-französische Jahrbücher* published in Paris in 1844. I was led by my studies to the conclusion that legal relations as well as forms of state could neither be understood by themselves, nor explained by the so-called general progress of the human mind, but that they are rooted in the material conditions of life, which are summed up by Hegel after the fashion of the English and French of the eighteenth century under the name 'civic

society'—the anatomy of that civic society is to be found in political economies.

In the "Preface" Marx identifies the date at which he felt that he could arrive at genuine independent judgments: "The study of the latter [political economy M.W.] which I had taken up in Paris, I continued at Brussels whither I emigrated on account of an order of expulsion issued by Mr Guizot". Marx completely dismisses the Paris writing, except for the "Introduction" which, as we have just seen, is reinterpreted as a precursor of his mature materialism. *On the Jewish Question* is ignored and the 1844 *Paris Manuscripts* lay forgotten and fortunately for Marx's account of himself, unpublished. Marx's account starts his economic writing with the work of the Brussels period, which comprise the jottings for self-clarification, the "Theses on Feuerbach", and their incorporation into *The German Ideology* written with Engels in 1845. If there is any doubt about what Marx conceived to be his adequately informed view, it should be removed by the "Preface" to the *Critique of Political Economy*; it is one of the classical statements of Marx's materialist view of history. In it we find the key concepts of the primacy of material conditions of production over ideological superstructure, the vision of inevitable advance of the forces of production and their discovery by scientific analysis, the division of history into definite stages defined by the mode of production, and the inevitability of ultimate revolution as a result of the breakdown of capitalism:

> The general conclusion at which I arrived, and which, once reached, continued to serve as the leading thread in my studies, may be briefly summed up as follows: In the social production which men carry on they enter into definite relations that are indispensable and independent of their will; these relations of production correspond to a definite stage of development of their material powers of production. The sum total of these relations constitutes the economic structure of society— the real foundation, on which rise legal and political superstructures and to which correspond definite forms of social consciousness. The mode of production in material life determines the general character of the social, political and spiritual processes of life. It is not the consciousness of men that determines their existence, but, on the contrary, their social existence determines their consciousness.

At a certain stage of their development, the material forces of production in society come in conflict with the existing relations of production, or—what is but a legal expression for the same thing—with the property relation within which they had been at work before. From forms of development of the forms of production these relations turn into their fetters. Then comes the period of social revolution. With the change of the economic foundation the entire immense superstructure is more or less rapidly transformed. In considering such transformation the distinction should always be made between the material transformation of the economic conditions of production which can be determined with the precision of natural science, and the legal, political, religious, aesthetic or philosophic—in short ideological forms in which men become conscious of this conflict and fight it out. Just as our opinion of an individual is not based on what he thinks of himself, so we can not judge of such a period of transformation by its own consciousness; on the contrary, this consciousness must rather be explained from the contradictions of material life, from the existing conflict between the social forces of production and the relations of production. No social order ever disappears before all the productive forces, for which there is room in it, have been developed and new higher relations of production never appear before the material conditions of their existence have matured in the womb of the old society. Therefore mankind always takes up only such problems as it can solve.[5]

Marx in Paris in 1844 was a long way from the author of the *Critique of Political Economy* in 1859. To be sure, he knew that economic relations would be central to his analysis but the focus of his enquiry was money and the exchange of goods for money, rather than the material relations of production.

Engels's revelations in the *Umrisse* must have come as a shock to Marx. He was not alone on the planet as a critic of the money fetish. Since Adam Smith, economic orthodoxy had denounced the mercantilist view that money was an end in itself. To arrive at that conclusion Smith had made the same eighteenth-century individualist point as Marx's *Critique of Hegel's "Philosophy of Right"*: social welfare was related to the welfare of individuals, rather than the state. While neither writer simplistically equated social welfare with the unadjusted sum of individual satisfactions, by and large it was to the individual, "empirical person" (as Marx would have it) that society ought to look for its public policy, rather than to the collective whole. Money, Smith pointed out, was only a measure of the relative exchange value of goods to individuals. It was to the welfare generated by those goods that society ought to look for its satisfaction. The real wealth of nations was the stock of factors of production—labour, land, and accumulated capital. These were the sources of production of goods and services which served to satisfy the individual welfare. The optimum division of labour of these productive factors took place, Smith argued, precisely in a civil society in which each man was free to maximize his own wealth and satisfaction. Competition was an "invisible hand" which produced the coordination of individual interest, and constrained it to serve the social purpose.

Marx had to see that it was the capitalist ideologues who were opposed to the money fetish, even while they pointed to the money function. Money serves to compare values embodied in disparate physical items. Money is liquid, an asset form that is most easily alienable. Liquidity provided a form of insurance against risk, by permitting easy transfer of wealth from one use to another. Peoples like the Jews, who were subject to persecution, often needed to hold their wealth in liquid form to avoid the caprices of their tormentors. Money simply was an expression of the market for better or worse.

Marx the humanist concentrated his fire on the "hucksterism", "egoism" and "competition" of the market-place, the very facility with which goods produced by some could be converted into satisfactions for others. The alienation of the products of labour from their immediate producers came to dominate his economic thinking during this period as the evil of private property. Money was an instrument and a symptom of this most fundamental disease, not so much the disease itself. Marx's shift of viewpoint was a matter of degree, of emphasis on the market more than on its phenomenal forms of money or the haggling and apparent hucksterism through which supply and demand operate. Accordingly, there is the beginning of a retreat from the extreme anti-semitism of *On the Jewish Question*. The jew-hatred is less explicit in the *Manuscripts*. In 1845, when he is further on his way to achieving the Brussels position, Marx and Engels polemicize again against Bauer in *The Holy Family*; they repeat the major premise identifying Jews with moneylending and hucksterism, nevertheless the tone is different.[6]

Increasingly, the theoretical issue that preoccupied Marx was the nature and origins of value in exchange, as well as its expression in money terms. Engels's *Umrisse* presented the matter as a counterposition of the English "cost of production" school of Smith, Ricardo and James Mill, and the French utility theorists such as J. B. Say. In characteristic Hegelian style, Engels attempted to rise above the substance of the debate by arguing that the opposition of views reflects a contradiction in reality. The separation of cost of production from utility, he contended, means that the determination of value is arbitrary and leads to unjust exchange.

Engels's own reconciliation attempts to retain both elements in the determination of value:

> The value of an object includes both factors, which the contending parties arbitrarily separate—and, as we have seen unsuccessfully. Value is the relation of production costs to utility. The first application of value is the decision as to whether a thing ought to be produced at all; i.e., as to whether utility counterbalances production costs. Only then can one talk of the application of value to exchange. The production costs of two objects being equal, the deciding factor determining their comparative value will be utility.[7]

It is possible to see in this passage a precursor of Marx's dismissal of utility in value determination in *Capital*; there the argument is that use value is a necessary qualitative condition for an article to constitute a commodity, but the quantitative expression of exchange value is determined solely by the labour content embodied in its production. Nevertheless, the main thrust of Engels's contradictory passage, is that the true value of a commodity is achieved by the balancing of costs on the one hand and utility on the other. Engels mistakenly views a one-sided approach of schools of political economists as reflective of the inability of the actual capitalist pricing mechanism to balance utility and cost which he intuits would maximize individual net satisfaction.

The basis of Engels's misunderstanding of functioning of a competitive market lies in his search for an interpersonal, objective measure of utility. He continues the previous passage by searching for a means of balancing costs and utility, unaware that this balancing requires only that each individual subjectively compare the usefulness of goods in his own mind; it does not require either that one party estimate the utility of goods to another, or that there exist some objective standard of utility binding on them both. Engels was not alone, at the time, in being unable to solve the problem. What is unfortunate was the tendency to project his own inability on the problem itself, a feature of the higher Hegelian criticism he shared with Marx. Giving it up as a bad job, Engels decides that the issue itself will be superseded by the elimination of private property: Utility, he says:

> is the only just basis of exchange. But if one proceeds from this basis, who is to decide the utility of the object? The mere opinion of the parties concerned? Then in any event one will be cheated. Or are we to assume a determination grounded in the inherent utility of the object independent of the parties concerned, and not apparent to them? If so, the exchange can only be effected by coercion, and each party considers itself cheated. The contradiction between the real inherent utility of the thing and the determination of that utility, between the determination of utility and the freedom of those who exchange, cannot be superseded without superseding private property; and once this is superseded, there can no longer be any question of exchange as it exists at present. The practical application of the concept of value will then be increasingly confined to the decision about production, and that is its proper sphere.[8]

By eliminating exchange in a communist society, Engels imagines that he has eliminated the need to decide what and how much to produce. In fact, as history has since shown, the problem of current communist societies (like all public choice systems) is precisely to define the collective measure of utility. Superseding private property has only transposed the coercion from the market to the state.

Engels finds an individualist conception of utility absurd in theory, and reflective of the absurdity of capitalism. It is impossible for him, and now for Marx, to accept an Epicurean hedonistic theory of human action. The consequences are a deviation of "real" value, objective utility, from the apparently chance-directed workings of supply and demand which determine price:

> But how do matters stand at present? We have seen that the concept of value is violently torn asunder, and that each of the separate sides is declared to be the whole. Production costs, distorted from the outset by competition, are supposed to be value itself. So is mere subjective utility—since no other kind of utility can exist at present. To help these lame definitions on to their feet, it is in both cases necessary to have recourse to competition; and the best of it is that with the English competition represents utility, in contrast to the costs of production, whilst inversely with Say it introduces the costs of production in contrast to utility. But what kind of utility, what kind of production costs, does it introduce? Its utility depends on chance, on fashion, on the whim of the rich; its production costs fluctuate with the fortuitous relationship of demand and supply.
>
> The difference between real value and exchange-value is based on a fact—namely, that the value of a thing differs from the so-called equivalent given for it in trade; i.e., that this equivalent is not an equivalent. This so-called equivalent is the price of the thing, and if the economist were honest, he would employ this term for "value in exchange". But he has still to keep up some sort of pretence that price is somehow bound up with value, lest the immorality of trade become too obvious. It is, however, quite correct, and a fundamental law of private property, that price is determined by the reciprocal action of production costs and competition. This purely empirical law was the first to be discovered by the economist; and from this law he then abstracted his "real value", i.e., the price at the time when competition is in a state of equilibrium, when demand and supply cover each other. Then, of course, what remains over are the costs of production and it is these which the economist proceeds to call "real value", whereas it is merely a definite aspect of price. Thus everything in economics stands on its head. Value, the primary factor, the source of price, is made dependent on price, its own product. As is well known, this inversion is the essence of abstraction; on which see Feuerbach.[9]

Probably the most important conclusion that Marx drew from Engels's *Umrisse* was that at least he did not know anything about the economic issues he was discussing, and had best learn. Evidently the first work Marx really studied was James Mill's *Elements of Political Economy*[10] (1821) in French translation. Marx's unpublished *étude* "On Mill" was written in the first half of 1844 as part of the series of notebooks which contain the *Economic and Philosophical Manuscripts*.

The *Elements* was the standard textbook of its day. Its didactic style was appropriate to the author's statement of intent, and almost designed to infuriate a passionate, prolix, rabid, Promethean revolutionary such as the young Marx:

> My object has been to compose a school-book of Political Economy, to detach the essential principles of the science from all extraneous topics, to state the propositions clearly and in their logical order, and to subjoin its demonstration to each. I am, myself persuaded, that nothing more is necessary for understanding every part of the book, than to read it with attention; such attention as persons of either sex, of ordinary understanding, are capable of bestowing.[11]

Patently Mill was neither a Jew nor a huckster, but he was a thoroughgoing individualist. Indeed the *Elements* is as much an exposition of Benthamite hedonistic psychology and ethics as it is of Ricardian economic theory. The standard of social choice for Mill is always "the greatest good for the greatest number". Mill might philosophize about the nature of the human creature and his work, but unquestionably he was in the service of individual men. Mill's theoretical arguments may certainly be criticized in retrospect. In Marx's mature works such as the *Critique of Political Economy* (1859)[12] as well as its proposed sequel which emerged posthumously as *Theories of Surplus Value*,[13] Marx seriously takes issue with Mill's presentation of value, wages, monetary theory and the like. But in Paris Marx was not capable of such criticism. In Mill he confronted an apparently clear-eyed, if somewhat sententious reformer. In his attack on rent as an unearned income and his critique of the Corn Laws, Mill was searching for realistic means of ameliorating the conditions of the poor.

The *Elements* was presented as an exposition of Ricardo. Undoubtedly it was true to him in spirit, even though it was at variance in significant ways from Ricardo's own, more sophisticated, *Principles of Political Economy of Taxation*. Mill was closer to

Ricardo's earlier *Essay on the Influence of Low Price of Corn on the Profits of Stock* which attempted to show that the dynamics of production and distribution of the national product were a product of natural forces: production of goods on the one hand, and the reproduction of human beings on the other. The overriding considerations in the economic life of society were "pre-institutional';[14] human arrangements of market and non-market societies had to conform to these physical and biological realities one way or another. In particular, the value of commodities and the income received by the owners of land, labour and capital were not capricious; they are simply the expression of natural relationships in market terms.

In the *Essay*, Ricardo took corn to be the sole item of consumption of the workers. The consumption level of the labourers in corn terms was limited to subsistence wages since any increase in wages above that level would induce increased population up to the margin of the food supply. Increases in population forced corn production on to less and less suitable land, as well as encouraging more and more intensive use of the land. The difference between corn product on the worst land called into production (or the margin of most intensive use of land) and more felicitous situations constituted the rent of the landowners. Profits were determined, again in corn terms, by the degree to which population growth pushed the extension of agriculture to successively poor soils, leaving a diminishing margin between the subsistence requirements of the workers and the total output on soils so poor that they paid no rent. The profits of the capitalist farmers were then consumed or saved in the form of the fund of subsistence to be advanced to workers in the next year. The agricultural rate of profit was determined by the ratio of profit income divided by the capital outlay.

Under competitive conditions, the canonical Ricardian argument proceeded, the natural conditions of agriculture were enforced on the non-agricultural industrial sector. Profit rates in industry could not differ from those in agriculture without engendering migrations of capital that would restore the equilibrium. Wage rates were everywhere given by the corn needs of the workers for subsistence. Trade certainly took place between the agricultural and industrial sectors. The analysis of the exchange value of commodities was certainly important, but it did not determine the distribution of income—the real wages of workers on the rate of profit of capitalists. Neither did value considerations alter the Malthusian predictions for the dynamic of the economy; these resulted from tendencies toward overpopulation relative to food producing capacity.

Ricardo himself retreated from his earlier simplistic view that decomposed the economy into a determining natural agricultural and a conforming industrial sector. In fact the latter consumed the products of agriculture as wage goods and capital, and contributed inputs to farming. Equalization of profit rates, as well as the definition of the subsistence wage, required that these key parameters of the economy be determined in all industries simultaneously in terms of some common unit. Exchange value replaced corn as the index. Although he did not hold to a pure labour theory of value in the sense in which Marx used it in *Capital*, Ricardo found it convenient to carry out his accounting in terms of the labour that was devoted to the production of commodities. Labour was certainly the most important element of the cost of production, and in any case was in accord with the generally held concept of human effort wresting a living from nature.[15]

Ricardo was at pains to point out that if an equal rate of return on capital per annum were to be maintained, it would be necessary to amend the labour theory of value. Processes of production that involved longer periods of time—or equivalently required a greater amount of previously produced capital[16] would have a greater exchange value than those of the same labour content which take a shorter period of time, or require less capital on hand. Even if one were to consider capital as a form of stored up labour, this difficulty would remain. While capital used up in the course of production might be said to transfer its labour content to the commodity as it wears out or is consumed, the existence of stocks of capital of different duration or amount would require that the new value added by production in the capital-intensive industry be greater than the labour expended directly and transferred through depreciated capital; the less capital-intensive industry would have an exchange value less than the labour expended directly or indirectly as depreciated capital. Emphasizing the relative nature of value, this "Ricardo effect" is expressed in terms of the effect of a change in the wage rate on relative prices. In the event of a rise in wages, goods with a higher than average capital-to-labour requirement would fall in price relative to those with a lower capital–labour ratio; equivalently, the second group would rise in price relative to the first.[16]

Despite the stated caveats, Ricardo used the labour theory of value to retain his vision of the dynamics of the economy as determined by the natural forces. With population growth, the increased labour expended on less fertile soils was translated into a rising value of subsistence goods, and a falling rate of profit, expressed in terms of the return on capital outlay. Agriculture was still dominant, for all practical purposes in Ricardo. The processes of production and distribution were logically prior to those of exchange.

The very organization of Mill's book makes it clear that this was his view as well. There is no doubt from the discussion in the *Theories of Surplus Value* that Marx continued to read Mill in this way. The order of "Topics" of political economy are listed in Mill's preface:

> It thus appears, that four inquiries are comprehended in this science.
> 1st. What are the laws, which regulate the production of commodities:
> 2ndly. What are the laws, according to which the commodities, produced by the labour of the community, are distributed:
> 3rdly. What are the laws, according to which commodities are exchanged for one another:
> 4thly. What are the laws, which regulate consumption.[17]

Mill's work resonated in the mind of the young revolutionary, anxious to find a political base in the proletariat. Expressing his concept of value in more simplistic terms than Ricardo, Mill had said that the value of commodities was determined by their labour content as an embodiment of human activity. Labour as the "agency of man" moved, separated, rearranged natural objects so as to "conspire with nature... The properties of matter perform the rest".[18] Yet, the conclusion to which Mill came was that this human activity was not free. Man was gripped by the compulsion of natural law from which he could not escape. The labour required to produce the elements of subsistence, compared to the wages of labour, was an expression of this natural law at work.

For all the difficulties pointed out by Ricardo, it seemed to Mill that there was no alternative to a monistic labour theory of value. Capital had to be treated as a sort of stored-up labour, and its cost limited to depreciation—excluding interest and profit. The only plausible alternative to such a reduction, would be a dualistic "cost of production" theory, summing the costs of capital along with the labour cost. This posibility, Mill felt, only compounded the difficulty for it would then be necessary to find some third, common means of valuation of both capital and labour. It was better to attempt to wish away the Ricardo effect as a semantic dispute over profit rates expressed as a percentage and as an absolute amount. Profits were simply another form of labour, Mill contended, whether expressed as an amount or a percentage.[19]

Mill, it should be remembered, had as much of a political axe to grind as Marx. Labour to the mind of the early British philosophical radicals was counterposed, not to capital, but to land. Man produced through his labour, direct and indirect, while the owners of land only extracted the differential usufruct of the soil. The notion that landlords reaped where they did not sow was an ideological cornerstone of the British reform movement since Adam Smith. To concede any claim to the owners of material property, even if ultimately explicable by the timing of indirect labour, would be to give the argument away. With more than a little anguish, Mill was impelled to rationalize profits as the simple pass-through of the value labour embodied in capital. Marx was not yet able to show that Mill's position was incapable of reconciling profits with the labour theory of value—there has to be more to profits than depreciation and capital consumption. But while an analytical critique had to wait, Marx was able to take Mill at his word; he could identify human activity with labour, and deny the claims of capital.

Mill could have had an easier time by reducing labour to the service provided by human capital, as the property of the proletarian. He could then have searched for a consistent set of prices of commodities, including both the human capital of the labourer and the material capital of the capitalist. It is possible to write a set of simultaneous equations for this purpose, provided one is willing to specify the inputs required to produce the labourer in the same sense as other produced goods. Had he had the mathematical intuition, this requirement should not have been morally repugnant to a Ricardian like Mill who reasoned in

terms of the corn subsistence of workers. Nevertheless the idea
seemed absurd. "It is nugatory", he said, "to include labour in
the definition of the word capital, and then to say that, capital
without labour, determines exchangeable value."[20] Confusing
simultaneous solution with circular reasoning, Mill expostulated
that it was impossible to determine the value of commodities in
terms of commodities:

> To say, indeed, that the value of commodities depends upon
> capital, implies one of the most obvious of all absurdities.
> Capital is commodities. If the value of commodities, then,
> depends on the value of capital, it depends upon the value of
> commodities; value in short depends on value. This is not an
> exposition of value. It is an attempt clearly and completely
> abortive.[21]

Despite his misgivings Mill is driven to the conclusion:

> It thus appears, that the quantity of labour, in the last resort,
> determines the proportion in which commodities exchange for
> one another.[22]

As far as Marx could tell, starting from his premises, Mill had
authoritatively reduced valuation to a mirror of natural processes: the niggardliness of nature on the one hand, which forced
increased output to be achieved under progressively more
arduous circumstances; and, on the other hand, the profligacy of
man with his seed, reproducing his kind at an accelerated rate
whenever incomes available to workers exceeded their subsistence.

If value were the passive mirror of natural law, then money
itself was merely its *numéraire*. Mill's *Elements* constituted an essay
on the inessentiality of money, in the face of the mercantilist
système monétaire. Marx had come to political economy with the
belief that the essential evil of civil society could be found precisely in exchange and money as the alienation of an otherwise
free Man. Mill had preached just the opposite: the bonds that
compassed mankind in a society of private property and free
competitive exchange were, in the last analysis, the immutable
working of natural law. The old regime of landed and commercial interests compounded the natural limitations by imposing

artificial constraints on trade and competition. Left to their own devices, hedonistic individuals in civil society would maximize the product of the partnership of man and nature. The product was not limitless. Man was not absolutely free. But his absence of freedom did not derive from his self-interest and the competition with his fellows. On the contrary, the limitations which the market imposed on the individual were not those inspired by the greed of other men, but were rigorously reflective of the ineluctably constrained, finite freedom which mankind might realistically hope to achieve.

How did Marx react? His mature view, signalled by the Brussels writings of 1845, would invent a new theory of natural law, embodying a theory of social development of production. But his first reaction in Paris in 1844, was to follow Engels's *Umrisse* and deny regularity to the working of civil society. Ephemeral supply and demand considerations cause exchange to be lawless—a matter of chance as Epicurus might have said:

> In the compensation of money and value of metal, as in his description of the cost of production as the only factor determining value, Mill commits the mistake—like the school of Ricardo in general—of stating the *abstract law* without the change or continual supersession of this law through which alone it comes into being. If it is a *constant law* that, for example, the cost of production in the last instance—or rather when demand and supply are in equilibrium which occurs sporadically, fortuitously—determines the price (value), it is just as much a constant law that they are not in equilibrium, and that therefore value and cost of production stand in no necessary relationship. Indeed, there is always only a momentary equilibrium of demand and supply owing to the previous fluctuation of demand and supply, owing to the disproportion between cost of production and exchange value... This *real* movement, of which that law is only an abstract, fortuitous and one-sided factor, is made by recent political economy, law is determined by its opposite, absence of law. The true law of political economy is *chance* from whose movement we, the scientific men, isolate certain factors arbitrarily in the form of laws.[23]

Marx expostulates that the system Mill describes leaves man unfree. Freedom, as we heard Marx say in *On the Jewish Question* consists in the purposive identification of the individual with the whole. Under a system of private property, Man does not consciously cooperate as a species, but inhumanly, egoistically:

> The mediating process between men engaged in exchange is not a social or human process, not *human relationship* it is the *abstract relationship* of private property to private property, and the expression of this *abstract* relationship is *value*, whose actual existence as value constitutes money. Since men engaged in exchange do not relate to each other as men, *things* lose the significance of human personal property.

Marx's complaint is not so much that Mill is wrong in his description of capitalism, but rather that he is right: the market reflects the physical realities in an impersonal way, overriding human will or intention.

Mill made Marx furious! Marx understood why political economists like Mill came to such conclusions: they are creatures of the institution of private property and the exchange mechanism which uses money as a medium of exchange. In the "*mediating activity* or movement, the *human*, social act by which man's products mutually complement one another is *estranged* from man and becomes the attribute of money, a *material thing* outside man". Man is put in the grip of objective forces. Marx declaims that Man

> ... is active here only as a man who has lost himself and is dehumanized; the *relation* itself between things, man's operation with them, becomes the operation of an entity outside man and above man. Owing to this *alien mediator*—instead of man himself being the mediator for man—man regards his will, his activity and his relation to other men as a power independent of him and them.[24]

What would Mill say to that? Simply that human experience with the market correctly leads people to face the reality of those forces beyond their control and those that can be amended. How would Marx disengage humanity from the law of diminishing returns in agriculture? What could he suggest in the face of the human propensity to reproduce? Marx would not, or could not, answer until he developed a competing doctrine of surplus value and "relative overpopulation" of the industrial reserve army of unemployed in *Capital*. In that book, the section "Fetishism of Commodities", Marx denounces the bourgeois economists for mistaking a relationship between men for a relation between things;[25] but the meaning is different from the earlier period. For by then he has developed his own compelling law of social evolution and, to his own satisfaction at least, has advanced a social exploitation theory of the poverty of the masses. It is not so much the fetishistic money and commodity veil that is the enemy, but the exploitation that the veil conceals.[26]

If we understand how Mill's writings pushed Marx back from the position taken in *On the Jewish Question*, then the economic commentaries "On Mill" and in the rest of the *Paris Manuscripts* can be understood as the transitional studies Marx said they were. Clearly it would no longer do to simply identify the market and the use of money with the image of the Jew—although this remained part of Marx's motivation and expression. Henceforth Marx cannot simply rest his case on the alleged worship of money as such, but rather is driven by the force of Mill's lessons to a discussion of exchange value. Despite his denial of the working of natural law behind the proximate supply and demand market phenomena, Marx is driven to seek a critique of private property under conditions in which goods are exchanged at equal exchange values as commodities.

Marx's monetary thought begins with his analysis of Mill's critique of mercantilism in general and bullionism in particular. Mill had made two points. First, gold and money were not identical. Any object of value, including paper promises, could serve as money. Second, society was harmed by policies which interfered with free trade in the misguided hope of amassing a greater national stock of money. Nothing but the misallocation of resources was to be gained from granting special privileges under the guise of achieving a favourable balance of trade. Money has no use except to measure the satisfactions derived from the flow of goods and services, whether produced internally or purchased abroad.

Marx retorted that Mill did not really break with the mercantilist system:

The opposition of modern political economy to the monetary system, the *système monétaire*, cannot achieve any decisive victory in spite of all its cleverness. For if the crude economic superstition of the people and governments clings to the *sensuous, tangible conspicuous* money-bag, and therefore believes both in the absolute value of the precious metals and possession of them as the sole reality of wealth—and if then the enlightened, worldly-wise economist comes forward and proves to them that money is a commodity like any other, the value of which, like that of any other commodity, depends therefore on the relation of the cost of production to demand, competition, and supply, to the quantity or competition of the other commodities—this economist is given the correct reply that never-the-less the *real* value of things is their *exchange-value* and this in the last instance exists in money, as the latter does in the precious metals, and that consequently money represents the true value of things and for that reason *money* is *the most desirable thing*. Indeed, in the last instance the economist's theory itself amounts to this wisdom, the only difference being that he possesses the capacity of abstraction, the capacity to recognise the existence of money under all forms of commodities and therefore not to believe in the exclusive value of its official metallic mode of existence. The metallic existence of money is only the official palpable expression of the soul of money, which is present in all branches of production and in all activities of bourgeois society.[27]

Marx reveals the degree to which he is embroiled in mercantilist preconception when he says that money is the "true value of things". Marx has advanced to the point of understanding the failings of bullionism, but like the somewhat more sophisticated mercantilists continues to insist that "as a result money is the most desirable thing". The point is not so much the absurdity of Marx's juvenile position, (How much money is a most desirable thing? If it were absolutely the most desirable good regardless of the amount held, then all men would be unthinkable misers who hoard money and survive on air. Why would a "most desirable thing" ever be exchanged? If it were not exchanged, how could it function as a medium of exchange?), but his failure to distinguish between money as liquid measure of wealth and wealth as a stock of productive assets.

The very basis for Marx's attack on the Jews was his own mercantilist preconception that profits arise from usurious moneylending, and hucksterism in trade. Mill saw profits as arising out of a competitive economic system; the opportunities for sharp dealing and usury were mercantilist symptoms of defects in the market system left over from the barriers and parochialism of the old regime. Mill advocated the more complete, perfect information market nexus, as a state of liberty. To be sure, it would be egoistical, but efficient in that the arbitrage functions of the "huckster" would be limited to small, self-liquidating margins arising out of minor market inconsistencies. Mercantilist limitation of the market, inhibited the division of labour and hence the growth of the wealth of nations.

Marx accepts Mill's explanation of non-metallic money, but finds its immateriality even more infamous:

> *Paper money* and the whole number of *paper representatives* of money (such as bills of exchange, mandates, promissory notes, etc.) are the more perfect mode of existence of *money as money*... In the *credit system* of which *banking* is the perfect expression, it appears as if the power of the alien, material force were broken the relationship of self-estrangement abolished and man had once more human relations to man... But this abolition of estrangement, this *return* of man to himself and therefore to other men is only an *appearance*; the self-estrangement, the dehumanisation, is all the more *infamous* and *extreme* because its elements is no longer commodity, metal, paper, but man's *moral* existence, man's *social* existence, the *inmost depths* of his heart, and because under the appearance of man's *trust* in man is the height of *distrust* and complete estrangement.[28]

Marx exclaims, "How vile it is to estimate the value of a man in money, as happens in the credit relationship". He means: How Jewish it is! One shows trust in "his fellow man not being a swindler but a 'good' man. By a 'good' man, the one who bestows his trust understands like Shylock, a man who is able to pay". Mill, in contrast, sees the "invention of bills of exchange, ascribed to Jews, in the feudal and barbarous ages" as merely an efficient means of international payment and division of labour as well as a precursor of other forms of paper money.[29] For Mill, libertarian and a friend of Ricardo, neither "Jew" nor trade was a term of opprobrium. "Dirty Jewish" is not an expression that occurs to him.

In search of the self-realization of Man, Marx rebelled against Mill's reduction of economics to a system of natural constraints. Overstating his case, Marx insisted that all the relations which limited men were social in character. Herein lay the basis for the unfreedom of a society based on private property mediated by exchange. In the market nexus, social intercourse does not appear to each individual as a conscious, free, unconstrained act of human cooperation. On the contrary, Marx said, it is founded on the compulsion of need.

There is, of course, no escape from restraint and compulsion on the individual. The desires and needs of others impinge on one socially, just as the physical realities limit absolute freedom materially. Freedom, for Marx, is the Hegelian identification of the individual with the whole. In his voluntary human cooperation, Man frees himself. Under a regime of private property, however, the individual does not subsume himself in the love of his species. On the contrary, he lives in a world of hedonistic wants and desires; and driven by scarcity—need—he strives for more material goods for egoistic satisfaction. The more men produce and consume, the more effectively do their efforts reach the boundaries of the possibilities available, both socially and physically. Man becomes less and less free in this paradoxical Hegelian sense. Insofar as the individual considers his own self-love, Marx is saying, he makes a prison for himself. Through universal love—as Hegel explained in his exegesis of Christianity—Man frees himself from his carnal egoism.

Marx translates this view of freedom into economics. Under a regime of private property:

Labour to earn a living involves: 1) estrangement and fortuitous connection between labour and the subject who labours; 2) estrangement and fortuitous connection between labour and the object of labour; 3) that the worker's role is determined by social needs which, however, are alien to him and a compulsion to which he submits out of egoistic need and necessity, and which have for him only the significance of a means of satisfying his dire need, just as for them he exists only as a slave of their needs; 4) that to the worker the maintenance of his individual existence appears to be the *purpose* of his activity and what he actually does is regarded by him only as a means; that he carries on his life's activity in order to earn a means of *subsistence*.

Hence the greater and the more developed the social power appears to be within the private property relationship, the more *egoistic*, asocial and estranged from his own nature does man become.[30]

Each individual man suffers, because he is driven. His work is not an expression of himself as an individual. Since it is work for another how can he express himself as an individual? Only by freely abandoning claims to illusory individual rights and submerging himself in the interest of the species. Work is then for Man, not individual men. "Hell", as Sartre told us in a similar humanist vein, "is other people."

Under private property Man is bounded by other men through the process of division of labour and the consequences of exchange:[31]

Just as the mutual exchange of the products of *human activity* appears as *barter*, as trade, so the mutual completion and exchange of the activity itself appears as division of labour, which turns man as far as possible into an abstract being, a machine tool, etc., and transforms him into a spiritual and physical monster.

It is precisely the *unity* of human labour that is regarded merely as *division* of labour, because social nature only comes into existence as its opposite, in the form of estrangement.[32]

What sort of world would eliminate the estrangement? What is Marx's image of the world of freedom beyond alienation?

Let us suppose that we had carried out production as human beings. Each of us would have in *two ways affirmed himself* and the other person. 1) In my *production* I would have objectified my *individuality*, its *specific character*, and therefore enjoyed not only an individual *manifestation of my life* during the activity, but also when looking at the object I would have the individual pleasure of knowing my personality to be *objective, visible to the senses* and hence a power *beyond all doubt*. 2) In your enjoyment or use of my product I would have the *direct* enjoyment both of being conscious of having satisfied a *human* need by my work, that is, of having objectified *man's* essential nature, and of having thus created an object corresponding to the need of another man's essential nature. 3) I would have been for you the *mediator* between you and the species, and therefore would become recognised and felt by you yourself as a completion of your own essential nature and consequently would know myself to be confirmed both in your thought and your love. 4) In the individual expression of my life I would have directly created your expression of your life and therefore in my individual activity I would have directly *confirmed* and *realised* my true nature, my *human* nature, my *communal* nature.

Our products would be so many mirrors in which we saw reflected our essential nature.

This relationship would moreover be reciprocal; what occurs on my side has also to occur on yours.

Let us review the various factors as seen in our supposition: My work would be a *free manifestation of life*, hence an *enjoyment of life*. Presupposing private property, my work is an *alienation of life*, for I work in *order to live*, in order to obtain for myself the *means* of life. My work is *not* my life.

Secondly, the *specific nature* of my individuality, therefore, would be affirmed in my labour, since the latter would be an affirmation of my *individual* life. Labour therefore would be *true*, *active property*. Presupposing private property, my individuality is alienated to such a degree that this *activity* is instead *hateful* to me, a *torment*, and rather the *semblance* of an activity. Hence, too, it is only a *forced* activity and one imposed on me only through an *external* fortuitous need, *not* through an *inner, essential* one.[33]

But the profane world of private property, of the awakening of individual desire, has expelled man temporarily from this economic Kingdom of God. Humanity makes itself the apparent master of the goods it produces, but in reality a slave to the desire for material things:

Although in your eyes your product is an *instrument*, a *means*, for taking possession of my product and thus for satisfying your need; yet in my eyes it is the *purpose* of our exchange. For me, you are rather the means and instrument for producing this object that is my aim, just as conversely you stand in the same relationship to my object. But 1) each of us actually *behaves* in the way he is regarded by the other. You have actually made yourself the means, the instrument, the producer of *your* own object in order to gain possession of mine; 2) your own object is for you only the *sensuously perceptible covering*, the *hidden shape*, of my object; for its production *signifies* and seeks to *express* the *acquisition* of my object. In fact therefore, you have become for yourself a *means*, and *instrument* of your object, of which your desire is the *servant*, and you have performed menial services in order that the object shall never again do a favour to your desire. If then our mutual thraldom to the object at the beginning of the process is now seen to be in reality the relationship between *master* and *slave*, that is merely the *crude* and frank expression of our *essential* relationship.

Our *mutual* value is for us the *value* of our mutual objects. Hence for us man himself is mutually of *no value*.[34]

The real world of bourgeois society is not the Christian ideal, but the rule of Judaism, Marx told us in his essay *On the Jewish Question*. There is no mistaking the same sense of disgrace, self-loathing in his description of present society:

The only intelligible language in which we converse with one another consists of our objects in their relation to each other. We would not understand a human language and it would remain without effect. By one side it would be recognised and felt as being a request, an entreaty, and therefore a *humiliation*, and consequently uttered with a feeling of shame, of degradation. By the other side it would be regarded as *impudence* or *lunacy* and rejected as such. We are to such an extent estranged from man's essential nature that the direct language of this essential nature seems to us a *violation of human dignity*, whereas the estranged language of material values seems to be the well-justified assertion of human dignity that is self-confident and conscious itself.[35]

One does not have to be psychiatrist to interpret such a passage, in light of what we know about the idealized image projected by Heinrich Marx, and the reality of his sycophancy. One has to feel compassion for his driven, compulsive son, attempting to escape from the web of shame.

Later Marx would look back at the concept of abstract man and comment that it was precisely a world of commodity exchange that gave rise to the concept. It was not that there existed an essential human nature violated by commodity production, but on the contrary it was the commodity form which gave rise to the cult of humanism. In *Capital*, Marx identifies the abstract man with Protestant Christianity as well as Deism as the essential religion of the bourgeoisie:

> The religious world is but the reflex of the real world. And for a society based upon the production of commodities, in which the producers in general enter into social relations with one another by treating their products as commodities and values, whereby they reduce their individual private labor to the standard of homogeneous human labor—for such a society, Christianity with its *cultus* of abstract man, more especially in its bourgeois developments, Protestantism, Deism, etc., is the most fitting form of religion.[36]

And for the Jews as a "trading nation", the mature Marx offers a bit of objectivity related to the primitive level of exchange in pre-capitalist societies. "Trading nations, properly so called, exist in the ancient world only in its interstices, like the gods of Epicurus in the Intermundia, or like Jews in the Pores of Polish society."[37] In *Capital* Marx avoids any denigration of the Jews, now placed in historical context. Ultimately the mysterious "fetishism of commodities" will be relieved, as a cumulative consequence of production rather than "emancipation from Judaism".

> The life-process of society, which is based on the process of material production, does not strip off its mystical veil until it is treated as production by freely associated men, and is consciously regulated by them in accordance with a settled plan. This however, demands for society a certain material groundwork or set of conditions of existence which in their turn are the spontaneous product of a long and painful process of development.[38]

For all its failings, Marx's earliest critique of James Mill did contain an element of meaningful criticism, in that Marx refused to believe that the basic determinants of the distribution of the

national product were given by technological and natural repro-
ductive considerations. The demand element had to enter into the
process of valuation; and value in turn was a key to the distribution of income to the owners of land, labour and capital.
Marx's ultimate solution in *Capital* is well known: he adopted the
labour theory of value as his own. Applying it to the market for
the worker's capacity to labour ("labour power") he arrived at a
subsistence concept of wages stated in value terms. The balance
of the value added to the product by labour in excess of subsistence requirements was "surplus value". In turn surplus value
was subdivided by the capitalists into profit, interest and rent.

In Paris, however, Marx's effort to avoid the mechanistic explanation offered by Mill led him to deny the existence of any law
of value as an operational feature of the market. In practice prices
were determined by chance, expressed as the apparent vagaries
of supply and demand, this despite the fact that his comments
pullulate with misconception and are couched in pejorative
language. Marx's thinking contains an intimation of the more
modern utility explanation of demand. His insistence that
exchange values are only an abstraction for money, while money
in turn is the expression of egoistic personal desire would in fact
lead to a subjective utility explanation of what actually happens
in capitalist markets. The sad fact is that, instead of following
this lead, Marx searched for a transcendental concept of value
opposed to the sufficient explanation of prices determined by
supply and demand.

Insofar as the economic portion of the *Economic and Philosophic
Manuscripts* is more than a repetition of the arguments already
encountered, it represents Marx's attempt to offer an explanation
of the distributive process. Marx argues that the market operates
contrary to the interest of the labouring class. In form the *Manuscripts* is a palimpsest of Adam Smith's earlier Wealth of Nations:
Marx attempts to use Smith's analytic machinery to deny his
conclusion that the hidden hand of competition benefits all elements of society. All are the victims of the alienation of man from
his essence, but the workers bear the main burden of this heart-
less and inhuman society.

Lacking a theory of value of his own, Marx makes use of
Smith's concept of natural and market price. By natural price,
Smith meant the long-term trend of the exchange value of com-
modities; natural price is given by the cost of production em-

bodied in the wages, interest and rents, required to produce a good. Presumably, Smith had in mind an ultimate reconciliation of these costs with the labour required to produce a commodity; but, as Ricardo pointed out, the ambiguity with which Smith clothed the labour theory of value makes this less certain. Market price, Smith explained, was the outcome of the short-term higgling and haggling of market supply and demand. In a condition of "perfect liberty", Smith held that market price would tend to converge to natural price "soon". However, Smith was willing to postpone the convergence for reasons of imperfection competition, information limitations, variation of "soil and situation" and ongoing technical and social change. In this he is to be contrasted with Ricardo and Mill, to whom long-run equilibrium was always immanent in the short-term movement of production and even population.

Smith applied his distinction to the labour market. Confronted by Ricardo's subsistence theory of wages, Smith might have been willing to concede that in the final analysis the market wage rate was tended to the natural price of labour: wages equal workers' subsistence measured in corn, prevented from rising by population growth increasing the labour supply at higher wage rates. Smith saw this only as a tendency, depending on the relative rates of growth of population counterbalanced by the increasing demand for labour through the accumulation of capital. Wages might tend to fall, owing to population growth, but they also tended to rise owing to the growth of the wealth of nations. Both labour and capital, therefore, had an interest in economic growth. Growth was engendered by the division of labour which, in turn, was engendered by the extension of the competitive market.

Marx attempts to make the interests of labour diverge from capital. He claims that labour will be alienated and impoverished by competition, the division of labour, and market exchange. Marx's first manuscript is divided into columns, "Wages of Labor", "Profit of Capital" and "Rent of Land". After Marx pursues these distributional categories in parallel he writes across the columns a passage which deals with "estranged labor". [This title is not in the original manuscript and has been provided by the editors.]

Marx's exposition of wages is a revision of Smith's Chapter VIII, "Of the Wages of Labour". Smith had argued that when the market price of commodities is reduced towards their natural price, the burden of the contraction frequently falls upon labour more than upon land or capital. Labour is at a bargaining disadvantage with respect to the capitalists. Capitalists can join forces easily in bargaining and are possessed of resources which permit them to "wait out" the workers who need constant employment. Marx repeats Smith's observation with added rancour:

> Wages are determined through the antagonistic struggle between capitalist and worker. Victory goes necessarily to the capitalist. The capitalist can live longer without the worker than the worker without the capitalist. Combination among the capitalists is customary and effective; workers' combination is prohibited and painful in its consequences for them. Besides, the landowner and the capitalist can make use of industrial advantages to augment their revenues, the worker has neither rent or interest on capital to supplement his industrial income. Hence the intensity of the competition among the workers... The separation of capital, rent and labor is thus fatal for the worker.[39]

Smith was no less indignant than Marx at the low wages inflicted on the workers. Yet it was clear to Smith that while wages were low, they were not at the biological minimum of subsistence. Moreover, in a progressive state of rapid economic growth, the market rate of wages would tend above their subsistence natural rate. The degree of flexibility which Smith allowed to the market, compared to his Ricardian descendants, permitted an increase in the labour standard of living rather than inevitable misery.

Marx felt compelled to turn every aspect of Smith's analysis against such a possibility, and hence was driven to attempt some serious economic analysis. The results were not particularly impressive; but the point is that Marx is driven toward attempting an economic science by the very force of the argument that classical economics implicitly presented against his viewpoint.

Marx asserts against Smith: "The worker need not necessarily gain when the capitalist does, but he necessarily loses when the latter loses".[40] He follows Smith's outline and comments briefly on the effect of "cheap" and dear years in the price of foodstuffs on wage rates, the degree to which monopolistic profits resulting from the excess of market over natural prices might be passed on to employees, and the degree of variability of wages compared to profits. These terse notes mainly serve to reveal that their author was not yet capable of precise economic argument. Marx misunderstood Smith both when he was right and when he was wrong.

Marx's main economic argument points to Smith's assertion that ties the rise in real wages to the rate of increase in the level of economic activity. Marx points to what he believes to be the costs of economic growth to show the misery of the workers even in Smith's progressive society. Marx asks: "When does a society find itself in a condition of advancing wealth? When the capitals and revenues of a country are growing".[41] "But these are only possible" under deleterious conditions which he lists under three headings:

> (a) As the result of the accumulation of much labour, capital being accumulated labour; as the result, therefore of the fact that more and more of his products are being taken away from the worker, that to an increasing extent his own labour confronts him as another man's property . . .

Marx is concerned to compare the stock of capital with the flow of current labour. Capital appears more powerful during periods of accumulation; the power of the alien force confronting labour seems enlarged. Yet he is not able to say here that either wages are lowered, or labour's share in national income is reduced. On the contrary, as Marx himself pointed out in *Capital*, vol. III, "The Absolute Overproduction of Capital", this is a period of labour shortage and wage rise; just as Smith had said the increased supply of capital, far from weakening labour as an "alien power" increases the demand for labour to utilize the capital.

> (b) The accumulation of capital increases the division of labor . . . Just as he is thus depressed spiritually and physically to the condition of a machine and from being a man becomes an abstract activity and a belly, so he also becomes ever more dependent on every fluctuation in market price, on the application of capital, and on the whim of the rich. Equally, the increase in the class of people wholly dependent on work inten-

sifies competition among the workers, thus lowering their price.

Marx makes one sensible and one silly remark in this passage. Like Smith, he makes good sense in pointing to the depressing effect of extreme division of labour, even though he is not willing to follow Smith and weigh social benefits along with costs by pointing to the higher real incomes which result. Such less spiritual desires reduce man to a "belly". The silly remark is the last sentence cited. It does not follow that, because increased wages induce additional labour-force participation, wages fall. It might be that wages do not rise as much as if no further labour is forthcoming at the higher wage rates, but the limitation of the wage increase is certainly not a fall.

Marx repeats the same error in the next passage, which compounds the mistake by asserting that interest incomes fall during cyclical upswings and the degree of monopolistic concentration increase during the same periods:

(c) In an increasingly prosperous society only the richest of the rich can continue to live on money interest. Everyone else has to carry on a business with his capital, or venture it in trade. As a result, the competition between the capitalists becomes more intense. The concentration of capital increases, the big capitalists ruin the small, and a section of the erstwhile capitalists sinks into the working class, which as a result of this supply again suffers to some extent a depression of wages and passes into a still greater dependence on the few big capitalists. The number of capitalists having been diminished, their competition with respect to the workers scarcely exists any longer; and the number of workers having been increased, their competition among themselves has become all the more intense, unnatural, and violent. Consequently, a section of the working class falls into beggary or starvation just as necessarily as a section of the middle capitalists falls into the working class.

Marx concludes:

Hence even in the condition of society most favourable to the worker, the inevitable result for the worker is overwork and premature death, decline to a mere machine, a bond servant of capital, which piles up dangerously over and against him, more competition, and starvation or beggary for a section of the workers.

In the very next sentence, Marx gives the game away. He concedes that Smith is right about the rising tendency of wages under the expansive phase of business activity, but argues that it induces workers to overwork, to seek higher incomes within the system. If wages increase, the voluntary labour supply response dehumanizes the labourer: it is the free working of the market again that is Marx's main concern. Civil society, the self-interest of the individual, even as seen by that person himself, dehumanizes his psychic and physical well being:

> The raising of wages excites in the worker the capitalist's mania to get rich, which he, however, can only satisfy by the sacrifice of his mind and body. The raising of wages presupposes and entails the accumulation of capital, and thus sets the product of labour against the worker as something ever more alien to him. Similarly, the division of labour renders him ever more one-sided and dependent, bringing with it the competition not only of men but also of machines. Since the worker has sunk to the level of a machine, he can be confronted by the machine as a competitor.[42]

The cyclical upswing, Marx believes, is self-limiting. The result is the termination of the condition of expansion which he holds to be so harmful for labour. The end of the situation, however, makes labour not better off but worse:

> Finally, as the amassing of capital increases the amount of industry and therefore the number of workers, it causes the same amount of industry to manufacture a larger amount of products, which leads to over-production and thus either ends by throwing a large section of workers out of work or by reducing their wages to the most miserable minimum.
>
> Such are the consequences of a state of society most favourable to the worker—namely, of a state of growing, advancing wealth.[43]

Heads I win, tails you lose!

For Marx, any wage is going to be too low. Marx proposes to avoid "the mistakes committed by the piecemeal reformers, who either want to *raise* wages, and in this way to improve the situation of the working class, or regard *equality* of wages (as Proudhon does) as the goal of social revolution".[44] The issue is the "estrangement of labor" inherent in the process of producing commodities for others. We shall return to this theme, after a brief view of Marx's comments on profits and rent, completing the Smithian triad.

Like his theory of wages, Marx's theory of capital in the *Manuscripts* is not very different in positive content from that of Smith and his expositors. His moral evaluation of the claims of capital are, of course, harsh in the extreme. Capital has as its "basis", Marx tells us "private property in the products of other men's labour".[45] From the outset, Marx's complaint is that the "governing power over labor and its products" due to the ownership of capital is the consequence of private property. The reader must be careful not to see this as the theory of surplus value: Marx is not holding forth about capital as a means to extract unpaid labour from the workers, as in his mature economics. Rather it is the ownership of stock of capital that permits the capitalist to direct the worker. Capital as the product of labour becomes an "alien power" over the worker. Marx's explanation of the profit of capital as a rate of return on the capital stock simply cites Smith. He follows Smith's discussion of the minimum rate of profit as that return on material, equipment, and the wages bill, necessary to compensate the capitalist for risk. Marx quotes Smith on the existence of monopoly profits. He repeats Smith's contention that capitalists have an interest different from society in that they would wish to limit competition.

Marx then attempts an economic argument against the legitimacy of profits. He points to the "concentration of capital in the hands of a few", and believes it to be the consequence of competition. There is the suggestion that competition leads to monopoly insofar as there are economies of large-scale production. The advantage, Marx says, goes to big capitalists in industries which employ a great deal of fixed capital. Profits, Marx is saying with Smith, are a consequence of the claims of the capitalist for a minimum rate of return, augmented by a monopolistic element associated with large-scale production and imperfections in the market. There really is no difference in their position except that Marx's distaste for "huckstering" on the market makes it impossible to understand that this competitive process is precisely the means by which monopolistic profits are eroded. He sees competition as the means by which firms with advantages of large-scale production can absorb the room on the market of smaller firms, but does not appreciate that the reverse process is at work as well. Competition also serves to divide the market among efficient smaller firms against large, bureaucratic or governmentally subsidized institutions.

Marx's discussion of rent is an amalgam of Smith's views of rent as a monopoly price, and his own additional concern with the social power of the landed aristocracy. He begins his *étude* on rent with long quotations from Smith establishing the monopoly character of rent income from land as a return to an unproduced input. The landlord is shown to "reap where he has not sown". He charges a rent equal to the excess over the wage bill and normal profit return to agricultural capital. Marx agrees also to Smith's exposition of the differential components of that rent depending on fertility and location. Marx balks at Smith's assertion that the landlord's interest is ultimately identical with that of the rest of society. Citing the "political economists"—presumably Mill—Marx concludes that even though the landlord gains rent from the increase in population and productivity, his share in the national product is a deduction from the amount available to other factors. Hence the "landlord's interest is inimically opposed to the interest of the tenant farmer— and thus already to a significant section of society".[46]

Moreover,

> the landlord can demand all the more rent from the tenant farmer the less wages the farmer pays, and as the farmer forces down wages all the lower the more rent the landlord demands, it follows that the interest of the landlord is just as hostile to that of the farm workers as is that of the manufacturers to their workers. He likewise forces down wages to the minimum.

Adapting the classical view Marx continues to emphasize the antagonism between labour and land. "Since a real reduction in the price of manufactured products raises the rent of land [in real terms by lowering the price of commodities M.W.], the landowner has a direct interest in lowering the wages of industrial workers.''[47] (Parenthetically, one ought to remark how completely Marx was writing within the Smithian framework of a cost of production theory of value. In later years Marx was to deny vehemently that wage rates determine prices given by the labour theory of value. Workers, to Marx's mature view, could increase wages by class struggle without increased prices.)

Marx then proceeds to argue that the special aspects of land in feudal society have been eroded by the competition with capitalists. In the end the landowning class has merged with the capitalist class as a result of the competition of the landowners with each other and through the comparison of rental incomes with interest incomes. Marx declines to shed "sentimental tears" over the passing of the old regime. He had long demanded an end to feudal privilege and immunity from the market. Although he shows a twinge of regret, he says it is mere romanticism to confuse the "shameful *huckstering of the land* with the perfectly rational consequence, inevitable and desirable within the realm of private property, of the *huckstering of private property*".

The division of the feudal estates, Marx argues, does not eliminate monopoly. Rather, insofar as land enters into the market place free from feudal restraint, it returns to monopoly "in a still more malignant form". As in the industrial sector, Marx sees economies of large-scale production which tend toward monopoly power. To be sure, the feudal social forms exacted a monopoly rent, but the capitalist organization of agriculture having passed through the division of estates, restores a new kind of monopolization based on property in general, rather than land alone.[48] In rents as profits, the source of injustice and lowered wages is the tendency toward monopolistic power of the propertied class, which can be exerted at the expense of labour. Marx sees this monopoly power in the market place as the basis of labour exploitation in the sense of low wages. "Eventually", Marx says, "wages which have already been reduced to a minimum, must be reduced yet further, to meet the new competition" of displaced agrarians. "This then necessarily leads to revolution.''[49]

Clearly, Marx's criticism of capitalism went deeper than a tenuous argument with Smith about the tendency of wages. Marx meant to establish on adequate economic and philosophic grounds the criticism of private property as anti-human. The inspiration of the economic portions of the *Manuscripts* remained Feuerbach. Private property and wage labour prevents man from achieving his full essence as a "species-being":

> Man is a species-being, not only because in practice and in theory he adopts the species (his own as well as those of other things) as his object, but—and this is only another way of expressing it—also because he treats himself as the actual, living species; because he treats himself as a *universal* and therefore a free being.[50]

Utilizing the Millian labour theory of value, Marx turns to a criticism of the alienation of this species essence in terms of the estrangement of labour:

> The object which labour produces—labour's product—confronts it as *something alien*, as a *power independent* of the producer. The product of labour is labour which has been embodied in an object, which has become material: it is the *objectification* of labour. Labour's realisation is its objectification. Under these economic conditions this realisation of labour appears as *loss of realisation* for the workers, objectification as *loss of the object and bondage to it*; appropriation as *estrangement, as alienation*.[51]

The purported decline in wages is a symptom of this estrangement. Marx asserts:

> So much does labour's realisation appear as loss of realisation that the worker loses realisation to the point of starving to death.
> So much does the appropriation of the object appear as estrangement that the more objects the worker produces the less he can possess and the more he falls under the sway of his product, capital.[52]

Marx has spiritual concerns at heart, his economic arguments being an inessential and weak reed. All the previous consequences, he tells us:

> are implied in the statement that the worker is related to the

product of his labour as to an *alien* object. For on this premise it is clear that the more the worker spends himself, the more powerful becomes the alien world of objects which he creates over and against himself, the poorer he himself—his inner world—becomes, the less belongs to him as his own. It is the same in religion. The more man puts into God, the less he retains in himself. The worker puts his life into the object; but now his life no longer belongs to him but to the object. Hence, the greater this activity, the more the worker lacks objects. Whatever the product of his labour is, he is not. Therefore the greater this product, the less is he himself. The *alienation* of the worker in his product means not only that his labour becomes an object, an *external* existence, but that it exists *outside* him, independently, as something alien to him, and that it becomes a power on its own confronting him. It means that the life which he has conferred on the object confronts him as something hostile and alien.[53]

Private property thus makes the labourer estranged from his free universal self. Instead both labourer and capitalist live their limited, finite, individual lives.

In estranging from man (1) nature, and (2) himself, his own active functions, his life activity, estranged labour estranges the *species* from man. It changes for him the *life of the species* into a means of individual life. First it estranges the life of the species and individual life, and secondly it makes individual life in its abstract form the purpose of the life of the species, likewise in its abstract and estranged form.

For labour, *life activity, productive life* itself, appears to man in the first place merely as a *means* of satisfying a need—the need to maintain physical existence. Yet the productive life is the life of the species. It is life-engendering life. The whole character of a species—its species-character—is contained in the character of its life activity; and free, conscious activity is man's species-character. Life itself appears only as a *means to life.*

The animal is immediately one with its life activity. It does not distinguish itself from it. It is *its life activity.* Man makes his life activity itself the object of his will and of his consciousness. He has conscious life activity. It is not a determination with which he directly merges. Conscious life activity distinguishes man immediately from animal life activity. It is just because of this that he is a species-being. Or it is only because he is a species-being that he is a conscious being, i.e., that his own life is an object for him. Only because of that is his activity free activity. Estranged labour reverses this relationship, so that it is just because man is a conscious being that he makes his life activity, his *essential being*, a mere means to his *existence*.[54]

The remainder of the *Manuscripts* is devoted to advancing this philosophy of labour, the subject of our next chapter.

7 Philosophy and Labour: The *Paris Manuscripts*

Marx's unpublished *Economic and Philosophic Manuscripts of 1844* was an *étude*, an exploration of the extent to which Feuerbach's critique of religion might be extended to the realm of private property. Marx hoped to find a validation of humanism by inserting Feuerbach's Man and his labour in place of Hegel's Idea, and then to argue for communism as the human society which should supersede the regime of private property. Marx ends, as we shall see, by returning full circle to idealism, dissolving Man into Idea. Marx cries out for revolutionary action and finds no guide in humanism. The *Manuscripts*, therefore, constitute the last stage in Marx's Feuerbachian Paris period. By pursuing humanism, Marx made himself ready to end it.

Feuerbach represented himself as a thoroughgoing empiricist—even a materialist. "I unconditionally repudiate", he asserted, "the *absolute* immaterial, self-sufficing speculation which draws its material from within." Repudiating Hegel, he continued, "I differ *toto coelo* from those philosophers who pluck out their eyes that they may see better; for my thought I require the senses".[1] Yet even while denying all abstraction, without question he assumed the existence of a human essence (*Wesen*): Man as Man. Man's species being (*Gattungswesen*) existed latent in men, regardless of their frequently egoistic, misanthropic behaviour, which, alas, the senses observe every day.

Man makes God in his own image, Feuerbach argued, and from this vantage point speculated about the nature of Man from his religious myth. Given his starting point in Man as a species rather than a diverse cultural product, it was inevitable that Feuerbach's image would be an idealization of his own culture. We can apply Feuerbach's method of the analysis of religious projection to Feuerbach himself to see that the essence of Man was drawn from German Protestant Christianity, revealing

Feuerbach's own idealized image of himself. "What then, is the nature of man ... the proper humanity of man?" he asks, "Reason, Will, Affection." They are "the perfections of the human being—nay, more, they are absolute perfections of being. To will, to love, to think, are the highest powers, are the absolute nature of man as man, and the basis of his existence".[2]

Other religions were preludes to Christianity, the religion of universal love that opened the way for the inversion of all religion into the love of species. In contrast, Judaism was the reflection of inherent Jewish egoism. The compact of the chosen people with God betrayed Jewish national exclusiveness. Jews were preoccupied with self, monetary gain and gastronomic excess. Albeit in alienated form, Christianity brought Man to the point of understanding himself as epitomizing universal Love, Reason, Will. Supersession of the alienation, would open the way for the worship of Man.

Having settled accounts with God, Feuerbach dared to confront Hegel. In his *Preliminary Theses for the Reform of Philosophy* and *Philosophy for the Future*, he contended that Hegel's Absolute Idea was God in philosophical guise. The Spirit of reason whose movement encompassed and determined the finite, myopic vision, of men, was a philosophical alienation of real Man. Man's fundamental task was to understand himself as the author of social institutions. Man's nature was to make the world over in his own image. Marx took this over completely. His only criticism was that Feuerbach declined to draw explicit political conclusions from his philosophy.[3]

The heart of the *Manuscripts*, then, is Marx's study of Hegel.[4] How far can he extend Feuerbach's transformation of Idea into Man? Can he find communism in the humanist inversion of Hegel? Marx begins by giving full credit to Feuerbach's philosophy rather than the religiosity of Bruno Bauer as the "true conqueror" of Hegel. Feuerbach, he says, made three essential contributions in the supersession of Hegel.[5] First, he showed that philosophy is

> nothing but religion ... another form and manner of the estrangement of the essence of man; Second, he called for the establishment of "true materialism" and "real science" by making the social relationship of "man to man" the basic principle; Thirdly, he counterposed Hegel's "negation of the

negation," to "the absolute positive, the self-supporting positive, positivity based on itself."

The Hegelian "negation of the negation" is the core of speculative reason, which Marx struggles to replace with the positive. Hegel's triad, he contends, starts from the abstract empty universal, then annuls its emptiness and posits the actual, sensuous, finite, particular. When this movement is taken as a whole, its concept "restores the abstraction, the infinite—the restoration of religion and theology".[6] Marx sees that Hegel surreptitiously imported contingent empirical information derived from sense experience by positing the sensuous and particular in the apparent march of pure reason. The importation is sometimes brilliant and anticipatory, and sometimes a crude forcing of the then current science into *a priori* schemata; but it always is an inadmissible speculation.[7]

If Hegel's speculative negations were unsatisfactory, what sort of positive account of knowledge could Marx accept which would be "self-supporting"? Feuerbach in his ambiguity had on the one hand led back to pure empiricism "sense certainty based on itself"[8] and on the other to a "true materialism" based on the humanist view of Man. Marx had finished with empiricism at an earlier stage, and so plunged on with the second alternative which Feuerbach had bequeathed him in search of a "real science".

Feuerbach himself was driven by the same imperatives and moved toward increasingly crude materialism. He finally blurted out: *"Mann ist was er isst!"* Marx strove for a middle course. He sought a "consistent naturalism or humanism" which is "distinct from both idealism and materialism, and constitutes at the same time the unifying truth of both".[9] Marx set himself the task of bridging the dualism. He would make Man the "subject". The relation of man to man would constitute the active principle; at the same time he would consider Man as an aspect of nature, in the objective materialist sense.

Marx's argument is a chain of identities: the Hegelian Absolute Idea in philosophy purported to be an account of the entire natural and human realm of Being. Feuerbach had shown that the Absolute was nothing but a philosophical code-word for God. He had also shown that God is nothing but Man. The fantastic conclusion to which Marx drove was that Being is at the same time Man. Marx states the conclusion and then feels a need for reinterpretation—perhaps circumlocution. If Nature is not identical with Man, then at least it is "for" Man in some sense; if Man is not identical with Nature, then at least he is "in" Nature as a "natural being."

With this schema in mind, Marx analyses Hegel's *Logic*. Hegel's dialectic has as its "coin of the realm" he says, abstract alienated thought, proceeding apart "from nature and from real man". The first part of the "double error" in Hegel consists in the opposition between objective reality and "self-consciousness" which Marx takes as the Hegelian term for Man. The estrangement is only overcome in alienated form in Hegel, Marx asserts, since both "self-consciousness" and the world of objects which it confronts are taken into the higher level of Consciousness.[10] Thus Man remains alienated from the universal concept which supersedes human will and purpose. Man is limited by Hegel's idealization of nature and other men. Consciousness—Idea or God—has appropriated what are "man's essential powers, which have become objects—indeed alien objects".[11] Hegel's Man is therefore finite, limited, and inherently unfree.

Marx believes that Hegel expresses the truth of the present human condition, albeit in fantastic forms of the movement of pure thought. Alienation in Hegel is but a reflection of the reality in which Man alienates himself from universal Man through labour within private property, as well as spiritually within religion. The issue to be confronted, Marx insists, is to make the world over for Man. Hegel's thought forms, subsisting in the imagination, are beyond the practical reach of the labour of Man. The finite human capacity alienates Man from his potential power over the alien world external to him as an unbridgeable chasm. Man is conceived by Hegel as a bounded, finite creature, eternally a slave to forces beyond his control. Hegel's unbounded conception is Consciousness. Freedom in him consists in identification of the finite with absolute, holistic, universal consciousness—Idea. We might say, Hegel's freedom consists in the subservience of individual thought and will to some authoritarian whole.[12]

Marx also intends to make Man free, not through subservience to the Absolute Idea but in practical affairs. In a practical way, Marx conceives of Man becoming the all-encompassing universal himself. The second part of the "double error" in Hegel is the overcoming of the opposition between Man and Nature as the product of "abstract mind" rather than Man's "essential powers put to work".[13]

Having rejected the all-encompassing Idea, what remains in Hegel for Marx is a dualism: Here is Man with his own innate species nature! There is the natural world of objects and men! In their relation all Hegel can find is the eternal "shuttling back and forth" between two abstract and mutually distinct entities.[14]

The dualism must be resolved, if Man is to be free. So long as Man is limited to mere self-consciousness, the world of nature will appear as "thinghood", external natural objects. To be sure "things" are objects of human activity; but this limited compass leads to the "positing of a *real* objective world, but within the framework of externality and, therefore, an overwhelming world not belonging to his own essential being". Man must be included in Nature. Nature must be included in Man. Both can be true, only if Man is Nature.

How is the actual world to be "vindicated" for Man? Marx replies that Hegel has already provided the answer in "Labor". "Hegel's standpoint", "is that of modern political economy." He grasps labour as the essence of Man. In the course of the labour process, as Man appropriates Nature, he appropriates himself as well. He becomes a universal species being, since the making over of the world for Man requires the conscious effort cooperative efforts of all men, and their orientation toward one another as a species. "Labor", Marx cites Hegel as saying, is "man's coming-to-be for himself." Since Hegel carried out his analysis of labour within the framework of alienation, the only labour he recognized was mental labour: the struggle of philosophy to surpass human limited self-consciousness. Nevertheless, the truth is implicit in Hegel. "The other philosophers" grasped at separate phases of nature and human life as phases of self-consciousness. What they did is "*known* to Hegel as the doings of *philosophy*. Hence his science is absolute".

"The outstanding achievement of Hegel's Phenomenology", we are told, is "the dialectic of negativity as a moving and generating principle."[15] The process involves the self-creation of man through his objectification at first as "loss of the object" which is overcome as a "transcendence of this alienation".[16] Marx explains that Hegel understands this process of the negation of the negation only as a mental principle of Consciousness, rather than the taking of the world into Man. For Marx, Man is not limited Self-consciousness, as Hegel would have it, but the equivalent of Consciousness itself. Despite himself, Marx is being driven back to pure Hegelian idealism by his desire for absolute freedom on the one hand, and his desire to find Man in the world of Nature and society on the other. Marx finds himself faced with two absolute unbounded universals, Man and Nature.[17] In the absence of a third common ground, Man is ... everything!

Later in life, having put aside dreams of absolute freedom, Marx as a materialist dwelt on the mutually limiting and transforming relation between human beings and their natural environment in the course of the labour process. Men are the products of their social structure, which in turn is the result of the historically constrained way in which the "forces of production" are capable of transforming nature at each stage in their evolution. Clearly the transformation of natural objects into items of human use cannot mean the repeal of the natural law, but rather constitutes the acceptance and utilization of that law. The whole point of the mature Marxian doctrine, is the continuing change in Man even after the elimination of class exploitation. Marx's positive contribution to the social sciences is his very insistence on the irrelevance of such "metaphysical" entities as Man's inherent essence.

So long as Marx persisted in positing the two universal elements, Man and Nature, he would remain a prisoner of the same dualism he saw in Hegel. If the human essence really was not determined by natural alien forces, then Man must have his own "positive" inherent spiritual characteristic. In essence then he is not a "natural being". But if he were not a natural being, how could he interact with his natural environment? How would his spiritual essence relate to his corporeal character, and through it to the rest of the physical universe? He must therefore be a "natural being". Inevitably Marx is led to self-contradiction: insofar as he places Man in Nature, Marx is led to a limited creature, the result of his own development and that of the world about him. He cannot at the same time be absolutely free.

Marx struggled to escape the contradiction between idealism and materialism, expressing their resolution as the identity of humanism and naturalism. It is worth reproducing Marx's argument in full to see the inner struggle in his mind:

> Whenever real, corporeal *man*, man with his feet firmly on the solid ground, man exhaling and inhaling all the forces of nature, *posits* his real, objective *essential powers* as alien objects by his externalisation, it is not the *act of positing* which is the subject in this process: it is the subjectivity of *objective* essential powers, whose action, therefore, must also be something *objective*. An objective being acts objectively, and he would not act objectively if the objective did not reside in the very nature of his being. He only creates or posits objects, because he is posited by objects—because at bottom he is *nature*. In the act of positing, therefore, this objective being does not fall from his state of "pure activity" into a *creating of* the *object*; on the contrary, his *objective* product only confirms his *objective* activity, his activity as the activity of an objective, natural being.

Here we see how consistent naturalism or humanism is distinct from both idealism and materialism, and constitutes at the same time the unifying truth of both. We see also how only naturalism is capable of comprehending the action of world history.

Man is directly a *natural being*. As a natural being and as a living natural being he is on the one hand endowed with *natural powers, vital powers*—he is an *active* natural being. These forces exist in him as tendencies and abilities—as *instincts*. On the other hand, as a natural, corporeal, sensuous, objective being he is a *suffering*, conditioned and limited creature, like animals and plants. That is to say, the *objects* of his instincts exist outside him, as *objects* independent of him; yet these objects are *objects* that he *needs*—essential *objects*, indispensable to the manifestation and confirmation of his essential powers. To say that man is a *corporeal*, living, real, sensuous, objective being full of natural vigour is to say that he has *real, sensuous objects* as the object of his being or of his life, or that he can only *express* his life in real, sensuous objects. *To be* objective, natural and sensuous, and at the same time to have object, nature and sense outside oneself, or oneself to be object, nature and sense for a third party, is one and the same thing. *Hunger* is a natural *need*; it therefore needs a *nature* outside itself, an *object* outside itself, in order to satisfy itself, to be stilled. Hunger is an acknowledged need of my body for an *object* existing outside it, indispensable to its integration and to the expression of its essential being.[18]

Alas, Marx's natural Man—this corporeal, even instinctive creature—is even closer to Feuerbach's crude material man who relates to the rest of reality by his hunger. Materialist man remains distinct from Marx's humanist man's "subjectivity for objective powers" who posits his "essential powers" by "externalization of them". In the end, the contradiction between naturalism and humanism, the tension between object and subject, the conception of an external world as the essential species power of Man—all of these expressions drove the Marx of the *Manuscripts* towards Man as an all-inclusive ideal entity.

Like the Hegelian universals upon which it is modelled, the term Man is devoid of content. Meaning is illicitly imported into the term by restatement in terms of process. Man does not simply equal Nature, he makes himself, vindicates himself, by the labour process through which he makes Nature his own. The meaning of Man as a universal now is not a fact but a potential; it takes on concrete meaning as a future communist organization of society:

It is now time to formulate the positive aspects of the Hegelian dialectic within the realm of estrangement.

(a) *Supersession* as an objective movement of *retracting* the alienation *into self*. This is the insight, expressed within the estrangement, concerning the *appropriation* of the objective essence through the supersession of its estrangement; it is the estranged insight into the *real objectification* of man, into the real appropriation of his objective essence through the annihilation of the *estranged* character of the objective world, through the supersession of the objective world in its estranged mode of being. In the same way atheism, being the supersession of God, is the advent of theoretical humanism, and communism, as the supersession of private property, is the vindication of real human life as man's possession and thus the advent of practical humanism, or atheism is humanism mediated with itself through the supersession of religion, whilst communism, is humanism, mediated with itself through the supersession of private property. Only through the supersession of this mediation—which is itself, however, a necessary premise—

does positively self-deriving humanism, *positive* humanism, come into being.[19]

For Marx, individual freedoms are egoistic in nature. Property rights separate the individual from the collective, just as religion, in positing God as an other being, makes men into finite creatures. Judaism makes a principle of this relationship, while Christianity only pretends to unify men with the Deity through spiritual communion. Property, religion, individual freedoms are the limited world of men who act as slaves rather than an omnipotent species. Labour as the "species activity" of Man is the means of the affirmation of the inherently free, universal nature of the species. Marx proclaims the universality of Man. Man includes Society as well as Nature in himself. At the same time, Marx contends Man is included in them:

Man is a species-being, not only because in practice and in theory he adopts the species (his own as well as those of other things) as his object, but—and this is only another way of expressing it—also because he treats himself as the actual, living species; because he treats himself as a *universal* and therefore a free being.

The life of the species, both in man and in animals, consists physically in the fact that man (like the animal) lives on inorganic nature; and the more universal man (or the animal) is, the more universal is the sphere of inorganic nature on which he lives. Just as plants, animals, stones, air, light, etc., constitute theoretically a part of human consciousness, partly as objects of natural science, partly as objects of art—his spiritual inorganic nature, spiritual nourishment which he must first prepare to make palatable and digestible—so also in the realm of practice they constitute a part of human life and human activity. Physically man lives only on these products of nature, whether they appear in the form of food, heating, clothes, a dwelling, etc. The universality of man appears in practice precisely in the universality which makes all nature his *inorganic body*—both inasmuch as nature is (1) his direct means of life, and (2) the material, the object, and the instrument of his life activity. Nature is man's *inorganic body*—nature, that is, insofar as it is not itself human body. Man *lives* on nature—means that nature is his *body*, with which he must remain in continuous interchange if he is not to die. That man's physical and spiri-

tual life is linked to nature means simply that nature is linked
to itself, for man is a part of nature.[20]

Marx characterizes the condition of estrangement in which
Man is constrained by his needs. Labour which expresses the
human species activity is not free but only a means to satisfy
other wants:

> Labour, *life activity, productive life* itself, appears to man in the
> first place merely as a *means* of satisfying a need—the need to
> maintain physical existence. Yet the productive life is the life of
> the species. It is life-engendering life. The whole character of a
> species—its species-character—is contained in the character of
> its life activity; and free conscious activity is man's species-
> character. Life itself appears only as a *means to life*.

Marx distinguishes Man from animals by virtue of his consciousness of himself as a species. He understands that labour as
the species essence is not a means to an end, but an expression of
his innate creative activity. Man produces universally and freely,
once having overcome his self-estrangement, and contains within
him the whole of nature. He is free—absolutely!

> The animal is immediately one with its life activity. It does not
> distinguish itself from it. It is *its life activity*. Man makes his life
> activity itself the object of his will and of his consciousness. He
> has conscious life activity. It is not a determination with which
> he directly merges. Conscious life activity distinguishes man
> immediately from animal life activity. It is just because of this
> that he is a species-being. Or it is only because he is a species-
> being that he is a conscious being, i.e., that his own life is an
> object for him. Only because of that is his activity free activity.
> Estranged labour reverses this relationship, so that it is just
> because man is a conscious being that he makes his life activ-
> ity, his *essential being*, a mere means to his *existence*.
> In creating a *world of objects* by his practical activity, in his
> *work upon* inorganic nature, man proves himself a conscious
> species-being, i.e., as a being that treats the species as its own
> essential being, or that treats itself as a species-being. Admit-
> tedly animals also produce. They build themselves nests,
> dwellings, like the bees, beavers, ants, etc. But an animal only

produces what it immediately needs for itself or its young. It produces one-sidedly, whilst man produces universally. It produces only under the dominion of immediate physical need, whilst man produces even when he is free from physical need and only truly produces in freedom therefrom. An animal produces only itself, whilst man reproduces the whole of nature. An animal's product belongs immediately to its physical body, whilst man freely confronts his product. An animal forms objects only in accordance with the standard and the need of the species to which it belongs, whilst man knows how to produce in accordance with the standard of every species, and knows how to apply everywhere the inherent standard to the object. Man therefore also forms objects in accordance with the laws of beauty.

It is just in his work upon the objective world, therefore, that man really proves himself to be a *species-being*. This production is his active species-life. Through this production, nature appears as *his* work and his reality. The object of labour is, therefore, the *objectification of man's species-life*: for he duplicates himself not only, as in consciousness, intellectually, but also actively, in reality, and therefore he sees himself in a world that he has created. In tearing away from man the object of his production, therefore, estranged labour tears from him his *species-life*, his real objectivity as a member of the species, and transforms his advantage over animals into the disadvantage that his inorganic body, nature, is taken away from him.[21]

Marx pursues his theme of alienated labour in the remaining portions of the *Manuscripts*. We will follow a bit further in this direction, as he amends and reinterprets his philosophic statement in apparently more concrete terms. Nevertheless, the true theme of the *Manuscripts* is more apparent now, undisguised. In attempting a transformative criticism of Hegel, making Idea into Man, Marx did the opposite. He has made Man into Idea. Marx has played the game out.

Writing many years later, Engels criticised Feuerbach in a way which we now see also applies to Marx's position at the stage of the *Paris Manuscripts*:

In form he is realistic since he takes his start from man; but there is absolutely no mention of the world in which this man lives; hence this "man" remains always the same abstract man who occupied the field in the philosophy of religion. For this man is not born of woman; he issues, as from a chrysalis, from the god of the monotheistic religions. He therefore does not live in a real world historically created and historically determined. It is true he has intercourse with other men, but each one of them is, however, just as much an abstraction as he himself is ... Feuerbach, to be sure, at long intervals makes such statements as: "A man thinks differently in a palace and in a hut." "If because of hunger, of misery, you have no food stuff in your body, you likewise have no stuff for morality in your head or heart." "Politics must become our religion," etc. But Feuerbach is absolutely incapable of achieving anything with these remarks. They remain purely figures of speech; for Feuerbach politics constituted an impassable frontier and the science of society, sociology, was *terra incognita* to him.

He appears just as superficial, in comparison with Hegel, in his treatment of the antithesis of good and evil. "One believes one is saying something great," Hegel remarks, "if one says that 'man is naturally good.' But one forgets that one says something far greater when one says 'man is naturally evil.'" According to Hegel, evil is the form in which the motive force of historical development presents itself. This, indeed, contains the twofold significance that while, on the one hand, each new advance necessarily appears as a sacrilege against things hallowed, as a rebellion against conditions which, however old and moribund, have still been sanctified by custom; on the other hand, it is precisely the wicked passions of man—greed and lust for power—which, since the emergence of class antagonisms, serve as levers of historical development—a fact of which the history of feudalism and of the bourgeoisie, for example, constitutes a single continual proof. But it does not occur to Feuerbach to investigate the historical role of moral evil. To him history is altogether a mysterious domain in which he feels ill at ease. Even his dictum: "Man as he sprang originally from nature was only a mere creature of nature, not a man. Man is a product of men, of culture, of history"—even this dictum with him remains absolutely sterile.[22]

The dualism between Man and Nature was only papered over in the *Manuscripts*. No amount of Hegelian word juggling could obscure the fact that Marx had not developed a real explanation of how social change would be brought about. Once having posited a transcendental human nature, intrinsic to Man as a species, rather than as an evolving social animal, there was no way of explaining the changing consciousness of men. If Man had an "essential" human spiritual nature, then the most one could do is to point to the disparity between this nature and the alienated position in which men found themselves in a private property, market economy. Yet this very fact implied the acceptance of "nonhuman" values by human beings. How did these come into being? How was a change of attitude to be brought about? What determined attitudes and changed them? Change was the point of the whole exercise, yet Marx had no conception of it any more than Feuerbach.

Proceeding from his grand conception of universal man and alienated labour, Marx attempts to deduce private property and the capitalist–worker relationship. How does the "concept of estranged, alienated labour" express itself in "real life"? Building on the labour theory of value of the classical economists, Marx took it as verified as a "fact of political economy" that labour is "estranged" from the worker. He asks: "If the product of labour is alien to me, if it confronts me as an alien power, to whom, then, does it belong?" He comes perilously close to the truth when he concludes that "the *alien* being ... can only be *man* himself". But then he reminds himself that if man were understood in the universal sense then his labour would not represent an alien power as he is sure it must. Therefore, "if the product of labour does not belong to the worker, if it confronts him as an alien power, then this can only be because it belongs to some *other man than the worker*". Who is he? He is the capitalist, "the master of this object" living "independent of" the worker. The capitalist is the reason labour "treats his own activity as unfree".[23]

The regime of private property in Marx's idealism is an expression of the finitude of the human individual. Marx makes this clear in pursuing the analogy with Feuerbach's view of religion as a product of the alienation of the human essence. Property is the practical consequence of self-estranged Man:

> Every self-estrangement of man, from himself and from nature, appears in the relation in which he places himself and nature to men other than and differentiated from himself. For this

reason religious self-estrangement necessarily appears in the relationship of the layman to the priest, or again to a mediator, etc., since we are here dealing with the intellectual world. In the real practical world self-estrangement can only become manifest through the real practical relationship to other men. The medium through which estrangement takes place is itself *practical*. Thus through estranged labour man not only creates his relationship to the object and to the act of production as to powers that are alien and hostile to him; he also creates the relationship in which other men stand to his production and to his product, and the relationship in which he stands to these other men. Just as he creates his own production as the loss of his reality, as his punishment; his own product as a loss, as a product not belonging to him; so he creates the domination of the person who does not produce over production and over the product. Just as he estranges his own activity from himself, so he confers upon the stranger an activity which is not his own.[24]

Under a regime of private property, Man is not *conscious* of producing for the species. Consciousness was central to Marx's earlier definition of Man as opposed to animals; and now we see it as the determinant of social systems. The failure of Man to be conscious of himself as a species produces the capitalist, not the reverse as he would insist later:

Through *estranged, alienated labour*, then, the worker produces the relationship to this labour of a man alien to labour and standing outside it. The relationship of the worker to labour creates the relation to it of the capitalist (or whatever one chooses to call the master of labour). Private property is thus the product, the result, the necessary consequence, of alienated labour, of the external relation of the worker to nature and to himself.[25]

It is now clear that distributive economics is not Marx's true concern. His struggle with economic theory is a means to express the alienation of man. The issue is not labour's share in the national product, but rather that the products of labour are "taken away from him" in the course of production for exchange. Marx is not now saying that the worker's recompense for his is inadequate, or less than the value of labour's product. The point is that the product of labour confronts him as an alien power, as the property of some other man, to command his labour. Never mind that the worker receives the products of the labour of others in return. Like an animal, alienated Man must respond to need, not higher purpose.

Marx says: "Political economy starts from labour as the real soul of production; yet to labour it gives nothing, and to private property everything". Marx cannot, and does not, mean that wages are nil and workers live on air. Rather his complaint is that workers do not control the product once it leaves their hands. Never mind that they receive goods on the same basis. The products of labour are destined for Man only through the capitalist and the market as an intermediary. "An enforced *increase of wages*", he says, "would therefore be nothing but better *payment for the slave,* and would not win either for the worker or for the labour their human status and dignity." Even further, the *"equality of wages* as demanded by Proudhon, only transform the relationship of present-day worker to his labour into the relation of all men to labour. Society is then conceived as an abstract capitalist".[26] The inhuman aspect of private property is that the "worker sinks to the level of a commodity and becomes indeed the most wretched of commodities".[27]

Marx goes on to express his ideas in monetary terms: "We have to grasp the intrinsic connection between private property, avarice, the separation of labour and capital and landed property; the connection of exchange and competition, of value and the devaluation of men, of monopoly and competition, etc.—we have to grasp this whole estrangement connected with the money system".[28] Marx attempts to turn the classical attack on mercantilism on its head to make the point:

> To this enlightened political economy, which has discovered—within private property—the *subjective essence* of wealth, the adherents of the monetary and mercantile system, who look upon private property *only as an objective* substance confronting men, seem therefore to be *fetishists, Catholics. Engels* was therefore right to call *Adam Smith* the *Luther of Political Economy.* Just as Luther recognised *religion—faith—*as the substance of the external world and in consequence stood opposed to Catholic paganism—just as he superseded *external* religiosity by making religiosity the *inner* substance of man—just as he negated the

priests outside the layman because he transplanted the priest into laymen's hearts, just so with wealth: wealth as something outside man and independent of him and therefore as something to be maintained and asserted only in an external fashion, is done away with; that is, this *external, mindless objectivity* of wealth is done away with, with private property being incorporated in man himself and with man himself being recognised as its essence. But as a result man is brought within the orbit of private property, just as with Luther he is brought within the orbit of religion. Under the semblance of recognising man, the political economy whose principle is labour rather carries to its logical conclusion the denial of man, since man himself no longer stands in an external relation of tension to the external substance of private property, but has himself become this tense essence of private property.[29]

Even in a non-monetary exchange economy, evidently, Man would be alienated still in this "Protestant" sense by the continuation of the commodity form. In its explanation of exchange, political economy denies Man. It bases itself on the hedonistic satisfactions of individual men. The truth of their explanation, according to Marx, is the real egoism of the individual in civil society. The political economy of Smith, Mill and Ricardo is an expression of the real alienation of the man from his essence:

> Society, as it appears to the political economist, is *civil society* in which every individual is a totality of needs and only exists for the other person, as the other exists for him, insofar as each becomes a means for the other. The political economist reduces everything (just as does politics in its *Rights of Man*) to man, i.e., to the individual whom he strips of all determinateness so as to class him as capitalist or worker.[30]

Classical political economy had shown how the cooperation of men could be achieved in civil society by the division of labour based on each individual seeking his own welfare. Nevertheless, Marx insisted that division of labour is cooperation only in estranged form, an aspect of the alienation of man from himself:

> The *division of labour* is the economic expression of the *social character of labour* within the estrangement. Or, since *labour* is

only an expression of human activity within alienation, of the manifestation of life as the alienation of life, the *division of labour*, too, is therefore nothing else but the *estranged, alienated* positing of human activity as a *real activity of the species* or as *activity of man as a species-being*.[31]

Again, on Marx's criterion for a non-alienated society, men must not only cooperate, they must cooperate consciously, freely, out of love of species. Man as the universal species, must supersede men as egoistic individuals. Adam Smith's alienated cooperation under division of labour, Marx asserts "rests on private property and exchange".[32] As Smith had said, the division of labour is limited by the extent market.

From the matrix of alienation—private property, division of labour, exchange—flowed all the evil consequences of society. The market confronted each person with an alien power standing above him. The increased productivity attendant on the division of labour, took place in estranged, alienated form. It produced mere things, different from Man. Men worshipped things instead of themselves. Wants were created by the market, further deepening the dependence of individuals on the alien power. Above all, capital as the product of human activity, stood hostile, overwhelming and opposed to man as labour.

All this is epitomized, Marx argued, in money. Money is the abstract, universal commodity. It stands for all things alien to Man himself, and like God is worshipped by Man, unaware that it represents his estranged self. Repeating the theme of *On the Jewish Question*, Marx says of money:

The distorting and confounding all human and natural qualities, the fraternisation of impossibilities—the *divine* power of money—lies in its *character* as men's estranged, alienating and self-disposing *species nature*. Money is the alienated ability of mankind.[33]

In contrast to Marx's mature economic theory, the Paris writing places the onus on the market mechanism, and its monetary medium of exchange. In *Capital* Marx observed that the relations of the market involve only the exchange of equalities. His formula for simple commodity exchange is: commodities are exchanged for equal value in money and exchanged again for different commodities. As an exchange of equals, the movement C—M—C excludes exploitation. The key to exploitation in *Capital* is found in the sphere of production outside the market. Surplus value is produced in the factory. Money is expended to purchase an equal value of commodities consisting of means of production and labour-power, the self-expanding source of value. The use of labour-power creates new value; the products of production are sold for money at their higher value. Consequently the formula for capitalist production is M–C–M'. To Marx's satisfaction in *Capital*, the riddle is solved by the production of additional, surplus value, by workers at the point of production. Goods are exchanged as equals on the market, yet capital appropriates an unearned income.

Yet here in the *Manuscripts*, Marx both stresses and misunderstands the C–M–C form. It seems to him inhuman that money should serve as a medium of exchange between different commodities. Human transactions, it seems to him, ought to be between like qualities:

> Since money, as the existing and active concept of value, confounds and confuses all things, it is the general *confounding* and *confusing* of all things—the world upside-down—the confounding and confusing of all natural and human qualities.
>
> He who can buy bravery is brave, though he be a coward. As money is not exchanged for any one specific quality, for any one specific thing, or for any particular human essential power, but for the entire objective world of man and nature, from the standpoint of its possessor it therefore serves to exchange every quality for every other, even contradictory, quality and object: it is the fraternisation of impossibilities. It makes contradictions embrace.
>
> Assume *man* to be *man* and his relationship to the world to be a human one: then you can exchange love only for love, trust for trust, etc. If you want to enjoy art, you must be an artistically cultivated person; if you want to exercise influence over other people, you must be a person with a stimulating and encouraging effect on other people. Every one of your relations to man and to nature must be a *specific expression*, corresponding to the object of your will of your *real individual life*. If you love without evoking love in return—that is, if your loving as loving does not produce reciprocal love; if through a *living expression* of

yourself as a loving person you do not make yourself a *beloved one*, then your love is impotent—a misfortune.[34]

But who would trade like use-values for like? Not even Marx's reciprocal lovers of opposite sex. The gains from trade lie precisely in the difference in qualities of goods acquired from those given up. Autarky is unthinkable even for nations, and incompatible with life as a prescription for individuals.

Later, of course, Marx took an historical view of the power of the market in rationalizing capitalist production. The *Communist Manifesto* accepted the corrosive effect which the market exerts on traditional, pre-capitalist, economic structures as part of progress. Viewed in these terms, the exchange of unlike commodities, and the division of labour it implies, is part of the unleashing of the forces of production by capital. In due course, the presumed satiation of those wants will provide "to each according to his needs" when the unfettered productive forces of communism hold sway. But this will not first be achieved by the release of the latent human spirituality attendant on the elimination of private property. On the contrary, in maturity Marx believed he had found in higher levels of productivity the ultimate means of making self-interest irrelevant. In the process Marx believed that society would create a new Man consonant with the productive levels achieved, just as in previous stages men were the creatures of class conflict spawned by the then-dominant "mode of production".

Alienation is neither a Marxian historical nor a material concept. It is a state of mind. The parameters of alienation—debased spiritual character, sense of helplessness, frustration of unfulfilled latent possibilities, a sense of isolation, the crudity of naked self-interest unrelieved by higher motivations—are all what Marx later characterized as the ideological aspect of a society that was moribund for reasons rooted in economic analysis.

What are the features of a non-alienated society? How did the Marx of the *Manuscripts* expect the individual to relate to the communist society of Man? Clearly the individual must be a social being; but not in the positive sense that he is a creature of social conditioning. To be thus determined would be to remain a finite slave to alien power. No, the free individual must be conscious of himself as a social being. He must see his individuality as an aspect of the totality of Man.

Like Hegel's Idea, Marx's Man contained its own contradiction. Man also had to be both singular and universal. Marx attempted to transfer the dichotomous figment of Hegel's imagination to a this-worldly society. He tells us that:

> Above all we must avoid postulating "society" again as an abstraction *vis-à-vis* the individual. The individual is the *social being*. His manifestations of life—even if they may not appear in the direct form of *communal* manifestations of life carried out in association with others—*are* therefore an expression and confirmation of *social life*. Man's individual and species-life are not *different*, however much—and this is inevitable—the mode of existence of the individual is a more *particular* or more *general* mode of the life of the species, or the life of the species is a more *particular* or more *general* individual life.
>
> In his *consciousness of species* man confirms his real *social life* and simply repeats his real existence in thought, just as conversely the being of the species confirms itself in species consciousness and exists for itself in its generality as a thinking being.
>
> Man, much as he may therefore be a *particular* individual (and it is precisely his particularity which makes him an individual, and a real *individual* social being), is just as much the *totality*—the ideal totality—the subjective existence of imagined and experienced society for itself; just as he exists also in the real world both as awareness and real enjoyment of social existence, and as a totality of human manifestation of life.
>
> Thinking and being are thus certainly *distinct* but at the same time they are in *unity* with each other.[35]

For Marx, as much as for Hegel, there is no doubt which will emerge triumphant in the contradiction between the individual and the species. Man as the eternal, universal category for Marx, is the dominant whole. Marx permits himself a remark which not only expresses this priority but, in its flirtation with death, suggests links to Germanic literary romanticism.

> *Death* seems to be a harsh victory of the species over the *particular* individual and to contradict their unity. But the particular

individual is only a *particular species-being*, and as such mortal.[36]

The ultimate outcome of the romantic dominance of the universal purpose had a tragic outcome for Germany a century later. Indeed death was the outcome for many. Marx's humanism, even his anti-semitism, cannot be said to be identical with the National Socialist movement; but they shared more than a common ancestor in Hegel's statism. The grip which National Socialism had on the German mind, was not fully accounted for by the standard Marxist account of fascism as the creature of the right wing of the bourgeoisie. German fascism drew its mass strength precisely from the alienated middle and lower classes.[37] It bade them identify with the "highest" elements of the human race and achieve their self-realization in relinquishing their individual claims.

In fact, the Nazi regime did provide more than the self-effacement of individual self-denial. It permitted a degree of social mobility of the alienated in both military and civilian life in a way which was not even attempted in the preceding democratic Weimar republic. Thus it became reasonable to conceive of the will and purpose of a new order which transcended even German nationalism, but extended to humanity as the term was defined. Who were to be excluded? The inhuman creatures, starting with the Jews. They were associated with greed, huckstering and commercial capitalism. Socialism in the National Socialist movement could be harnessed to Hitler's purposes by identifying the inhuman with the Jews and, through them, any opponents of the regime. At the same time the relative social mobility that adherence to the Nazi party afforded suggested the semblance of a social order which transcended private property and traditional status.[38]

There was deadly peril in the ideas which intrigued Marx in Paris: for all his pretensions to the contrary, someone must speak for Man even as a species; someone must administer resources and enforce consent. The danger of any universalism is the unlimited, "free", extent of that power.

As a philosopher of the universal, Marx necessarily opposed liberal British empiricism. Standing as he did for the primacy of Man in general, he still had to explain individual experience in its positive and normative aspects: he had to account for individual sense perceptions of the external world; and he had to show how the hedonic personal satisfaction of individual desires ought to be subsumed in universal species activity.

His answer to the first, epistemological question, is designed to show "how subjectivity and objectivity, spirituality and materiality, activity and suffering, lose their antithetical character".[39] The senses themselves, Marx asserts, take on a social character, becoming human "though the objectively unfolded richness of man's essential being". Reasoning from the analogy of the arts, Marx argues that "just as music awakens in man the sense of music, and just as the most beautiful music has *no* sense for the unmusical ear—is no object for it", it follows that the "object can only be the confirmation of one of my essential powers".[40]

Following from his conception of the external world as becoming included in Man, Marx argues that as Man becomes less finite, less restricted to egoistical concerns, his perceptions broaden. In the end the problem of an outside, alien, world, which is the external object of perception by the senses of the individual observer, is simply eliminated by making "human" sense all-encompassing:

> The forming of the five senses is a labour of the entire history of the world down to the present. The *sense* caught up in crude practical need has only a restricted sense. For the starving man, it is not the human form of food that exists, but only its abstract existence as food. It could just as well be there in its crudest form, and it would be impossible to say wherein this feeding activity differs from that of *animals*. The care-burdened, poverty-stricken man has no *sense* for the finest play; the dealer in minerals sees only the commercial value but not the beauty and the specific character of the mineral: he has no mineralogical sense. Thus, the objectification of the human essence, both in its theoretical and practical aspects, is required to make man's *sense human*, as well as to create the human sense corresponding to the entire wealth of human and natural substance.[41]

Man who is identical with Nature has no problem of perception: there is no external world to perceive, for it is already included in his species powers. Marx's solution is the classic response of the philosophers of Universal Spirit, from Spinoza to Hegel.

Marx's universalism is, of course, the antithesis of empiricism. Attempting to come to terms with Feuerbach's assertion that "sense perception must be the basis of all science", Marx attempts to grapple with the dualism by accepting it. In Hegelian fashion he changes his universe of discourse and includes the universality of Man in terms of an evolving process, becoming. He says, "History itself is a *real* part of *natural history*—of nature developing into man. Natural science will in time incorporate into itself the science of man just as the science of man will incorporate into itself natural science; there will be *one* science".[42] Driven by the dichotomy between Man and Nature, Marx clearly is moving toward a monistic theory of perception; it will take a year of further reflection before he breaks with Feuerbach's dualism and arrives at the materialism of his maturity.

Normatively, Marx had to negate Bentham's individual utility calculus. Satisfactions, humanly considered, are social in character. Man consumes collectively when functioning as Man, renouncing the egoism of private property. Identifying private property with any system of individual utility maximization Marx argues:

> Private property has made us so stupid and one-sided that an object is only *ours* when we have it—when it exists for us as capital, or when it is directly possessed, eaten, drunk, worn, inhabited, etc.,—in short, when it is *used* by us. Although private property itself again conceives all these direct realisations of possession only as *means of life*, and the life which they serve as means is the *life of private property*—labour and conversion into capital.[43]

Private property which Marx "derived" as a consequence of the alienation of Man now becomes its cause. With the abolition of private property the individual freely merges his desires and his efforts in the collective interest, without calculation of compensation. His efforts, his senses, his desires and satisfactions all are merged with the whole Man!

The abolition of private property is therefore the complete *emancipation* of all human senses and qualities, but it is this emancipation precisely because these senses and attributes have become, subjectively and objectively, *human*. The eye has become a *human* eye, just as its *object* has become a social, *human* object—an object made by man for man. The *senses* have therefore become directly in their practice *theoreticians*. They relate themselves to the *thing* for the sake of the thing, but the thing itself is an *objective human* relation to itself and to man, and vice versa. Need or enjoyment has consequently lost its *egoistical* nature, and nature has lost its mere *utility* by use becoming *human* use.[44]

With the elimination of private property, men will enter into the millennial Kingdom of Man.

8 Breakout from Humanism

By the summer of 1844, Marx had come full circle back to Hegelian spiritualism. The next year witnessed the breakout from the trap in which he had enmeshed himself. The transitional period begins in Paris, in the fall of 1844 and reflects discussions with Proudhon. The shift is recorded in *The Holy Family*,[1] which Marx wrote together with relatively minor contributions by Engels. Here Marx identifies himself as a humanist—but also a materialist and an empiricist. Marx's confusion of these philosophical schools is testimony to the fact that he had not yet broken with Feuerbach. This schism was to come later with the *Theses on Feuerbach* and *The German Ideology*. The point made in *The German Ideology* was that Feuerbach could be lumped together with Bauer as spokesmen for pretentious, petty-bourgeois German idealism. His doctrine was *impuissance mise en action*, as Engels said a year later.[2] In *The Holy Family*, Marx aims his shafts at the neo-Hegelian form of humanism represented by Bruno Bauer and his coterie.

Marx had signalled his disenchantment with Bauer already in the *Paris Manuscripts*, but in *The Holy Family* new dimensions of Bauer's thought are opened up for criticism. Bauer's capacity for hyperbole was more than Marx could take. But more than literary style was at stake: the title of Marx and Engels's book makes clear that Bauer's form of humanism is nothing but Christian doctrine expressed in extravagant philosophical guise. "Real humanism", Marx tells us in the Foreword, "has no more dangerous enemy in Germany than *spiritualism* or *speculative idealism* which substitutes '*self-consciousness*' or the '*spirit*' for the *real individual man* and with the evangelist teaches: 'It is the spirit that quickeneth; the flesh profiteth nothing'."[3] Marx goes on to specifically identify the religious content of Bauer's views, and in the Feuerbachian mode to identify them with Hegelian speculation although he is not willing to compare Bauer's capacities with those of Hegel: "Bauer's criticism is precisely *speculation* reproducing itself as a caricature ... the most complete expression of the Christian-Germanic principle, which makes its last effort by transforming "criticism" itself into a transcendent power ... In Bauer's criticism ... the nonsense of German speculation in general has reached its peak".[4]

As a rejection of the extreme speculative wing of his humanist colleagues, *The Holy Family* represents a step toward Marx's ultimate materialism. It is Marx's last attempt to refashion humanism into a more meaningful doctrine before giving it up altogether. The concept of the "human essence" is not yet expunged from Marx's vocabulary, but he struggles to reinterpret it in terms of individual men rather than a universal. Marx realizes that the consequence of positing any abstract universal concept as if it had *a priori* reality, trivially made the singular individual entity which exhibited the quality appear as essence is alienated from the prior universal term. This is at root the source of the Hegelian spirit against which Marx properly rebelled in his earliest *Critique of Hegel's "Philosophy of Right"*. Hegel's error, he contended there, was his inversion of predicate and subject. Now Marx contends that humanism, in Bauer's hands at least, is guilty of the same inversion of Man. "By changing the predicate into the subject, all the attributes and manifestations of human nature can be critically transformed into their *negations* and into alienations of human nature."[5]

Significantly for its religious implications, Marx singles out for ridicule Edgar Bauer's analysis of love; for Marx it reduces the concept of alienation to absurdity. Bauer has changed the *"man who loves"* into "the love of *man*, into a man of *love"*, as a result, "making 'love' a being apart, separate from man and as such independent".[6] Bauer's man is constrained, finite, alienated by human sexual love. Another person becomes the object of love outside the subject, according to Bauer, thus limiting his universal character. Such sexual love, Marx comments with heavy irony, is an "un-Critical, un-Christian materialist",[7] Marx pours venomous sarcasm on the universalization of the subject, in Bauer's hands at the expense of contingent objective reality:

Object! Horrible! There is nothing more damnable, more profane, more mass-like than an *object—à bas* the object! How could absolute subjectivity, the *actus purus*, "pure" Criticism, not see in love its *bête noire*, that Satan incarnate, in love, which first really teaches man to believe in the objective world outside himself, which not only makes man into an object, but even the object into a man![8]

The whole suggestion of alienated love seemed as silly to Marx at the end of his year in Paris as it had seemed profound at its beginning. Common sense seems to have crept in a bit, aided by the propensity of Marx's erstwhile associates to push the notion beyond all reasonableness. Egoism, selfishness, self-interest, far from being alien to human nature for Marx, suddenly seemed intrinsic to it. At least that is the way Marx reacted to Edgar Bauer who played the humanist game to the hilt, denying all the practical concerns in the name of the search for unalienated absolute freedom. "Criticism", Marx snapped, "is so *free* from all *selfishness* that for it the whole range of human essence is exhausted *by its own self.*"[9]

Marx was undoubtedly helped along the way in his escape from humanism by the contact with Proudhon. This famous French revolutionary is favourably discussed in *The Holy Family*. His *What is Property?* is defended against the Bauer group. Marx had earlier written to Proudhon suggesting collaboration in Paris. Proudhon's reply was wary, pleading the press of time in the preparation of his *System of Economical Contradictions*, better known by its later subtitle, *The Philosophy of Poverty.*[10] Proudhon confessed his concern, in any future collaboration, that they should not go about setting up a new dogma to replace the old. Nevertheless, the two men spent a great deal of time together in Paris. Proudhon claimed that Marx had taught him the Hegelian dialectic employed in the *System of Contradictions*. After their rupture in Marx's *The Poverty of Philosophy* (1847) Marx insisted that Proudhon did not understand either Hegel or economics. Undoubtedly both men were right about each other.

Nevertheless, despite Marx's polemical exploitation of even the minutiae in Proudhon's work, he did not rebut its critique of humanism which, we surmise, was included in their extensive discussions in Paris. In *The Holy Family*, Marx invoked what he took to be Proudhon's Gallic materialism and political activism in opposition to the philosohical and religious reveries of Bruno and Edgar Bauer. Proudhon does not mention Feuerbach by name, but his humanist materialism is the subject of criticism. Proudhon insists that materialism entails a dualism between idea and matter. Matter itself is unobservable by the senses, he says, but is itself a creature of "conscience". It is a metaphysical *a priori* ... unverified hypothesis of spirit". If one posits an essential human essence, Proudhon continues, "the *me*, an incomprehensible nature, feeling itself free, distinct and permanent", constructs a *"not-me"* which is "equally incomprehensible, but also distinct and permanent".[11]

Attempts to resolve the dualism, Proudhon continues, lead back to God, perhaps with another name. He says,

> whether philosophy, after having overthrown theological dogmatism, spiritualizes matter or materializes thought, idealizes being or realizes ideas ... it everywhere substitutes ... phrases ... which explain and signify nothing,—it always leads us back to this everlasting dualism, and, in summoning us to believe in ourselves, compels us to believe in God, if not in spirits. It is true, that in making spirit a part of Nature ... it has been led to this famous conclusion, which sums up nearly all the fruit of its researches: in man spirit *knows itself*, while everywhere else it seems *not to know itself*.[12]

Granted that "atheism, sometimes called humanism" has shown God to be a human affirmation of itself as something other than its own conceptions of itself, as all mythologies and theologies show", does it follow, Proudhon asks, that, "humanity, considered as a whole ... satisfies the Divine idea after eliminating from the latter the exaggerated and fanciful attributes of God"?[13] "Modern philosophers" have not provided an empirical "scientific" demonstration, of their conclusions. Moreover, Proudhon concludes, they proceed from the conception of God to describe Man, under the guise of using Man to describe God. Thus they have themselves conceded the notion of the Deity as meaningful *a priori*.

Proudhon's criticism is effectively destructive of the position taken by Marx and Feuerbach. The idea of God persists in humanism in the very conception of Man, "more tenacious, more pitiless than ever". Concluding in a vein that is certainly applicable to the Marx of the *Manuscripts*, Proudhon writes: "We have reached one of those prophetic epochs when society, scornful of the past and doubtful of the future, now distractedly clings to the present, leaving a few solitary thinkers to establish the new faith; now cries to God from the depths of its enjoyments and asks for a sign of salvation, or seeks in the spectacle of its revolutions, as in the entrails of a victim, the secret of its destiny".[14]

Out of a growing, still half-formed need to find a new philosophic basis Marx is led to re-examine the identity of humanism with materialism which Feuerbach had led him to. In the constructive portions of *The Holy Family*, when his thought is not preoccupied with polemic, Marx considers different forms of humanism which he identifies by national tradition. Germanic speculative humanism forever bears the stamp of Hegelian metaphysics. Feuerbach's contribution is contrasted with French materialism and its English variant. These western forms are seen as preoccupied with practical matters of property ownership leading to communism as well as atheistic elimination of religion.[15]

The practical question is: How to make revolution? Bauer is prepared only to talk and philosophize among the coffee-house intelligentsia, scorning the "masses". Marx intuits, at least, that Feuerbachian materialism–humanism is not very different. Marx needs a programme for humanism which will have a practical material base, and an effective communist economic programme for the reformation of society. All he can do so far in *The Holy Family* is to vacillate between humanism and a watered-down materialism, not distinguishable from empiricism.

Marx applies the term materialism to empiricism as well as materialism proper. There are two strands of French materialism that originate from Descartes, he tells us. "The former, *mechanical materialism*, merges with French natural science proper."[16] It arrives at geometry, physics, and, in human affairs, mechanical and physiological notions even of the soul. The book which expressed the "second strand" of materialism was Locke's treatise *An Essay Concerning Human Understanding*. It "came from across the channel as if in answer to a call. It was welcomed enthusiastically like a long awaited guest".[17] Locke supplied the proof, Marx comments, of "Bacon's fundamental principle, the origin of all human knowledge and ideas from the world of sensation".[18]

Marx reaches backward from Locke to identify his sensationalism[19] with his materialist expressions even though inconsistent with each other. He declines to go forward in the clarification of the method particularly in Hume. In some passages Marx clings only to the name of materialism; the substance of his concern is the strict priority of the senses which will lead him further away from Hegelian concepts as transmuted by the German ideologists until he can construct a materialism of his own. In the antecedents of Lockean empiricism, Marx also finds the nominalist key to escape from the tyranny of abstract concepts: "Materialism is the *natural-born* son of Great Britain. Already the British schoolman, *Duns Scotus*, asked, '*whether it was impossible for matter to think?*'" Then he adds: "Moreover, he was a *nominalist*. Nominalism, the *first form* of materialism, is chiefly found among the English schoolmen".[20]

Marx is clearly floundering. Under the name of materialism, he has convinced himself that he can speak of the primacy both of the individual and of society; he can think both of man as *tabula rasa* and of man as "truly human". For him man is a creature of self-interest and man is a social being. Man is educated by the processes of associative psychology, and man realizes his own essence. Man is the creature of his environment, and Man, when placed in a human environment, develops his "true" nature. Consider the passage in *The Holy Family* where he convinces himself that the second "trend of French materialism leads directly to socialism and communism":

> There is no need for any great penetration to see from the teaching of materialism on the original goodness and equal intellectual endowment of men, the omnipotence of experience, habit and education, and the influence of environment on men, the great significance of industry, the justification of enjoyment, etc., how necessarily materialism is connected with communism and socialism. If man draws all his knowledge, sensation, etc., from the world of the senses and the experience gained in it, then what has to be done is to arrange the empirical world in such a way that man experiences and becomes accustomed to what is truly human in it and that he becomes aware of himself as man. If correctly understood interest is the principle of all morality, man's private interest must be made to coincide with the interest of humanity. If man is unfree in the materialistic sense, i.e., is free not through the negative power to avoid this or that, but through the positive power to

assert his true individuality, crime must not be punished in the individual, but the anti-social sources of crime must be destroyed, and each man must be given social scope for the vital manifestation of his being. If man is shaped by environment, his environment must be made human. If man is social by nature, he will develop his true nature only in society, and the power of his nature must be measured not by the power of the separate individual but by the power of society.[21]

Marx has not yet realized that making man human by education and environment involves an infinite regress. Human society was seen as created by the conscious decision of men dedicated to human values. The insight that "the educator himself must be educated" is coming but must wait for the *Theses on Feuerbach*. In *The Holy Family*, he convinces himself of the "connection of eighteenth-century materialism with English and French *communism* of the nineteenth century". He cites—of all people—Jeremy Bentham[22] whom he later excoriated in *Capital* as the "leather-tongued oracle of the bourgeoisie". Indeed the passage he cites is Bentham's defence of the individual interest as opposed to the collective "*intérêt général*". He praises Bentham for his service as a predecessor of Robert Owen: "*Bentham* based his system of *correctly understood interest* on Helvétius' morality, and *Owen* proceeded from Bentham's *system* to found English communism".[23] Even Mandeville's *Fable of the Bees* is evidence of the "socialist tendencies of materialism".[24]

Seeking a lever to use against the speculative constructions of Bruno Bauer, Marx reaches out for the same empiricist elements he used against Hegel in his earliest critique. Now, of course, his doctrinal situation is much more difficult. Marx has more clearly drawn on empiricist and nominalist conceptions, and at the same time he is more concerned to label them as materialism. Whatever the name he gives to this brief return to empiricism, it is a position he cannot maintain at the end of his stay in Paris any more than he could at the beginning. Karl Marx was not to be John Stuart Mill. Benthamite calculations of individual utility do not, in fact, lead to communism and the conscious collective interest, but to private property and self-interest. The concept of Man was in danger of becoming a vacuous platitude in Marx's mind—or worse, a euphemism for the Christian God; but at the same time, the calculation of individual interests which he saw as the alternative in this portion of *The Holy Family* had at their end civil society and what Marx took to be the God of the Jews. The middle ground of dividing society into classes based on a materialist philosophy was not yet at hand.

In looking for a new philosophic ground in *The Holy Family* Marx had the advantage of a sound training in that discipline. In economics, where he had achieved only a first reading of the classics, he was less sure-footed. Marx turned towards Proudhon to suggest a way, even while cognizant of the faulty economic analysis that characterized *What is Property?*[25] Marx defended the "French" practical Proudhon against the "German" Bauer, even to the point of quarrelling over the details of translation from French to German. Proudhon is at least the equal of Feuerbach, Marx says, because he had a programme: equality. Proudhon would translate Feuerbach's German philosophy into French practice:

> Proudhon conceives equality as the creative principle of private property, which is in direct contradiction to equality. If Herr Edgar compares French *equality* with German "self-consciousness" for an instant, he will see that the latter principle expresses *in German*, i.e., in abstract thought, what the former says *in French* that is, in the language of politics and of thoughtful observation. Self-consciousness is man's equality with himself in pure thought. Equality is man's consciousness of himself in the element of practice, i.e., man's consciousness of other men as his equals and man's attitude to other men as his equals. Equality is the French expression for the unity of human essence, for man's consciousness of his species, for the practical identity of man with man, i.e., for the social or human relation of man to man. Hence, just as destructive criticism in Germany, before it had progressed in *Feuerbach* to the consideration of *real man*, tried to resolve everything definite and existing by the principle of *self-consciousness*, destructive criticism in France tried to do the same by the principle of *equality*.[26]

What is Property? retains its value even though "Proudhon's treatise will be ... scientifically superseded by a criticism of *political economy*, including Proudhon's conception of political economy". All previous "treatises on political economy take *private property* for granted",[27] whereas Proudhon had declaimed that "Property is theft!" Although Marx later came to the judgment that Proudhon's "equality" represented the petty-bourgeois and peasant interest, the charge that Proudhon was not a genuine opponent of property rights is largely absent from the present work. In *The Holy Family*, Marx sees Proudhon as generalizing the attacks on landed claims to income to other property forms.[28]

Property, Proudhon had argued, was "impossible" for a number of reasons, not all of which need detain us.[29] Marx's patience with Proudhon's bowdlerization of a dialectical contradiction as the "impossibility" of a state of affairs which is evidently extant, is testimony to his belief that his pupil in German philosophy was converging to his own view of Hegel. Marx's repetition of Proudhon's economic arguments, however, is testimony to his own lack of preparation in this area. Marx repeats with approval the charge we met earlier in Engels' *Umrisse* that "value is determined in the beginning in an apparently rational way, by the cost of production of an object and by its social usefulness. Later it turns out that value is determined quite fortuitously".[30] In particular Marx agrees with Proudhon that the hostile relations of wages and profit make for a crisis of underconsumption. The workers are unable to "buy back their product", since they create all its value, and yet only receive a portion of it as wages. Marx rejected this crude underconsumptionism in *Capital*, precisely because it proved too much.[31] It made capitalism impossible altogether, instead of being subject to the more dialectical sort of contradiction which would make a hitherto operant system into a disfunctional one.

Property was impossible, Proudhon told his readers because it was "unjust". Marx paraphrases Proudhon's position with respect to the wage bargain:

> The size of wages is determined at the beginning by *free* agreement between the free worker and the free capitalist. Later it turns out that the worker is compelled to fix it as low as possible. *Freedom* of the contracting parties has been supplanted by compulsion. The same holds good of trade and all other economic relationships.[32]

It is this compulsion Proudhon had contended, that makes for inequality. Ultimately property is theft, Proudhon argued, because exchange under compulsion gives rise to inequality. As one reads Proudhon's argument, it dawns on the reader that it is inequality which is regarded as unjust, rather than property as such. Indeed there is nothing wrong with "contracting parties", so long as they do not operate in "ignorance" or under "compulsion". In fact, Proudhon argues, and Marx cites him, that the institution of private property was "originally" at the time of the social contract, a necessary device for protecting equality, the weak against the strong, but like other human institutions it has become perverted into an instrument of injustice.

Proudhon has led Marx further on his way, despite both their intentions. When the market mechanism, Proudhon's "commercial operation of exchanging products or services", works under conditions of liberty, there is net gain to each participant through the division of labour and the specialization of individuals according to their diverse powers or training. Proudhon imagined that this would not be "repugnant to equality" since he considered the labour effort of each person from Homer to the simple herdsman to be equal. To arrive at this conclusion Proudhon had to consider the special skills of some labourers as an element of inequality, entailing neither scarcity nor sacrifice in their acquisition. Wages should be equal regardless of skill. He had also to neglect the principle of demand for scarce labour of various types under the assumption of unlimited provision of skills. This permitted him to reject the principle of "to each capacity according to its results"[33] in favour of equal distribution of the national product.

Bizarre as these assumptions may have been, Marx did not challenge them on economic grounds even though they led to the conclusion that liberty was perfectly consistent with commerce. If Marx wanted to find the deleterious effects of property on labour, he either had to follow Proudhon in exploring the imperfections of the market due to privilege, oppression and ignorance, or he had to look elsewhere in the economy for exploitation rather than alienation. Marx had actually done the first in his attack on the economic influence of the old regime in his *Critique of Hegel's "Philosophy of Right"*, and had arrived at precisely the radical petty-bourgeois egalitarian view as Proudhon.[34] He was not ready to do the second.

At this transitional stage, Marx would dearly have loved to

construe Proudhon to be a humanist. Proudhon "is himself a proletarian", Marx believes, and "his work is a scientific manifesto of the French proletariat":

> Proudhon asks himself why equality, although as the creative principle of reason it underlies the institution of property and as the ultimate rational foundation is the basis of all arguments in favour of property, nevertheless does not exist, while its negation, private property, does. He accordingly considers the fact of property in itself. He proves "that, in truth, property as an institution and a principle, is *impossible*", i.e. that *it contradicts itself* and abolishes itself in all points; that, to put it in the German way, it is the existence of alienated, self-contradicting, self-estranged equality.

Yet he must concede Proudhon's argument for the original functional aspects of property in defence of Proudhon's true goal of equality:

> While negating private property, Proudhon feels the need to justify the existence of private property historically. His argument, like all first arguments of this kind, is pragmatic, i.e., he assumes that earlier generations wished consciously and with reflection to realise in their institutions that equality which for him represents the human essence.[35]

The fact remained that Proudhon was a stubbornly individualistic, anarchist peasant. Not only was he opposed to any sort of communist collectivism, but the very aspect of private property which he did not call into question was the exchange of equal values in a market characterized by perfect information. The problem with property institutions was privilege and power not the humanist notion that the exchange process confronted Man with an alien objective process outside his control. Extreme as Proudhon's means were, his goals were stated in terms of the common-sense man of individual motivations—the petty bourgeois, the peasant. Somewhat ruefully, Marx is forced to concede that Proudhon at least is led by his concern for liberty and equality to continued estrangement of Man:

> Proudhon did not succeed in giving this thought appropriate

development. The idea of *"equal possession"* is the economic and therefore itself still estranged expression for the fact that the *object* as *being for man* as the *objective being of man,* is at the same time the *existence of man for other men,* his *human relation to other men,* the *social behaviour of man to man.* Proudhon abolishes economic estrangement *within* economic estrangement.[36]

Even while Marx saw Proudhon's underlying view of property as leading away from humanism and communism, Marx turned toward him in economics just as he flirted with empiricism in-philosophy *faute de mieux.* Marx evidently realises that this individualist line of thought will bring him back to his starting point at his father's knee. Yet he also realises by now that there is something terribly wrong with philosophical humanism. Bauer is a mouther of empty words. Alienation is not a statement of the social process, but leads back to theology and Hegel. Proudhon brought him to the brink of a rupture with Feuerbach's legacy. Marx will not be able to advance until he makes that break and, as he says, "supersedes Proudhon" in a more thoroughgoing materialist philosophy of history.

That break is not to come in this work. But all the groundwork has been laid. The contradictions Marx sees in Proudhon really represent the theoretical crisis in Marx's thinking. For all his sound and fury about impossibilities. and contradictions, Proudhon was asking that the bourgeois slogans of the French revolution, liberty, equality, fraternity, be put into practice. The civil society, which that revolution represented, accepted men as self-seeking on one hand, and equal before the law on the other in accordance with the social contract. Proudhon meant to update the social contract to deal with economic inequalities that had arisen after the end of feudalism because of the special privilege of unequal distribution of stocks of wealth in the form of human and material capital. Ignorance and oppression still remained after the successful storming of the Bastille. Difficult as it might be to implement, Proudhon argued that a revised social contract to bind civil society together was still both possible and necessary. It was essential to eliminate the imperfections in individual liberty rather than attempt to supersede individualism altogether. This was the essence of Proudhon's quarrel with Marx, even before they set eyes upon each other.

Since the end of the Kreuznach period with the *Critique of*

Hegel's "Philosophy of Right" (which bears such a striking resemblance to Proudhon), Marx had been arguing that it was not the imperfections in, but the essence of, civil society that brought about the dehumanization of Man. The very perfection of civil society permitted the separation between the "political" issue of making actual civil society fully consistent with its concept of individual equality, and the "human" question of the integration of individuals into their collective species. The distinction was central to Marx's critique of Bauer in *On the Jewish Question*. Marx could therefore advocate civil rights for Jews within "the democratic representative state, the perfected modern state",[37] and yet attack both Jews and the modern state for their anti-human character. Proudhon was right against Bauer. "All the contradictions in the political essence expounded by Herr Bauer in *Die Judenfrage*", Marx tells us, "are of this kind—contradictions in constitutionalism, which is, in general the contradiction between the modern representative state and the old state of privileges."[38]

Neither Bauer nor Proudhon was seen by Marx as capable of dealing with modern society. The victory of the modern representative state is epitomized in the "North American States", where the destruction of privilege, and its replacement by a competitive market economy based on private property unleashes the forces of industry and trade.[39] In the passage we cite Marx is aiming his shafts at Bauer's "Criticism". Nevertheless, his remarks show why Proudhon's alternative to the German philosophers will never do for Marx, even while he is absorbing the lessons which Proudhon offered:

The modern "public system", the developed modern state, is not based as *Criticism* thinks, on a society of privileges, but on a society in which *privileges have been abolished* and *dissolved*, on developed *civil society* in which the vital elements which were still politically bound under the privilege system have been set free. Here no *"privileged exclusivity"*, stands opposed either to any other exclusivity or to the public system. Free industry and free trade abolished privileged exclusivity and thereby the struggle between the privileged exclusivities. They replace exclusivity with man freed from privilege—which isolates from the general totality but at the same time unites in a smaller exclusive totality—man no longer bound to other men even by the *semblance* of a common bond. Thus they produce the universal struggle of man against man, individual against individual. In the same way *civil society* as a whole is this war against one another of individuals, who are no longer isolated from one another by anything but their *individuality*, and the universal unrestrained movement of the elementary forces of life freed from the fetters of privilege. The contradiction between the *democratic representative state* and *civil society* is the completion of the *classic* contradiction between public *commonweal* and *slavery*. In the modern world each person is *at the same time* a member of slave society and of the public commonweal. Precisely the *slavery of civil society* is in *appearance* the greatest *freedom* because it is in appearance the fully developed *independence* of the individual, who considers as his *own* freedom the uncurbed movement, no longer bound by a common bond or by man, of the estranged elements of his life, such as property, industry, religion, etc., whereas actually this is his fully developed slavery and inhumanity. *Law* has here taken the place of privilege.[40]

The resolution of the question by Proudhon, was the abolition of law. Marx's response was that anarchy does not overcome the separation of Man from society, but merely restates his individualism in extreme terms:

Anarchy is the law of civil society emancipated from divisive privileges, and the *anarchy of civil society* is the basis of modern public system, just as the *public system* in its turn is the guarantee of that anarchy. To the same great extent that the two are opposed to each other they also determine each other.[41]

The best course for Marx, seems to be to pursue philosophical humanism which, *The Holy Family* shows, reduces itself to coffeehouse fantasy. It is almost time for Marx to become a Marxist.

Marx must perform certain tasks to break out from humanism and still avoid a return to the substance of individualism: first, he must distinguish more clearly between materialism and empiricism than he was able to do in *The Holy Family*. Marx could not have helped knowing that the history of empiricism has as its outcome the denial of matter as an unobservable entity, just as it was the denial of the existence of God. Even Locke described the material object as "something I know not what". Hume and Kant had shown the term to have the same transcendental character as Spinozist pantheistic Substance. Indeed Marx directly quotes Hegel's "supposed explanation" of the identification of matter with "Absolute Being" as a "predicateless Absolute" in the course of quibbling with Bauer over the interpretation of Spinoza's influence on contemporary thought.[42]

Empiricism looks to the facts of sense experience as the source of all knowledge without fixed preconceptions. That is not to deny that an *a priori* synthetic is the conceptual prerequisite for observation; nevertheless these "models" are all hypothetical in character. The social scientist would be as free to generalize from attitudinal states of mind as well as physical relations to construct hypotheses explanatory of observed human behaviour. Saying the same thing in Marxian terms, empiricism would accept ideology is as adequate explanation of events as material or physical relations. For example, the modern economist considers the attitudes of individuals toward the consumption of goods which underlie demand as of equal significance as the technological capacities to produce embodied in supply. The interaction of the subjective and objective elements—neither being primary— is required to explain the prices of goods and services, their allocation among alternative uses, the distribution of income, and the like.

Marxist materialism establishes a hierarchy of fact. Materialism regards matter—or at least the physical labour relation of men in opposition to nature—as the *explicans*, the substratum; individual or collectively held ideas are the consequence, the superstructure, the *explicandum*. Marx's *a priori* synthetic concept is that the real condition of men is not given by what they feel or what they believe about their social condition, but by what they do in the course of the labour process. In *The Holy Family* Marx has not yet reached this point, but it is becoming clear to him that Man's essence will not do as the *explicans*. The end of that line of thought is the rococo mysticism of Bauer's holy family.

The second task that Marx must yet accomplish is to link his philosophy with an historical sense of progressivity which will not only remedy the defects of his previous thought, but will also encompass the revolutionizing industrial development he saw all around him. To bury capitalism, he first must be able to praise the system for its accomplishments. His previous humanist stance contrasted the present existence of man with the ideal human essence, and called for a reconciliation which would make society more philosophical. Despite the frequent use of such terms as "must" and "necessity", in the Paris period Marx appealed to philosophical necessity rather than to ongoing processes in the physical and social world. Marx's appeal to the proletariat announced in the "Introduction" to the *Critique of Hegel's "Philosophy of Right"*, of course foreshadowed an historical process. But even in this respect, Marx simply noted that the proletariat was growing in numbers and had no vested interest in property. Therefore they were the likely candidates to implement the liberation of humanity from its state of alienation.

Now, at the point of putting humanism behind him, Marx must construct a theory of history which will be consistent with the material relations of the labour process, rather than with the derivative attitude or ideology. Indeed, the ideological sense of alienation of oppressed classes from society, is to be taken as the consequence of the economic breakdown of a pre-existing mode of production. If the materialism which Marx is striving for is not to retain the same static aspect as his humanist analysis of Man, then the material relations themselves must be shown to contain an inherent dynamic of their own which will drive the workers to their destiny.

It has to be shown that the sense of alienation is not the bootless cry of otherwise free Man in the grip of natural and social processes which appear to them as the coils of an "alien power". On the contrary, the estrangement of the revolutionary classes from society, is to be shown as the consequence of a natural social—as opposed to conscious, purposive "human"—process. It represents the "ideological superstructure" of a system of production which is in its dying phase. The society which for a certain mode of production seemed not only rational, but inevitable, is suddenly contrasted with a new concept of rational order thrown up by advances of the forces of production. Marx's mature social dynamic is, at its core, the process of evolving class relationships under the pressure of advances in production and the consequent evolution of class consciousness.

Marx's final labour which was to consume the rest of his life was to find a materialist economic basis for his criticism of capitalism. Up to this point, his focus has been on the market. Alienation as a critique of private property had been carried on in terms of the inhumanity of the impersonal exchange of labour or the products of labour. Yet exchange in a competitive market is one of equal market values and, as Say was pointing out in his extension of Smith, net gains in use value to all the parties involved. Proudhon had really conceded that point in attacking the injustice of property insofar as that did not permit true equality of exchange owing to the market power of the wealthy and landed.

Marx ultimately was to say in *Capital* that the source of exploitation was not in the pure exchange of commodities (C–M–C, commodities–money–commodities), but in the extraction of surplus value from the worker at the point of production (M–C–M', money–commodities–more money value.) Money buys labour-power and the means of production which produce commodities for sale at an enhanced value. To be sure, for Marx, cheating and sharp dealing, the market power of the wealthy, and the planning power of monopolies, still played a part in making the market imperfect. Yet it was not the imperfection of the market that was crucial to the critique of capitalism. What marked capitalism as an exploitative system to Marx was the extraction of surplus labour above subsistence in the workplace even at competitive market values.

This conception of exploitation was based on the labour theory of value which was at once materialist and historically relative. Value had a materialist base in labour time spent in production. Moreover, the extraction of surplus value under capitalism placed it in the historical context of previous class societies where surplus labour was extracted from slaves and serfs. In these earlier exploitative societies, the market relation lay at the social periphery, according to Marx. Value and surplus value were the specific historical capitalist ways of exploiting labour consistent with commodity form of production of goods for exchange. The exchange of equal values on the market, C–M–C, appears central to the system only in the unhistorical minds of the "vulgar", "bourgeois economists" who speak of the "market system" as a euphemism for capitalism. For Marxism the production of surplus value is the essential aspect of capitalism as a stage in the historical process. The schema which historically differentiates capitalism from the C–M–C feature of all exchange systems is M–C–M'. That is why Marx's major work is called *Capital* rather than "Commodities", and capitalism is said to be historically obsolete rather than intrinsically inhuman.

Let us say this somewhat differently. Marxism in its maturity is on the side of increased productivity—economic growth. The end of division of labour and the process of exchange comes as the finale of an episode of "lower" communism in which production becomes adequate to satisfy workers' needs. The society which Marx advocated in the *Paris Manuscripts* would, in the absence of an era of capitalist economic growth based on further division of labour, have been a no-growth or low-growth economy. Indeed that is why the arguments of the *Manuscripts* have been attractive to many willing to dress in blue denim—out of either affectation, or religious and secular self-denial. Indeed, for some of this last group, opium has served as the religion of the alienated children of the middle classes.

How could a poverty-stricken utopia be maintained? If people had unfulfilled desires, could they at the same time view their labour as a game, as a pleasurable expression of their human activity? It is easy to see that given the choice they would work harder, longer, specialize more even in spite of the inhumaneness of the division of labour, if it would get them more good which they desire. After all if labour is fun, and goods are good, why not have more fun and more goods? It is as simple as that. Clearly people would work until the additional amount of labour was no longer fun. At least at the margin work has to be unpleasant if goods are scarce.

Of course goods do not have to be scarce, if people's wants are satiated—if that is possible. Seeing the vast burst of industrial production and the absorption of the consumer goods produced by the burgeoning economic machine, it became more and more implausible to say that the satisfactions derived from those goods were just egoistic "false consciousness". The view that the utopia of freely given labour has to be a high productivity situation became plain to Marx; therefore an intermediate stage was needed in which communist institutions would remove the "fetters" on the forces of production rather than squelch them.

One would expect that anti-semitism would become less central to his doctrine *pari passu* with his shift away from exchange and alienation. Indeed this is the case. In *The Holy Family* the transition is most obvious. After all, Marx could not defend Benthamite individualistic hedonism as communism and materialism on one hand, and denounce the Jews as egoists and hucksters on the other.

In fact Marx continues to repeat this denunciation of the Jews in the portion of *The Holy Family* which constitutes a rejoinder to Bauer's response to *On the Jewish Question*. Nevertheless the slander is muted in tone if not in content. In these sections the Jews are still identified with the "money system", and the villain of the piece is still exchange; but there is a flicker of sympathy in the choice of words which puts the onus on society for the reform of Jews rather than on the Jews themselves.[43] Moreover, with his budding historical sense, Marx sees the Jews to be the product of history, not simply the epitome of civil society. Even more important for the theory that was to follow, the Jews symbolize practical economic activity, and hence are one of the forces which have moved historical development forward.

Herr Bauer has no inkling that real *secular* jewry, and hence *religious* Jewry *too,* is being continually produced by the *present day civil life* and finds its final development in the *money system*. He could not have any inkling of this because he did not know Jewry as a part of the real world but only as a part of *his* world, *theology*; because he, a pious, godly man, considers not the active *everyday Jew* but the hypocritical *Jew of the Sabbath* to be the *real* Jew. For Herr Bauer, as a theologian of the *Christian faith,* the *world-historic* significance of Jewry had to cease the *moment* Christianity was *born.* Hence he had to repeat the old orthodox view that it has maintained itself *in spite* of history; and the old theological superstition that Jewry exists only as a *confirmation* of the divine curse, as a *tangible proof* of the Christian revelation had to recur with him in the *Critical-theological* form that it exists and has existed only as *crude religious doubt* about the supernatural origin of Christianity, i.e., as a *tangible proof* against Christian revelation.

On the other hand, it was proved [in *On the Jewish Question* м.w.]that Jewry has maintained itself and developed *through* history, *in* and *with* history, and that this development is to be perceived not by the eye of the theologian but only by the eye of the man of the world, because it is to be found, not in *religious theory,* but only in *commercial* and *industrial practice.* It was explained *why* practical Jewry attains its full development only in the fully developed *Christian world itself.* The existence of the *present-day* Jew was not explained by his religion—as though this religion were something apart, independently existing— but the tenacious survival of the Jewish religion was explained by practical features of civil society which are *fantastically* reflected in that religion. The emancipation of the Jews into human beings, or the human emancipation of Jewry, was therefore not conceived, as by Herr Bauer, as the special task of the Jews, but as a general practical task of the present-day world, which is *Jewish* to the core. It was proved that the task of abolishing the essence of Jewry is actually the task of abolishing the *Jewish character of civil society*, abolishing the inhumanity of the present-day practice of life, the most extreme expression of which is the *money system*.[44]

Referring still to *On the Jewish Question,* Marx stresses his arguments for civil emancipation of the Jews, and puts the blame for selfishness on civil society.

It was shown that the *recognition of the rights of man* by the *modern state* has no other meaning than the *recognition of slavery* by the *state of antiquity* had. In other words, just as the ancient state had slavery as its *natural basis,* the *modern state* has as its *natural basis* civil society and the *man* of civil society, i.e., the independent man linked with other men only by the ties of private interest and *unconscious* natural necessity, the slave of labour for gain and of his own as well as other men's *selfish* need. The modern state has recognized this its natural basis as such in the *universal rights of man.* It did not create it. As it was the product of civil society driven beyond the old political bonds by its own development, the modern state, for its part now recognized the womb from which it springs and its basis by the *declaration* of the *rights of man.*[45]

Marx then goes on to say that the rights of Man apply to all men. He seconds the argument by Riesser[46] that Bauer's argument is asymmetrical. Either Jews *and* Christians should be "hanged" for behaving like egoists, or they both should get civil rights; but in their rights before the law one group should not be treated one way and the second in another fashion.[47] Yet he cannot restrain himself from transferring his Jew hatred to society even while making this point:

Herr *Riesser* correctly expresses the meaning of the Jews' desire for recognition of their free humanity when he demands, among other things, the freedom of movement, sojourn, travel, earning one's living, etc. These manifestations of *"free humanity"* are explicitly recognized as such in the French Declaration of the Rights of Man. The Jew has all the more right to the recognition of his "free humanity" as "free civil society" is of a thoroughly commercial and Jewish nature, and the Jew is a necessary member of it.

Despite this nastiness, the stress in *The Holy Family* is the granting of civil rights to Jews as a political question, even though it will not solve "human" problems. There is a suggestion of putting the Jews in historical perspective. Marx notes, albeit with some disdain, "the polemic of a few liberal and rationalist Jews" against Bauer. These "poor opponents" not only pointed to the asymmetry of Bauer's view on civil rights between religions, but that the Jews have served to make the "modern times".[48]

Marx even blurts out his carefully protected sensitivity to the effect of the social ostracism on the Jews. He is discussing Bauer's attempt to save his thesis by substituting the word "society" for the "state": "Society behaves just as exclusively as the state, only in a more polite form: it does not throw you out, but it makes it so uncomfortable for you that you go out of your own will".[49] Marx makes clear that it is not only an abstract "you" that he is talking about in this passage.

> Absolute Criticism itself has argued that the state excludes Jews because and in so far as they exclude the state and hence exclude *themselves* from the state. If this reciprocal relationship has a more polite, a more hypocritical, a more insidious form in the *Critical* "society", this only proves the "Critical" "society" is more hypocritical and less developed.[50]

Anti-semitism was everywhere, and Marx did not escape it by writing *On the Jewish Question*. His enlightened friends, as well as the less *avant-garde* society thought of him as a Jew. One can see in these pathetic passages a glimpse of how they must have feared his intellect, sniggered behind his back, and salted the wounds of his sensitivity.

These shifts of emphasis away from anti-semitism, and bits of sympathy for the plight of the Jews, certainly reflect the real pressures of Marx's personal situation. He was in exile in Paris. His anti-semitism had only served to limit whatever psychological or material succour he could hope for from his family. Paris was as pullulant with anti-semitism as Germany. Proudhon, for instance, is characterized by *Encyclopedia Judaica* as a virulent anti-semite. Marx was befriended by Moses Hess the "red rabbi"; and through Hess, he became closely associated with Heinrich Heine, who shared his Jewish origin and alienated upbringing.

Apart from personal considerations, anti-semitism wanes during this period in Marx because it ceases to have the same function in his changing ideology. As he shifts the locus of oppression from trade to industrial production, there is even less rationale for identifying exploitation with Jews. They certainly did include in their number moneylenders and traders, but very few industrial capitalists.

As Marx begins to view history as the class struggle between classes of owners and non-owners of the means of production at the workplace, it is clear that the Jewish stereotype put them outside of this central exploitative relationship. They lived as traders, Marx said later, in the "pores" of old Polish society. Insofar as they contributed to trade and commerce, they served to undermine the economic basis for feudal society, the *ancien régime* and the Reaction even while doing business with it.

All these changes were embryonic in 1845 when Marx and Engels wrote *The Holy Family*. It was still necessary to bring a new philosophy, history and economics into existence. It is to this process that we turn our attention next.

9   A New World View

Marx needed a change of scene. The opportunity was provided in February 1845, by the order of the French government which expelled him to Brussels. Removed from the immediate and constant interaction with his colleagues, Marx was compelled to limit his political activity to that level of discretion which would permit him to retain his asylum.[1] Despite himself, Marx was provided with the occasion to review his commitment to humanism. Engels reported that when he joined Marx in Belgium later in the spring, he was presented with the "germ of a new world view" in the jotted notes which have become famous as the *Theses on Feuerbach*.[2] Together they spent the next year and a half spelling out the consequences of that view. Their product was a polemical work against their former colleagues, *The German Ideology*.[3] This effort virtually completed the break with the past—with a lapse or two.

At the end of his stay in Paris, Marx had embraced two diametrically opposed views of Man: one was Feuerbach's human essence, known through its projection in Christianity; the other was Locke's *tabula rasa*, devoid of any innate ideas, and entirely the creature of the individual's unique personal experience. Marx had to find his own passage between them.

Feuerbach is first rejected in the *Theses*, as a defective materialist. (In *The German Ideology* Marx goes further, and his former idol is held up to ridicule along with Bruno Bauer and Max Stirner as an idealist speculative philosopher, antithetical to materialism.) Marx had learned from Locke that man is not a static entity, an abstraction. He accepted Locke's teaching as the "materialist doctrine concerning the changing of circumstance and upbringing" in the formation of human character.[4]

Marx says that Feuerbach "resolved the essence of religion into the essence of man. But the essence of man is no abstraction inherent in each individual. In its reality it is the ensemble of the social relations."[5] To understand Man as a social product, it is necessary to jettison the notion of Man as a natural species, and investigate the historical changing of circumstances that forge Man as he exists in a particular form of society.[6] "Feuerbach", Marx argued, "does not enter upon a criticism of this real essence." He is "obliged: 1. To abstract from the historical process and to define the religious sentiment by itself and to presuppose an abstract—*isolated*—human individual. 2 Essence, therefore, can be regarded only as 'species', as an inner, mute, general character which unites many individuals *in a natural way*".[7] This "natural" way of regarding Man is to be contrasted with the social and historical moulding of human beings and their institutions. "Feuerbach, consequently does not see that the 'religious sentiment' is itself a social product, and that the abstract individual which he analyses belongs to a particular form of society".[8] Marx has concluded that it is meaningless to talk of Man in a state of nature in either the sense of Feuerbach or Rousseau.

Yet for Marx, Locke's so-called materialism is static in a way which is only slightly better than that of Feuerbach. Certainly Locke's associationist psychology left room for the alteration of human behaviour. In the hands of the Victorians to follow, the use of education and exhortation was seen as the means of amelioration of the human condition; social problems would yield, in the younger Mill's words, to the progressive "improvement of mankind". It seemed to Marx, however, that the programme of progressive reform involved its proponents in an infinite regress. If indeed all men are the product of their social conditioning, then those who would manipulate this process are themselves the product of their education. "The materialist doctrine concerning the changing of circumstances and upbringing", Marx says, "forgets that circumstances are changed by men and the educator must himself be educated".[9] In the spirit of the Kantian antinomy, Marx points out that the manipulation of men to higher purposes "must, therefore divide society into two parts, one of which is superior to society"[10]—an uncaused cause.

Marx was certainly right. The infuriating self-righteousness of all the Victorian reformers was the product of their need to place themselves above society to be effective as educators. Perhaps, it would be more fair to describe this as the character of all educators (parents?) who must function to infuse values by conditioning, all the while knowing that these norms are neither absolute, nor logically demonstrable, but the product of their own conditioning. Marx was, of course, unscarred by the present ethical ambivalence which refuses to inculcate what it cannot rationally justify, and ends by inculcating its ambivalence. The view of the *Theses* is the search for a positive theory of social conditioning, endogenous to the system of historically changing circumstances. The purposive action of individuals was seen as both determined by, and determinant of, the working of circumstances. For Mill the historical process was the cumulative "improvement of mankind" toward unquestioned moral goals as a result of education. Marx saw the social process as the cumulative development of the material practical capabilities of men in the social labour process.

Marx's necessary first step is to distinguish his concept of materialism from its faulted earlier versions in Feuerbach and Locke. "The chief defect of all previous materialism (that of Feuerbach included)", he wrote, "is that things, reality, sensuousness are conceived only in the form of the *object, or of contemplation,* but not as *sensuous human activity, practice,* not subjectively."[11] This is a double-edged sword for Marx. He believed that practice in this sense, epistemologically justified statements about material reality, and also provided a basis for a meaningful theory of man as the active participant in this reality.

Marx's practical justification for the use of the term "matter" parallels Kant's practical belief in God. In the *Critique of Practical Reason* Kant had argued the practical necessity for dealing with ethical judgments requires us to act as if there were a God. God is a necessary precondition for the moral experience which Kant took as the essential practical feature of human life: What ought I do? Kant's theory of God, was in fact a theory of Man, a moral creature acting in response to the "categorical imperative".

Marx came to the conclusion that it was necessary to believe in a material natural universe, as a prerequisite to practical human activity. Marx's purpose, like Kant's, is to understand Man, and to set out a course of action for him. Man can be understood, Marx is saying, as a product of his conditioning in his practical activities, labouring in a material world of nature. To understand Man, it seems to Marx, it is necessary to posit a material world. "The question whether objective truth can be attributed to human thinking", Marx concludes, "is not a question of theory but is a practical question."[12] It is not possible to justify the existence of matter as Feuerbach had, as a "sensuous object". Materialism as an explanation of human practice is a necessity for a theory of progressive "changing circumstances" which will not depend on an educator standing above society bringing about the improvement of mankind. "Man must prove the truth, i.e., the reality and power, the this-worldliness of his thinking in practice. The dispute over the reality or non-reality of thinking which is isolated from practice, is a purely *scholastic* question."[13]

The trouble with Feuerbach, Marx tells us, is that while "Feuerbach wants sensuous objects as distinct from conceptual objects, but he does not conceive human activity itself as objective activity. In *Das Wesen des Christentums* he regards the theoretical attitude as the only genuine human attitude."[14] Thus Feuerbach is led to see practice "in its dirty-Jewish form of appearance", Marx continues in the same thesis. Marx does not really decry Feuerbach's anti-semitism as such, but he points out that it is misplaced. It is precisely the this-worldliness of practical activity which explains Man. To focus on its "dirty-Jewish" aspect is to miss its essential significance in defining Man.

Marx is not prepared to provide us with a theory of how we may know the material world any more than Kant was prepared to describe the Deity. There is no answer here to the epistemological question posed by Democritus: Do the sensations produced by the presumably existent atoms, correspond to images of the way the world really is? Does the truth lie in the bottom of a deep well? Marx offers no theory of the method and extent by which valid inferences can be drawn from experience. In its place, he presents us with a sociology of knowledge. That is to say, he accounts for human ideas as derivative of the practical aspects of social material activity in the same sense that Hegel accounted for the "doings" of philosophy as the dialectical working of Idea. Knowledge is to be explained as are other ideas, such as religion, as a "social product"—later an ideological superstructure. Matter like Idea remains undefined, but is a means of expressing Marx's preconception about the order of causation in human affairs. It has no meaning beyond this.

A reconsideration of the third *Thesis* will illustrate the point. Does the statement that men are changed by circumstances and circumstances are changed by men involve its Lockean proponents in a hopeless antinomy? Certainly it does, in the sense that any "educator" can only reflect his own conditioning, and has no ultimate claim to legitimacy. Education—conditioning—is a creature of its own education. Does the statement that men are changed by circumstances and circumstances are changed by men mean that conditioning is not an adequate positive explanation of human events? Are its proponents forced to posit a portion of society which is superior to society to avoid an infinite regress of social causes?

In fact neither the general Kantian theory of causation, nor the Lockean theory of conditioning in particular, are subject to that rebuke unless one is looking for an ultimate, original, uncaused cause. The notion of social causation by conditioning of individuals, leads to an account of history as a sequence of singular events, each of which is caused by the antecedent conditioning circumstances surrounding interaction of human beings and their physical and social environment. The difficulty arises when one looks for an explanation which will not make the sequence dependent on the circumstances pertinent to each event (as well as uniformities common to them all), but insists on what Karl Popper[15] called an "historicist" complete explanation of those particulars from general principle. Then certainly, to attempt to explain all events simply from the fact that men are product of their circumstances and conditioning, falls victim to the fact that these circumstances are product of men. If, however, one is concerned with particular circumstances it is perfectly reasonable to explain how they shape men and give rise to new circumstances.

The significance of the third *Thesis* is that Marx is seen to assume the existence of an overriding principle which can explain both circumstances and men, and which he therefore must take outside the chain of circumstances in place of the educator. Instead of the education of men by circumstances, it is the practical activity of men which at the same time is the basis of the circumstances in which men find themselves. "All social life is essentially practical", Marx says, "All mysteries which lead theory to mysticism find their rational solution in human practice and in the comprehension of this practice."[16]

Marx is now fully aware that there is an unbridgeable gulf between his new point of view of the British empiricist tradition from Locke to Bentham. Only a few months earlier, he was prepared to call them communists; but now he sees that their "contemplative materialist" viewpoint is faulty: they are prepared to accept all sense information, including the state of ideas, on an equal footing with practical material relations; they insist on sense information as the source of all meaningful statements, which is as antithetical to materialism in Marx's sense as it is to theism; most important for Marx, as the practical consequence of "contemplative materialism", is its individualism in both perception and the calculus of social values. For him all these issues are conjoined. For perception is a practical activity, itself collective and social, as was already signalled in *The Holy Family*. In the ninth *Thesis* Marx explicitly relates the individual's role in the act of perception to the individualism of civil society. "The highest point reached by contemplative materialism, that is, materialism which does not comprehend sensuousness as practical activity, is the contemplation of single individuals and of civil society."[17]

Still not able to advance a class theory of history, and dissatisfied with the category of Man, Marx realizes that the individualist conception of society is incompatible with his new conception of collective practice. He is certain in the tenth *Thesis* that "the standpoint of the old materialism is civil society", and not knowing quite what to put in its place he continues, "the standpoint of the new is human society, or social humanity"[18]

From our present vantage point, we can see how, in each stage of his development, Marx has taken a distinctly different view toward the legitimacy of the individualist definition of welfare. In his first stage, individualism in perception and social purpose were part of the defence of democracy in civil society. Despite its waverings and Feuerbachian language, this was the message of the *Critique of Hegel's "Philosophy of Right"*, as well as related journalistic writings. The second, humanistic, stage, regarded hedonism as egoistic, "dirty-Jewish", anti-human. In the opening statements of his mature viewpoint, he used empiricist and hedonist artillery as a way to batter down the metaphysics of "the holy family", but remained unwilling to use these individualist concepts in a constructive rather than critical way. Marx has come to his final view that the social truth which can explain—and bring about—change is not the viewpoint of individuals, but the practical activity in which they are engaged. To the "old materialism", capitalism is simply civil society. Marx is to say very soon after the *Theses* that hedonism is simply the viewpoint of capitalism, expressing its ideological superstructure, and concealing its mode of production which is the essence of the system. The *Theses on Feuerbach* initiate Marx's turn towards a deterministic science of society. There are some signs that he might have relented in later years. Certainly he always did hedge on the deterministic aspect of the theory by referring to short-term ideological influences, especially in the analysis of concrete political circumstances. Nevertheless, the core of Marxism is its belief in the objective nature of the progression of history toward communism. Yet the *Theses* make clear that there is an equal element of activism along with determinism in bringing social change about. Marx is saying more than that practical activity in the labour process develops social forces which will change the world. He is also saying that practical activity includes the conscious bringing about of a social revolution.

This dual theme of objective determinism on one hand, and subjective revolutionary purpose on the other, intertwine at every turn. The ringing final thesis, "the philosophers have only *interpreted* the world in various ways; the point is to change it",[19] only encapsulates the active theme which is evident from the start. The first thesis chides Feuerbach for not appreciating the importance of "revolutionary" "practical–critical" activity. The significance of the active "subject" was "set forth abstractly by idealism", but must be integrated in the new revolutionary materialism.

It is in the third *Thesis*, however, that we best can appreciate how Marx views the matter. We have already discussed the first brief paragraph of this thesis in which Marx reasons from the requirement that the "educator must be educated" to an infinite regress of causation on the one hand, and the unjustifiable arrogation to itself of wisdom by the educating elite on the other. How is this regress to be resolved? Marx answers in the second paragraph: "The coincidence of the changing of circumstances and of human activity or self-change can be conceived and rationally understood only as *revolutionary practice*".[20] What does Marx mean by revolutionary practice? Certainly it includes more than the objective, unconscious hand of the history of production. It entails conscious "self-change" through political and economic revolutionary action. Engels's version of the *Theses* presented as an appendix to *Ludwig Feuerbach and the Outcome (Ausgang) of Classical German Philosophy* omits the word "self-change", and the

German for revolutionary practice" (*revolutionäre Praxis*) is transmuted to "revolutionizing practice" (*umwälzende Praxis*). Contrasted with *revolutionäre, unwälzende* literally means "turning
around" and only figuratively means revolutionary. "Revolutionizing" is a reasonable translation of Engels's alteration since
it suggests drastic objective change as much as purposive action.
Engels's choice of words comes from an entirely different root
from the one chosen by Marx, a fact not apparent in translation.[21]

The issue that the thesis raises goes far beyond the emendation
that Marx's scribe might have made. Indeed, Engels's importation reflects the shift of emphasis that he tried to achieve. For
insofar as the second paragraph of the *Thesis* relies on conscious
revolutionary activity as its instrument for self-change, it falls
victim to the infinite regress posited in the first paragraph. The
revolutionary cannot stand "superior to society" if the "educator" cannot; if the educator must be educated, the potential revolutionary must be revolutionized. Of course revolutions are
implemented by the practical actions of revolutionaries, but they
have to be either self-generating actions by persons above the
masses, or themselves caused by a process greater than their personal intent.

Whatever difficulty Engels may have had with the persistent
dualism in the doctrine, Marx had none. It was possible for him
to accept Engels's emphasis on consistency and operational
mechanisms—especially when they were together—and yet
insist on the element of consciousness and purpose in revolutionary practice. Marx could ridicule the notion that the truth of a
social system lay in what its participants thought of it themselves, and yet spend his whole life attempting to convince
anyone who would listen of the failings of the system, and urging
them to implement its demise. He could minimize the importance of individuals in making history, and yet in his towering ego
considered himself as such a force.

There is no complete resolution of the dualism which remains
a fatal flaw in Marxism, but there is a model for it in the role of
prophets in the Old Testament. The dualism that runs through
the Hebrew Bible is the omnipotence of God on the one hand,
and the freedom of the will of men implicit in the injunction to
obey the commandments of the Covenant. If God really determined the universe and its inhabitants in every dimension, then

it would be pointless to call upon men to obey the Law since they would be the determination of the Deity. Indeed, it was to this conclusion of predestination which Calvin drove from his reading of Old Testament scripture. Equivalently, if divine support and mercy were contingent upon voluntary obedience to the law of the Pentateuch, God would have abdicated His control over men and their future.

In fact, the Old Testament lays claim to both alternatives. The key is the role of the prophets.[22] These aggressive non-conformists were distinguished, at least in principle, from ecstatics and necromancers forbidden by the Scripture. Rather they were lay individuals who had been commanded to act as the messengers of the Omnipotent; they were to expound and repeat his commandments, and to relay his message of condemnation to the transgressors of the Law. The prophet foretold the future in both the contingent and positive sense. If Israel persisted in breaking the Covenant, in exploiting the poor, in lavish display (even in ritual), in allying itself with earthly false powers, and in blasphemous worship of man-made fetishes, then divine retribution was in store. While there may have been room for repentance, nevertheless the main point of, say, Amos and Hosea was that, for the most part, repentance was not to be, and in any case was too late. Jehovah had finally lost patience. Defeat, destruction and exile awaited the inhabitants of Israel and Judah. Isaiah emphasized the working of history—the expansion of the Assyrian and Babylonian power—as the instruments of divine retribution. Nations were on courses predetermined by Gods power, they were his instruments even though they were to be punished for the evil they inflicted on the Hebrews. All the punishment inflicted on the Jews followed from their own sins; at least in the short term, divine grace was contingent on their behaviour. In the end, however, God would not be denied his omnipotence by signing over pure free will to men to practise evil indefinitely. Jeremiah and Ezekiel both expounded the doctrine of a new covenant, arising as a result of the spiritual discipline of Babylonian exile. God's word would re-enter the spirit of man, and the once-breached Covenant would be renewed. The message of the prophets was of the unity of the contingent and necessary view of human action. Divine necessity, working in the history of the people, would ensure that Israel would fulfil the requirements of renewed succour. In the final analysis God would redeem the

Jews and, through them, all of mankind, out of his own transcendental necessity.[23] Practice and necessity were themes that the Old Testament sought to unite in the transcendental being of God, just as Marx did in the materialist science of society which he intuited in his own exile.

Despite his intention, Marx had reached for the Jewish paradigm, and cast himself in the role of prophet. The prophet's injunction is not pure faith, good works, or universal love, as ends in themselves, but as part of obedience to divine commandments. The struggle of the pious against the unrighteous was right because it was the divine will which was to work itself out with inexorable finality. The very definition of moral behaviour in Marx is expressed in terms of the workings of the inexorable historical process, just as it was defined for the Jews as the commandments of God, ultimately to be obeyed. The prophet serves to expound God's will, to be his instrument, to denounce iniquity. He serves as one of the means by which Israel will internalize the Law in their ethical behaviour, and convince God to support Israel and, through her, the rest of mankind. Eschatology, morality and prophecy in the Old Testament, reappear in Marx as historical materialism, activism and the new science of society. For both the key is not Pauline faith, but earthly practice. That practice reflects human purpose—perhaps free to err in the short term—but ultimately to conform to divine or historical law.

It is, of course, true that Old Testament conceptions had been embodied in the Evangelical religion in which Marx had been educated, and certainly the notion of history as the instrumentality of the Absolute was a leading Hegelian thesis, to which Marx acknowledged his indebtedness. Nevertheless it is the emphasis on practice by human beings, and the immediate response of God to the activity of men that serves to underline the Hebraic element in Marx's construction. The whole point of the prophetic injunction to Israel was that the ultimate criterion was neither sacrifice nor even worship at the temple, both of which implied belief in the existence and power of God. The basis for God's judgment was the practical behaviour of the Jews. The instrumentality of God's response was practical earthly retribution, say, in the form of Assyrian invasion.

While it certainly is the case that these Jewish viewpoints could have reached Marx through any number of non-Jewish intermediaries, the point is that in Brussels he opted for them

against his earlier secular Christianity. It is not likely that he consciously conceived of his evolving viewpoint as converging to the
Jewish paradigm. Yet it is also the case that he did not reject it as
Jewish as he had done in the past. Feuerbach had been mistaken
to think of practice as "dirty-Jewish"; for Marx practice was the
means by which humanity was forged in history, and (expressing
the same inconsistency as Scripture) the means by which man
made himself. In the years that followed, Marx would stress one
or other aspect of the ancient dilemma. When pushed—either by
the presence of Engels or the need to confront his pretensions to
rigorous political economy—Marx moved to the determinist
view. Yet for each law of history or economics he offered "coun-
teracting causes". These served to preserve the possibility of purposive action as a moving force of history, at least in the short
run.

Especially the political writings of Marx have permitted the
introduction of such "ideological" elements whenever realism or
convenience required. The consequence for Marxism is that the
acceptance of the scriptural dualism has reduced the doctrine to
meaninglessness; while its rejection in favour of materialist determinism has led to conclusions so dogmatic, and so palpably false,
that Marx himself was seen to squirm at what he and his colleagues had wrought. Notwithstanding his occasional squea-
mishness, it would be a mistake to imagine that Marx did not
really believe in the ultimate triumph of his laws of history, any
more than the Hebrew prophets doubted the ultimate triumph of
Jehovah. To blame this view, and the dogmatism it generated, on
Frederick Engels's influence is both to overestimate his personal
influence, and to ignore the pressure for internal consistency that
was placed on Marx's evolving thought. The point is not that
Engels was the more mechanical advocate of materialism, but
that Marx was always driven in that direction in the course of
their interaction.

10 The End of Ideology

Together in Brussels, Engels and Marx laboured for over a year to work out the consequences of the *Theses*. Their first coherent statement of their world view was the verbose, *The German Ideology*, left to the "gnawing criticism of the mice" after attempts to find a publisher ended in failure. Its main purpose, according to the young authors, was self-clarification: breaking decisively with the Young Hegelian humanists, while at the same time advancing a materialism genuinely distinct from British empiricism.

The German Ideology hardened Marx's distinction between practical action and abstract thought, into the philosophical dichotomy between materialism and idealism. Reflecting, perhaps, Engels's increased influence, the deterministic strand in Marx's materialism assumed a more prominent role in this work, in comparison with the greater conscious voluntarism of *"revolutionäre Praxis"* in the *Theses*. The two young authors proceed to the notion that all the social aspects of human thought and institution—collectively considered as ideology—are derivative of the historically evolved material relations of production. Marx and Engels argue for a complete schism in philosophy between the material and ideal viewpoints. Those who argue for the primacy of self-subsistent ideas, even in the realm of human affairs, are damned and consigned to the latter camp.

On this basis, Marx and Engels lump all the Young Hegelians together as the German ideologists: with Bruno Bauer, Max Stirner and the old hero, Ludwig Feuerbach. What they all have in common is a belief in a transcendental category inherited from Hegel, or derived from him. Marx now claims that the notion of "the essence of Man" is merely a restatement of the Hegelian doctrine of the primacy of universal Idea in a parochial Germanic context. He accuses his colleagues of sins which amount to treading the same ground he trod in the Paris *Manuscripts* a year earlier. Among other things *The German Ideology* is an exercise in self-criticism projected, as usual, on the ineptitude of his former associates.

At the very outset, after establishing the division between idealism and materialism as their main theme, Marx and Engels contend that the Young Hegelians are not only idealists in philosophy but also specifically German ideologists. The German viewpoint is, like that of other idealists, a projection of their own real condition. In Marx's new conception, this is taken to mean their class situation, rather than the human condition. Feuerbach, Bauer and Stirner are representatives of the pusillanimous German petty bourgeoisie, who only imagine themselves to be spokesman for humanity in general:

Hitherto men have always formed wrong ideas about themselves, about what they are and what they ought to be. They have arranged their relations according to their ideas of God, or normal man, etc. The products of their brains have got out of their hands. They, the creators, have bowed down before their creations. Let us liberate them from the chimeras, the ideas, dogmas, imaginary beings under the yoke of which they are pining away. Let us revolt against this rule of concepts. Let us teach men, says one, how to exchange these imaginations for thoughts which correspond to the essence of man; says another, how to take up a critical attitude to them; says the third, how to get them out of their heads; and existing reality will collapse.

These innocent and child-like fancies are the kernel of the modern Young-Hegelian philosophy, which not only is received by the German public with horror and awe, but is announced by our *philosophic heroes* with the solemn consciousness of its word-shattering danger and criminal ruthlessness. The first volume of the present publication has the aim of uncloaking these sheep, who take themselves and are taken for wolves; of showing that their bleating merely imitates in a philosophic form the conceptions of the German middle class; that the boasting of these philosophic commentators only mirrors the wretchedness of the real conditions in Germany. It is its aim to ridicule and discredit the philosophic struggle with the shadows of reality, which appeals to the dreamy and muddled German nation.[1]

At last Marx sees the ethnocentrism of the humanist view he espoused only a year earlier. Purporting to find the universal nature of Man, the Young Hegelians have merely repeated the German Christian ideal in secular form. Purporting to criticize Hegel from the humanist left, they never really escaped from Hegelian idealism. They simply replaced the idealist and theological terms in Hegel with humanist and secular names, and set one or another of these against the Hegelian totality:

> Their polemics against Hegel and against one another are confined to this—each takes one aspect of the Hegelian system and turns this against the whole system as well as against the aspect chosen by the others. To begin with they took pure unfalsified Hegelian categories such as "substance" and "self-consciousness" later they secularized these categories by giving them more profane names such as "species", "the unique", "man", etc.[2]

As we have explained, this last is precisely what Marx himself did in the *Economic and Philosophic Manuscripts*; he substituted "Man" for "self-consciousness" and struggled to make this category play the universal role which Hegel had ascribed to Idea. Now Marx sees that this procedure is worse than muddle-headed; it leads to a static view of the nature of Man, rather than pointing to the practical, material, means of revolutionizing society and changing Man himself:

> Since the Young Hegelians consider conceptions, thoughts, ideas, in fact all the products of consciousness, to which they attribute an independent existence, as the real chains of men (just as the Old Hegelians declare them the true bonds of human society), it is evident that the Young Hegelians have to fight only against these illusions of consciousness. Since, according to their fantasy, the relations of men, all their doings, their fetters and their limitations are products of their consciousness, the Young Hegelians logically put to men the moral postulate of exchanging their present consciousness for human, critical or egoistic consciousness, and thus of removing their limitations. This demand to change consciousness

amounts to a demand to interpret the existing world in a different way, i.e. to recognise it by means of a different interpretation. The Young-Hegelian ideologists, in spite of their allegedly "world-shattering" phrases, are the staunchest conservatives...

It has not occurred to any one of these philosophers to inquire into the connection of German philosophy with German reality, the connection of their criticism with their own material surroundings.[3]

The inherent conservatism of the humanist model is apparent from the political absurdity of philosophical appeals to workers to take up arms to make themselves more human by abolishing private property. The ridiculous nature of the demand in practice according to Marx, follows from a conception of humanity which reflects the mawkish ideals of the petty bourgeoisie rather than the practical requisites for proletarian revolutionary action. Humanism is unwilling to take practical revolutionary action and lapses instead into dreams of good wishes and good will. Furthermore, Marx sees the inherent conservatism in the ethnocentric nature of Man as a philosophic category. The idealised view of man is, like all other ideology, the viewpoint of the ruling class. Hence Man appears to the German ideologists as possessed of an inherent, eternal, essential nature, while to Marx, Man has no such innate human nature except in the broadest biological sense. Human nature is the ideological reflection of historical conditioning, and as such is essentially transitory in its characteristics. The revolutionary language of the German ideology, Marx concludes, is mere bombast.

"As an example", Marx writes, "of Feuerbach's acceptance and at the same time misunderstanding of existing reality which he still shares with our opponents, we recall the passage in the *Philosophie der Zukunft* where he develops the view that the being of a thing or man is at the same time its or his essence, that the determinate conditions of existence, the mode of life and activity of an animal or human individual are those in which its "essence feels itself satisfied."[4] What happens if the human does not live as specified by its essence? Marx answers that Feuerbach views "every exception" as an "unhappy chance, an abnormality which cannot be altered".[5] As an alternative the anarchist Stirner views this situation for moralizing that "you *should be* dif-

ferent from what you *really are*. This entire separation of consciousness from the individuals who are its basis and from their
actual conditions, this notion that the egoist of the present day
bourgeois society does not possess the consciousness corresponding to his egoism is an old philosophical fad".[6] By saying that
one's "appearance" was "not appropriate to his essence ... the
philosopher ... admits that a definite consciousness is appropriate to a definite people and definite circumstances. But at the
same time he imagines that this moral demand of people—the
demand that they should change their consciousness—will bring
about this altered consciousness, and in people who have
changed owing to changed empirical conditions and who, of
course, now also possess a different consciousness, he sees
nothing but a changed consciousness".[7]

The point Marx is making is that ideology, including the
feeling of alienation, is not the product of an inherent essence, but
a social product. One cannot moralize alienation out of existence
by criticism of society which does not happen to match the
"essence of man". New social conditions generate new "human"
characteristics which do not jibe with the old society from which
the oppressed classes are now alienated. Indeed the Feuerbachian position is itself an expression of the German conditions of
the petty bourgeoisie. The overtly political bourgeois ideology of
France and England, reflects their more complete division of
labour and the existence of a large, independent bourgeois class.[8]
The idealization of Man by the German ideologists takes human
social behaviour safely out of the domain of possible alteration.
The result of their efforts is a high-flown restatement of the ideals
of the present, rather than a doctrine by which one might
"change the world".

Marx explicitly aims this criticism at Feuerbach, and by extension against the views he expressed himself in the 1844 period in
Paris:

> Certainly Feuerbach ... realizes that man too is an "object of
> the senses". But apart from the fact that he only conceives him
> as an "object of the senses", not as "sensuous activity",
> because he still remains in the realm of theory and conceives of
> men not in their given social connection, not under their exist-
> ing conditions of life, which have made them *what* they are, he
> never arrives at the actually existing, active men, but stops at

the abstraction "man", and gets no further than recognizing "the actual, individual, corporeal man" emotionally, i.e., he knows no other "human relations" "of man to man" than love and friendship, and even then idealized. He gives no criticism of the present conditions of life. Thus he never manages to conceive the sensuous world as the total living sensuous *activity* of the individuals composing it; therefore when, for example, he sees instead of healthy men a crowd of scrofulous, overworked and consumptive starvelings, he is compelled to take refuge in the "higher perception" and in the ideal "compensation in the species", and thus to relapse into idealism at the very point where the communist materialist sees the necessity, and at the same time the condition, of a transformation both of industry and of the social structure.

As far as Feuerbach is a materialist he does not deal with history and as far as he considers history he is not a materialist. With him materialism and history diverge completely.[9]

Marx goes on to develop his criticism of the unhistorical character of Feuerbach's work:

Feuerbach's "conception" of the sensuous world is confined on the one hand to mere contemplation of it, and on the other to mere feeling; he posits "Man" instead of "real historical man". "Man" is really "the German". In the first case, the *contemplation* of the sensuous world, he necessarily lights on things which contradict his consciousness and feeling, which disturb the harmony he presupposes, the harmony of all parts of the sensuous world and especially of man and nature. To remove this disturbance, he must take refuge in a double perception, a profane one which perceives "only the flatly obvious" and a higher, philosophical, one which perceives the "true essence" of things. He does not see that the sensuous world around him is not a thing given direct from all eternity, remaining ever the same, but the product of industry and of the state of society; and, indeed (a product) if the sense that it is an historical product, the result of the activity of a whole succession of generations, each standing on the shoulders of the preceding one, developing its industry and its intercourse, and modifying its social system according to the changed needs.[10]

In Paris Marx thought he was putting Feuerbach on sounder ground by enlarging his critique of religion to include a critique of property. Marx now sees in Feuerbach the same fault that we have pointed to in the *Manuscripts* and *On the Jewish Question*: Marx was asking men to give up their "Jewish" egoism by overthrowing the regime of private property in favour of the rule of Man. Marx's Man in Paris, like Feuerbach's creature, was an idealization of the German Christian ideal. Historical process and social causation are as absent in the *Manuscripts* as they are in *The Essence of Christianity*.

Convinced now that "Man" is a chimera, Marx must now show how men are the historical social products of their practical activity. The materialist theory must explain how the ideas ascribed to Man by the Germans "got into the heads" of men at a given stage of history. With this new perspective in mind, Marx comes as close as he ever could to recanting his previous "philosophical" language. His old associates, he contends, did not understand that the "trend" of the earlier work was diametrically opposed to their humanism:

> Owing to the fact that Feuerbach showed the religious world as an illusion of the earthly world—a world which in his writing appears merely as a *phrase*—German theory too was confronted with the question which he left unanswered: how did it come about that people "got" these illusions "into their heads"? Even for the German theoreticians this question paved the way to the materialistic view of the world, a view which is *not without premises*, but which empirically observes the actual material premises as such and for that reason is, for the first time, *actually* a critical view of the world. This path was already indicated in the *Deutsch-Französische Jahrbücher*— in the *Einleitung zur Kritik der Hegelschen Rechtsphilosophie* and "*Zur Judenfrage.*" But since at that time this was done in philosophical phraseology, the traditionally occurring philosophical expressions such as "human essence", "species", etc., gave the German theoreticians the desired reason for misunderstanding the real trend of thought and believing that here again it was a question merely of giving a new turn to their worn out theoretical garment ... Philosophy and the study of the actual world have the same relation to one another as onanism and sexual love.[11]

Marx is well aware that he too is starting his social enquiry with materialist preconceptions imported from philosophy. These "premises from which we begin, he asserts, "are not dogmas, but real premises from which abstraction can only be made in the imagination". His premises refer to "the real individuals, their activity and the material conditions of their life, both those which they find already existing and those produced by their activity. These premises can thus be verified in a purely empirical way".[12] The account Marx is to give of history is presumed to substantiate the view that "activity and the material conditions of life" are fundamental to explaining human behaviour.

What is the role of ideology in Marx's system of premises? Are not institutions, traditions, religion, politics, aesthetics also part of the facts of social existence? Marx responds by describing the manner in which humans and human society differs from other creatures:

> The first premise of all human history is, of course, the existence of living human individuals. Thus the first fact to be established is the physical organization of these individuals and their consequent relation to the rest of nature... Men can be distinguished from animals by consciousness, by religion or by anything else you like.

But in terms of material activity, Marx claims, the key to human activity is social production: he continues: "They themselves begin to distinguish themselves from animals as soon as they begin to *produce* their means of subsistence, a step which is conditioned by their physical organization. By producing their means of subsistence men are indirectly producing their material life".[13]

The universal characteristics of all the descendants of Cain, in Marx's version as well as the scriptural original, is the need to labour to earn their living. In opposition to his idealist opponents, Marx the materialist asserts the primacy of production in the logical as well as the archaeological sense:

> The way in which men produce their means of subsistence depends first of all on the nature of the means of subsistence

they actually find in existence and have to reproduce.

This mode of production must not be considered simply as being the reproduction of the physical existence of the individuals. Rather it is a definite form of activity of these individuals, a definite form of expressing their life, a definite *mode of life* on their part. As individuals express their life, so they are. What they are, therefore, coincides with their production, both with *what* they produce and with *how* they produce. Hence what individuals are depends on the material conditions of their production.[14]

It is hard to imagine how some recent readers of Marx can believe that this sort of statement, which recurs over and over again in *The German Ideology*, is consistent with the spiritualism of the 1844 documents. Marx is perfectly explicit in his meaning. He views the primacy of material relations of production as simply a fact, a verified premise. He makes clear the social determinism he has in mind by the iteration of the word "definite" in connection with production, as contrasted with the variable, dependent nature of the individual consciousness: "definite individuals who are productively active in a definite way enter into these definite social and political relations.[15] Marx makes crystal clear his view of the order of causation:

The production of ideas, of conceptions of consciousness, is at first directly interwoven with the material activity and the material intercourse of men—the language of real life. Conceiving, thinking, the mental intercourse of men at this stage still appear as the direct efflux of their material behavior. The same applies to mental production as expressed in the language of the politics, laws, morality, religion, metaphysics, etc., of a people. Men are the producers of their conceptions, ideas, etc., that is, real, active men, as they are conditioned by a definite development of their productive forces and of the intercourse corresponding to these, up to its further forms. Consciousness (*das Bewusstsein*) can never be anything else than conscious being (*das bewusste Sein*), and the being of men is their actual life-process.[16]

The materialist Marx is able to understand Feuerbach's inversion of religion in a new light. It is now evident to Marx that both the belief in God and the humanism which Feuerbach counter-poses to religion are founded on illusion. The mistake lies in iden-tifying reality as caused by the forces of consciousness rather than the practical processes of production. True, Feuerbach was able to invert the philosophy of religion, but Marx asserts that he was unable to relate his own construct of Man as a species-being to its materialist basis. "If in all ideology", Marx says, "men and their relations appear upside-down as in a *camera obscura*, this phenom-enon arises just as much from their historical life process as the inversion of objects on the retina does from their physical life process."[17]

More than an error is involved in the German ideology, Marx claims. By their concern with "morality, religion, metaphysics" as the dimensions of the alienation of Man, they have concerned themselves with the ideological efflux of his consciousness. But these are neither the real practical concerns of the proletarians, nor is the self-contemplation of his inner self by Man the means to effective social change. Rather the preoccupation with these issues is the symptom of the impotence of the German bourgeois society and the evidence of its superficial discontent. Lacking a material basis and an historical process for change, the German ideology persists in the inversion which substitutes the dreams of ideal human society for a science of society to change the material existence of mankind in an effective, revolutionary way.

Marx is explicit in his comparison:

In direct contrast to German philosophy which descends from heaven to earth, here it is a matter of ascending from earth to heaven. That is to say, not of setting out from what men say, imagine, conceive, nor from men as narrated, thought of, im-agined, conceived, in order to arrive at men in the flesh; but setting out from real, active men, and on the basis of their real life-process demonstrating the development of the ideological reflexes and echoes of this life-process. The phantoms formed in the brains of men are also, necessarily, sublimates of their material life-process, which is empirically verifiable and bound to material premises. Morality, religion, metaphysics, and all the rest of ideology as well as the forms of consciousness corresponding to these, thus no longer retain the semblance of independence. They have no history, no development; but men, developing their material production and their material intercourse, alter, along with this their actual world, also their thinking and the products of their thinking. It is not consciousness that determines life, but life that determines consciousness. For the first manner of approach the starting-point is -consciousness taken as the living individual; for the second manner of approach, which conforms to real life, it is the real living individuals themselves, and consciousness is considered solely as *their* consciousness.[18]

No longer are Marx and Engels the Paris existentialist philosophers, seeking to elevate man's existence above the mundane. If ever they were the wistful dreamers for a communism of meagre wants, this is no longer the case. Such conceptions are derived from the German petty-bourgeois mind, attuned to small production:

> We shall, of course, not take the trouble to explain to our wise philosophers that the "liberation" of "man" is not advanced a single step by reducing philosophy, theology, substance and all the rubbish to "self-consciousness" and by liberating "man" from the domination of these phrases, which have never held him in thrall. Nor shall we explain to them that it is possible to achieve real liberation only in the real world and by real means, that slavery cannot be abolished without the steam-engine and the mule jenny, serfdom cannot be abolished without improved agriculture, and that, in general, people cannot be liberated as long as they are unable to obtain food and drink, housing and clothing in adequate quality and quantity. "Liberation" is a historical and not a mental act, and it is brought about by historical conditions, the [level] of industry, com[merce], [agri]culture, [intercourse...] then subsequently, in accordance with the different stages of their development, [they make up] the nonsense of substance, subject, self-consciousness and pure criticism, as well as religious and theological nonsense, and later they get rid of it again when their development is sufficiently advanced. In Germany, a country where only a trivial historical development is taking place, these mental developments, these glorified and ineffective trivialities, naturally serve as a substitute for the lack of historical development, and they take root and have to be combated. But this fight is of *local* importance.[19]

The desire of people for material advancement, egoism in this sense, is not "dirty Jewish", but rather the motivation for the advance of the forces of production. The satisfaction of material wants is the ultimate source of the salvation of mankind through communism.[20]

The German Ideology is the first place wher. Marx and Engels suggest that the transition from one social order to another is made historically necessary by the need to remove the fetters of the older order on the forces of production. Once freed from capitalist limitations, communism would constitute a higher level of productivity. This idea comes through very clearly in the following passage, even though Marx's identification of the limiting nature of capitalist relations is vaguely expressed as the "destructive forces" of "machinery and money":

> In the development of productive forces there comes a stage when the productive forces and the means of intercourse are brought into being which, under the existing relations, only cause mischief, and are no longer productive but destructive forces (machinery and money); and connected with this a class is called forth which has to bear all the burdens of society without enjoying its advantages, which is ousted from society and forced into the sharpest contradiction to all other classes; a class which forms the majority of all members of society, and from which emanates the consciousness of the necessity of a fundamental revolution, which may, of course, arise among the other classes too through contemplation of this class.[21]

The chosen class, responding to the call of history, is not opposed to production. On the contrary, Marx concedes that there are advantages as well as burdens even to capitalist productivity. The point is that the working of history represents itself by the workers being forced to bear the burden of production, and being denied its advantages. The economic development of the forces of production sets the stage for the seizure of political and social power by the proletariat.

Marx explains that each stage in the development of the productive process defines its own class structure and political organization of the state. He says that, "the conditions under which definite productive forces can be applied are the conditions of the rule of a definite class of society, whose social power, deriving from its property has its *practical*–idealistic expression in each case in the form of the state, and therefore every revolutionary struggle is directed against a class which till then has been in power". The future is with a classless society brought about by the workers' seizure of power. "In all previous revolutions the mode of activity always remained unchanged and it was only a question of a different distribution of this activity, a new distribution of labor to other persons, while the communist revolution is directed against the hitherto existing *mode* of activity, does away with *labor*, and abolishes the rule of all classes with the classes themselves." Gone is talk of a realization of the essence of Man, a recapturing of a prior existent true self. On the contrary, the very point of the Marxian exercise is "the production on a mass scale of this communist consciousness and for the success of the cause itself, the alteration of man on a mass scale" by the "practical movement" of revolution.[22] Human nature not only can be changed, Marx claims, it needs to be changed and it will be changed.

Each stage in the process of social change is identified by its class structure appropriate to the methods of production. The definition of class is whether it has the "means of material production" or whether it is propertyless.[23] At such time as the growth of the forces of production come into conflict with the institutional structure associated with an earlier era, the stage is set for a revolution which reorganizes the social organization of human intercourse to become congruent with the demands of the materialist productive relations. "The whole internal structure of the nation itself", the authors tell us, "depends on the stage of development reached by its production and its internal and external intercourse. How far the productive forces of a nation are developed is shown most manifestly by the degree to which the division of labor has been carried." The development of production and the division of labour are mutually supportive as "each new productive force, insofar as it is not merely a quantitative extension of the productive forces already known (for instance the bringing into cultivation of fresh land), causes a further development of the division of labor."[24]

It is at this point that Marx and Engels introduce the famous schematization of history into stages of the mode of production, later codified as primitive communism, slavery feudalism, capitalism, and communism in its lower and higher phase. This schema was to undergo modification in the nearly forty years in which Marx and Engels used it as their frame of reference. The deterministic aspect of the model was hardened in *The Communist Manifesto* in 1847; it was modified in application in Marx's political writing and correspondence—sometimes to the point of amending it out of practical significance; it became the theoretical basis for *Capital*, where Marx tried to express the mechanics justifying his belief in the transitory nature of capitalism and its continued exploitation of the propertyless even under conditions of free market competition; and, it was made the subject of anthropological comments in Engels's *Origin of the Family, Private Property and the State*. Nevertheless, the basic paradigm offered in *The German Ideology* remained central to Marxism.

In this earliest formulation, Marx and Engels take as their point of departure the division of labour which the classical economists had identified with the advance of productivity. "The various stages in the division of labor are just so many different forms of property, i.e, the existing stage in the division of labor determines also the relations of individuals to one another with reference to the material, instrument and product of labor."[25]

Pre-capitalist society is divided into three stages. The first is "tribal property" which primarily is based on "hunting, fishing and cattle raising". The division of labour is "still very elementary" and is confined to an "extension of the natural division of labor existing in the family. The social structure is, therefore, limited to an extension of the family" headed by "patriarchal chieftains". Slavery "develops gradually" toward the end of this period along with population growth, trade and war. The "second form" has as its exemplar classical Greek civilization in which a city is the centre of the union of several tribes; slaves and land are owned by the city as "communal and state property". Here the "class relations between citizens and slaves are now completely developed". The conversion of land into private property, especially in Rome, modifies the class structure into "propertied citizens and slaves" and the transformation of the "plebeian small peasantry into a proletariat".

"The third form is feudal or estate property" which has its base in the country as opposed to the town. Marx and Engels identify the Middle Ages with the disruption of agricultural production attendant upon the decline of the Roman Empire. This is as close as they come to consideration of the possibility of a retrograde motion in the forces of production, although even here they explain the development of small-scale agriculture as having been prepared by the Roman conquests and conditions of rural dispersal, disruption of the market and the "influence of the Germanic military constitution". Their commentary describes the technology of small-scale strip farming in the countryside and craft production in the towns, but indicate that there was "little or no division of labor". As a consequence "property during the feudal epoch primarily consisted on one hand of landed property with serf labor chained to it, and on the other of the personal labor of the individual who with his small capital commands the labor of journeymen. The organization of both was determined by the restricted conditions of production".[26]

It appeared to Marx and Engels that they had provided evidence to the effect that (1) there is a direct correspondence between the dominant form of production and division of labour on the one hand, and the form of social organization on the other; and, (2) that the order of determination is from production to social organization:

> The fact is, therefore, that definite individuals who are productively active in a definite way enter into these definite social and political relations. Empirical observation must in each separate instance bring out empirically, and without any mystification and speculation, the connection of the social and political structure with production. The social structure and the state are continually evolving out of the life-process of definite individuals, however, of these individuals, not as they may appear in their own or other people's imagination, but as they *actually* are, i.e., as they act, produce materially, and hence as they work under definite material limits, presuppositions, and conditions independent of their will.[27]

It is clear that the answer to the question as to what people "actually" are, is given in terms of the determining power of the economics of production.

Marx and Engels then go on to develop their account of the rise of capitalism as part of the saga of the expansion of the division of labour. They divide the process into three stages.[28] The "most important division of material and mental labor is the separation of town and country". This separation is the basis for the authors' account of the rise of the town as the centre of crafts carried on by freed and escaped serfs. Theirs was a system of craft-exclusive guild labour organization.[29]

The second stage of the division of labour was the separation of production and commerce, the formation of a special class of merchants. This division of labour arose out of the heritage of the towns of the earlier period, and "among other things with the Jews". Repeating what he learned from Smith and Mill, Marx explains how the division of labour was extended by the growth of the market.[30] Mercantile capitalism was only an intermediate stage; while it served to stimulate the division of labour, it was itself dependent on protectionism and feudal restriction, and hence upon the imperfection of the market. The final stage of industrial capitalism arose, Marx and Engels recount, as

the concentration of trade and manufacture in one country, England, developing irresistably in the seventeenth century, gradually created for this country a relative world market which could no longer be met by the industrial productive forces hitherto existing. This demand, outgrowing the productive forces, was the motive power which, by producing large scale industry—the application of elemental forces to industrial ends, machinery and the most extensive division of labor.[31]

Industrial capitalism swept all before it through the force of competition. All the vestiges of feudalism, national difference, traditional and craft skills were overturned by the new manufacture and its attendant world market. In the end, however, "large scale industry created a class which in all nations has the same interest, and for which nationality is already dead; a class which is really rid of all the old world and at the same time stands pitted against it. For the worker it makes not only his relation to the capitalist, but labor itself, unbearable".[32]

Marx and Engels's account is not yet complete. It is still unclear, in the historical passages we have been reviewing, whether the authors are simply presenting the reader with an account of the past succession of changes in the dominant forms of production and their consequent social formations, or whether the economics of production has an inner drive of its own which will not only determine social arrangements, but drive them along a predetermined historical path with the "iron necessity" Marx spoke of in *Capital*. As a consequence, the necessity of the communist revolution in relation to the historical process is likewise unsure. Certainly there is the remark mentioned previously to the effect that at a certain stage in the development of "the productive forces and means of intercourse are brought into being, which, under the existing relations only cause mischief and are no longer productive but destructive forces (machinery and money)", but by and large the burden of the message is that the proletariat is brought into existence by capitalism. This new class suffers and is driven by its misery to destroy capitalism in favour of communism.

What is missing—or at least not emphasized to the degree that appears later—is the theory of the breakdown of each social order as a result of its own internal contradictions. Thus it appears in each of the preceding stages as if exogenous forces, such as population growth, trade and war, were as important as the endogenous elements of economic breakdown inherent within each system. Moreover, the identification of the division of labour as the dynamic element, tended to stress the significance of the market and the exchange process in the actual account of the stages, contrary to the materialist premise of the primacy of production.

Read without regard for Marx's intent to develop a general dynamic explanation of history, the account of Western European experience given in this part of *The German Ideology* would seem simply to stress the significance of economic relations and insist that every society must have its institutions consistent with the economic arrangements. Marx makes the claim in these passages to have shown the determination of social institutions is by material economic relations; that is, however, only his premise. He certainly has shown the need for consistency but not causation.

Thus, in contrast to *The Communist Manifesto's* forward drive of the forces of production, Marx and Engels offer the reader of *The German Ideology* the instance of a retrogression in the forces of production occasioned by the fall of the Roman Empire. The *Manifesto* only alludes to pre-feudal class formations, but its account of economic development starts with the Middle Ages and represents the historical development as the steady progress of production. In the *Manifesto*, exchange is itself regarded as part of the social formation created by the advance of production under nascent capitalism. Most important, the proletarian revolution becomes an historical necessity in the *Manifesto*; it is a consequence of the breakdown of capitalism. The symptoms of exploitation and economic crises are themselves a result of the growth of social productive forces becoming incompatible with the private ownership of the means of production. The consequence of the contradiction is revealed in terms of increasing disfunction.

The direction toward greater monism in the progression from *The German Ideology* is indicated by the changes in terminology. In *The German Ideology*, the forces of production are said to come into conflict with the *Verkehrsform*, while he later speaks of the conflict of the forces of production (*Produktivkräfte*) with the relations of production, *Produktionsverhältnisse*. The word *Verkehr* is ambiguous in the German language, meaning commerce and exchange in some contexts, and the more generalized notion of intercourse or relation in others. The use of the term *Verkehrsform*, we can see, is more than a terminological awkwardness to be replaced by the nicety *Produktionsverhältnisse*; *Verkehrform* reflects Marx's identification of exchange becoming inconsistent with the division of labour, resulting as much from the development of the former as the latter. The later use of *Produktionsverhältnisse* includes the forms of exchange—indeed the possibility of exchange—as features of a production-determined social system.

In the absence of either a fully developed theory of historical development which will speak to the future of the capitalist order, or an adequate economic analysis of exploitation and crises, Marx and Engels cannot fully emancipate themselves from their earlier forms of normative exhortation to proletarian revolution. Thus there remain passages in which the authors justify communism simply by inveighing against the division of labour as such, the existence of an alien power in society and the like. In the economic sense, they ask, how can men "gain control of exchange and production"? In inverted commas, Marx and Engels refer to "this 'estrangement' (to use a term which will be comprehensible to the philosophers)"; they look forward to the "world-historical, empirically universal individuals in place of the local ones". None of this is strictly incompatible with his mature view of the ultimate state of classless society. Indeed it is precisely at this point in *The German Ideology* where Marx and Engels look to the "practical premises" for the abolition of the "estrangement" and find them in the "rendering of the great mass of humanity propertyless, and moreover in contradiction to an existing world of wealth and culture; both these premises presuppose a great increase in productive power". While this represents a drastic reinterpretation of the doctrine of estrangement as a situation to be overcome in the eschatological communist future, nevertheless Marx is aware of the danger of pursuing this line of argument back in the direction of a voluntarist view of social change. Marx inserts a comment in the jointly authored manuscript in a space before the word "estrangement" that discloses his concern and the direction in which he feels his analysis must go:

> Communism is for us not a *state of affairs* which is to be established, an *ideal* to which reality will have to adjust itself. We call communism the *real* movement which abolishes the present state of things. The conditions of this movement result from the now existing premise.[33]

Later in the work, Marx and Engels denounce the anarchist, Max Stirner (dubbed Saint Sancho), for just this voluntarist approach. Marx and Engels specify that the productive forces must be advanced enough to permit a communist society; they also insist that capitalism cannot be abolished until the development of those forces has reached a pitch at which the regime of private property becomes a "restricting fetter" on production:

> "If, if if!"
> "If" Saint Sancho had for one moment set aside the current ideas of lawyers and politicians about private property, and also the polemic against it, if he had once looked at this private property in its empirical existence, in its connection with the productive forces of individuals, then all his Solomon's wisdom, with which he will now entertain us, would have been reduced to nothing. Then it would hardly have escaped him (although like Habakkuk he is *capable de tout*) that private property is a form of intercourse necessary for certain stages of development of the productive forces; a form of intercourse that cannot be abolished, and cannot be dispensed with in the production of actual material life, until productive forces have

been created for which private property becomes a restricting fetter.[34]

Marx and Engels's writing of this time took over a year, during which time the authors' views were evolving towards increased determinism. The change of emphasis we have reviewed here suggests that they were right in later viewing the main achievement of *The German Ideology* as self-clarification.

While Marx was driven towards historical determinism, it is clear that he was uncomfortable with his formulation through the rest of his life. From time to time he attempted to avoid the mindless applications of his "historical sketch of the genesis of capitalism in western Europe into a historico-philosophic theory of the general path every people is fated to tread whatever the historical circumstances in which it finds itself". Marx makes this remark in the same letter to a Russian revolutionary in which he cites the passage in *Capital* where having long since abandoned his opposition to the "negation of the negation" he wrote: "The historical tendency of production is summed up thus: that it 'itself begets its own negation with the inexorability which governs the metamorphoses of nature' ... that capitalist property, resting already, as it actually does, on a collective mode of production, cannot but transform itself into social property".[35]

In *The Communist Manifesto* as well as *The German Ideology*, the Marxian account of "stages" is presented as retrospective. It does indeed tell the history of western European economic development, and represents itself as opposed to those "self-sufficient" philosophies which excogitate laws of history derived from the development of consciousness. In *The German Ideology* Marx sets forth a modest proposal of purportedly inductive empirical research:

> Where speculation ends, where real life starts, there consequently begins real, positive science, the expounding of the practical activity, of the practical process of development of men. Empty phrases about consciousness end, and real knowledge has to take their place. When the reality is described, a self-sufficient philosophy loses its medium of existence. At the best its place can only be taken by a summing-up of the most general results, abstractions which are derived from the observation of the historical development of men. These abstractions in themselves, divorced from real history, have no value

whatsoever. They can only serve to facilitate the arrangement of historical material, to indicate the sequence of its separate strata. But they by no means afford a recipe or schema, as does philosophy, for neatly trimming the epochs of history. On the contrary, the difficulties begin only when one sets about the examination and arrangement of the material—whether of a past epoch or of the present—and its actual presentation.[36]

Yet if this were all that Marx were to do, he would be hard put to defend the view that the material relations of production were the ultimate determinants of the social structure. After all, the account given in both the *Manifesto* and *The German Ideology* is of changing economic arrangements and changing social structures. If it is the former which is the fundamental element, what explains its own evolution? Is it the result of random technical ebb and flow of progress and retrogression? Is it the creature of fortuitous events such as the barbarian invasion of Rome? Or, is it the consequence of "ideological" changes which take place, such as the religious element stressed by such persons as Bruno Bauer and, later, Max Weber? If any of these explanations are accepted, then it really is impossible to assert that the economic relations are primary. Unless the forces of production advance *sui generis*, they are as much the consequence of the social structure as its cause. Consciousness would be no less significant than material relations of production in a view of history which consists of a series of events; if each event were caused by the singular, unique conjuncture of events that preceded it, there would be no warrant for any general explanation of history at all. This may well be the most sensible way to regard history, but it is not the method of Marx. If there is to be a primary element in history, then its change must be explained in terms exogenous to the system itself. An endogenous description of the "forces of production" leaves them determined as much as determining, in a system of simultaneous evolution of technology, capital accumulation and consciousness. In this latter alternative, a communist outcome would be problematic in each country and situation; it might well depend precisely on a "conscious decision" to change or not to change the existing state of affairs. Historical necessity was a political necessity to the Marxian system.

It seemed to Marx that he could encompass the ideological and institutional elements of superstructure into the conjuncture of production-determined systems. The manner in which this inclusion is accomplished gives us a clue to the way in which he hoped to avoid a rigidly formulated stages-of-history theory. In the *Manifesto* as well as *The German Ideology* the defence of what has come to be called historical materialism is in fact stated in terms of the history of western Europe. Yet at the same time it cannot be merely a history; it is an illustration, perhaps an exemplar, of the working of the materialist presupposition. Marx says so himself:

This manner of approach is not devoid of premises. It starts out from the real premises and does not abandon them for a moment. Its premises are men, not in any fantastic isolation and fixity, but in their actual, empirically perceptible process of development under definite conditions. As soon as this active life-process is described, history ceases to be a collection of dead facts, as it is with the empiricists (themselves still abstract), or an imagined activity of imagined subjects as with the idealists.[37]

If anything, the translation makes the *a priori* nature of the Marxian method more innocuous than in the original. The word "premise" is in German *Vorraussetzung*, translatable as "supposition" or "presupposition" as well as "premise". Whatever the emphasis in translation, Marx is not pursuing the method of empiricism, whose belief in the primacy of "dead facts" leads away from any theory or philosophy of history.

As we noted in previous chapters, the heart of the Kantian message was that some sort of presupposition given *a priori* is a necessity for perception. The mere fact of a "premise" is not what characterizes Marx's historical necessity, rather it is his formulation of his premises in such a way as to include in his historical account precisely those ideological elements which the theory denies are the causative elements. Telling the story of history including forces and counter-forces may appear as less dogmatic, but it merely makes the theory empirically vacuous; there is no event which can put to test the contention of the underlying dominance of the material forces of production, when its working is described in illustration which in each instance give equal weight to the ideological opposite.

Thus Marx's account of the social history of western Europe

points to the concordance between the economic and the social. Yet Marx does not say explicitly that all social systems go through the same evolution. Nor could he justify such an induction based on a sample of one. There is no empirical warrant for the uniqueness of the stages in the forces of production, nor for the belief that the correspondence between these forces and the social integument is necessarily one to one.

Nonetheless there remains a crucial element of universality in his message. Every historical event contrary to the European pattern has to be rationalized away. The reasons for the development in other locales of deviations from the canonical form must be shown to be sufficient. In his letters to early Russian revolutionaries, we have noted, Marx rejected an interpretation that would require that Russian agrarian society go through the complete cycle of stages from primitive communism to capitalism. Why? It is because the forces of production suitable for a communist collectivism have already arisen as a result of industrialization in western Europe. The Russian *mir* need not go the way of the German *mark* because feudal and capitalist productive forces have evolved elsewhere and might simply be taken over. If capitalism had not evolved elsewhere, what might have happened? Marx does not say. Marx's pretensions to concreteness do not leave room for hypothetical alternatives.

More is involved in this matter than Marx's ability to explain—or explain away—discrepancies between events and his faith in the ultimate communist outcome derived from the schematic view of history. Marx portrayed events as having a dialectical logic of their own, in which the transcendental, underlying, universal element is contradicted by the immediate particular reality we empirically observe. The course of history is the reassertion of the unity of the two. The universal element reasserts itself through conflict with its own negation. The deterministic evolutionary negation of the negation which Marx rejected in the ahistorical *Manuscripts* reappears as the centrepiece of his analysis. Marx takes the western European experience to be more than an account of the past because he believes that there exists a single, fundamental law inherent in social history. The series of events are but an illustration of the universal inherent in the particular. Now the universal is no longer the static concept of Man, but the historical evolution of the material laws of society.

The immediate paradigm for Marx's conception of history was, of course, Hegel. Marx credited him with the dialectical conception in which events proceed through the primary principle of internal self-contradiction. Hegel's logic needed only to be stood on its head, Marx said, and shown to be a material rather than a speculative element inherent in the universe.[38] Nevertheless, the conception itself originates in the Old Testament, and it can be seen that Marx is in many ways closer to that original than he was to the speculative philosopher in Berlin. Marx's rationalization that his thesis was an inversion of Hegel, rather than a reversion to the more ancient paradigm, is a not uncommon feature of persons who repeat their cultural preconceptions all the more strongly when they cannot see their working in themselves. In any case, as Marx aged, it seems from recent research that he retained and revived association with Jewish relatives and acquaintances, all the while unaware of the influence of their common heritage on his social thought.[39] Marx could therefore express himself in vulgar anti-semitic terms, even at the same time as he reflected Jewish premises.

In Marx, as we have noted, neither the existence of material reality, nor the working of the immanent materialist laws of motion of history are inductively established through observation. Like the God of Israel in Hebrew scripture and tradition, existence is never the point at issue. The point of both is to illustrate their working in history through interaction with their opposites. Events are not to be simply set right by divine fiat, or indirectly, say, through redeeming faith in Jesus. The God of the Hebrews causes his will to work itself out through the practical life and struggles of Israel. The objective truth of God's purpose is the reality which underlies the struggles of the Hebrews with their gentile neighbours. In their "empirical life", the Hebrews moral transgressions contradict the Deity, even though they are his product and his chosen people. Thus they are led into conflict with oppressing nations who act as God's historical agent. God in the Jewish theology generates his own contradiction, and overcomes that contradiction. He is immanent in events, not as a static perfect entity, but through the process of the negation of himself and the supersession of that negation ultimately to the eschatological triumph of his will.

Through bitter experience and struggle with their enemies, the Hebrews are driven to a higher level of consciousness of the objective omnipotence of God, and the process he is generating through their lives. The enemies of Israel are, in fact, the enemies of the people of God. They are punished—defeated and destroyed by the outstretched arm of Jehovah—yet they are a necessary agent in the purification and tempering of the Jews through suffering and struggle. The oppressing nations are part of the objective reality of God in the history of Jew and gentile.

There are no short-cuts in the Old Testament. The lesson of history, as interpreted by the prophets—from Amos to Marx—is not to demonstrate to the disbeliever the existence of God, or to measure the virtue of his laws. Rather, while purporting to be an historical account, the point of the scripture is an evocative statement, calling upon the Jews to lead mankind to unity with Jehovah through precept, example and struggle. To understand the objective power of God is to accept his laws as revealed in the Torah. The moral injunction is stated in positive terms. One accepts the laws revealed in the Torah not because one "ought" to do so as a result of ethical argument, but because they are in fact the laws he establishes. For both the believing Jew and the materialist philosopher, a hortatory historicist *Haggadah* is sufficient.

The Hebraic paradigm is, of course, a complex and often pluralistic one, even though the main tenets are so pervasive as to permit summary. One of the significant divisions within it, is the degree to which the prophetic injunctions apply to individuals, or to Israel as a collective. With Ezekiel, in contrast to the earlier work of, say, Amos and Isaiah, a powerful impetus towards individualism is added to the collective fortunes of Israel which we have identified with Marx's prototype for the proletariat. Thus the distinction between the virtuous and wicked in Ezekiel suggested that a remnant of Israel will be saved from the ordeal of the Babylonian conquest. Even so, the ultimate ingathering of the elect, the resurrection of the dead and restoration of Jerusalem to the Jews, are all to emphasize that it is the history of Israel as a collective that is at stake. On the day of triumph for God as for Marx's history, Israel, like the proletariat Marx drew in its image, will unite individuals, classes and nations under the aegis of the chosen.[40] The basis for the eternal "new covenant" which Ezekiel predicted, is the elimination of the divisions within Israel, the purification of its sins, and the ultimate return of David to Israel as "My servant to rule forever".

Marx's *Haggadah* treads a similar path between the role of the collective and the individual. The latter achieves his identification with humanity only in the ultimate, when the proletarian revolution brings the "pre-history of mankind" to a close. The achievement of the universal cohesion of all of humanity takes place not through the relaxation of conflict, of progress towards peace with one's enemies, but by bringing the contradictions to their ultimate climax. The class-conscious proletariat, operating in the secular equivalent of pre-messianic time, purifies its ranks, defeats its enemies, and prepares itself thereby to rule as the representative of mankind. Individual participation is a prerequisite for human salvation, but it acquires meaning only as it affects the class interests already objectively present through the working of history.

Marx's telling of the story of history purports to be different from the Hegelian manipulation of categories. It is real history, Marx believes. It is an account of the practical and mundane. In its premises, however, it reveals that the basis for belief and action are based on supermundane considerations. Insofar as Marx manipulates the empty term "material" to account for events after the event, he does not differ from Hegel's manipulation of Idea, or the Old Testament account of the will of Jehovah. In none of these doctrines is a forecast made which would permit a critical test before the end of historical time (or before the communist programme is put into effect). The theory is defined so as to be beyond human verification. A first reading of Marx suggests that he has empirical verification of his doctrine in mind, but we have seen that this is a delusion—of Marx's as well as of some of his readers. No such test is intended in scripture—where it would amount to blasphemy; nor is it the point of Hegel's philosophy which interprets events after the fact when the "Owl of Minerva" has departed.

Evidence of Marx's evolving attitude towards empirical enquiry is to be found in his changed attitude toward Bentham, after his unstinting praise in *The Holy Family*. The utilitarian notion of an index measuring individual satisfactions now seems patently absurd to Marx. It only acquires apparent meaning, he says, because it is the bourgeois method of evaluation, the "monetary–commercial" relation in disguise.[41] "Political economy", he tells us, "is the real science of this theory of utility."

As his argument progresses, Marx discovers, and presents as a reproach, that what are involved in utility calculations are the facts of individual satisfactions (ordered in a consistent fashion). He is right, of course. Utility means nothing more than this. He concludes that the main fault of utilitarian principles is the individualism which it focuses upon. By its very nature, attention to individual desires limits one to consideration of the capitalist stage of history. Utilitarianism, he now concludes, played a positive role against feudalism by presenting the capitalist viewpoint as if it were a universal statement of both truth and justice. However, the utility analysis of individual attitudes cannot rise beyond the bourgeois vision:

> Remaining within the confines of bourgeois conditions, it could criticise only those relations which had been handed down from a past epoch and were an obstacle to the development of the bourgeoisie. Hence, although the utility theory does expound the connection of all existing relations with economic relations, it does so only in a restricted way... From the outset the utility theory had the aspect of a theory of general utility, yet this aspect only became fraught with meaning when economic relations, especially division of labor and exchange were included... The economic content gradually turned the utility theory into a mere apologia for the existing state of affairs.[42]

Marx is not saying that utilitarianism is false, contrary to observed behaviour, conceptually faulty as an non-empirical construct. On the contrary, its main fault is that it is an accurate picture of bourgeois society. For Marx, science has to transcend the evidence of the known, and extrapolate into the unknown.

With his historical perspective on the meaning of truth thus developed, Marx is able to look back at the issues of the alienation of Man from society in a new light. He has rejected the conception that there exists a human essence discovered by philosophy to which the social organization ought to conform. He has decided that he needs a materialist science of society to replace these pontifical good wishes. Yet, on reflection, it became apparent to him that such a science cannot be built on the observation of individuals as they view themselves, and the satisfactions they claim to receive from society. To do so would be to see man only in terms of capitalist society, one founded on the divergence between individual and social interests.

This divergence is inevitable under the stage of development of the forces of production marked by the division of labour. In this "natural" rather than human relationship, human beings are faced with social forces beyond their control, an alien power:

> Just because individuals seek *only* their particular interest, which for them does not coincide with their common interest, the latter is asserted as an interest "alien' to them, and "independent" of them, as in its turn a particular and distinctive "general" interest; or they themselves must remain within this discord, as in democracy.... The division of labor offers us the first example of the fact that, as long as man remains in naturally evolved society, that is, as long as a cleavage exists between the particular and the common interest, as long, therefore, as activity is not voluntary, but naturally divided, man's own deed becomes an alien power opposed to him, which enslaves him instead of being controlled by him. For as soon as the division of labor comes into being, each man has a particular, exclusive sphere of activity which is forced upon him and from which he cannot escape.[43]

Marx's language is still reminiscent of his earlier position, but we shall see there is a crucial distinction: the alien power of society which faces each individual as the "natural" division of labour is itself a symptom of limited productive forces. His argument starts from the assertion:

> The social power, i.e., the multiplied productive force, which arises through the cooperation of different individuals as it is caused by the division of labor, appears to these individuals, since their cooperation is as an alien force existing outside of them, of the origin and goal of which they are ignorant, which they thus are no longer able to control, which on the contrary passes through a peculiar series of phases and stages independent of the will and action of man ... Whereas with the abolition of the basis, private property, with the communistic regulation of production (and, implicit in this the abolition of the alien attitude of men to their own product), the power of the relation of supply and demand is dissolved into nothing,

and men once more gain control of exchange, production and the way they behave to one another.[44]

In this passage Marx is thinking about alienation as the product of specific forms of division of labour which pass through a series of "phases and stages independent of the will and action of man". Marx now believes that alienation is a state of mind, corresponding to the materially based impossibility of men to voluntarily cooperate during pre-communist stages of production.

Now that Marx is approaching the question of alienation from an historical point of view, he dares to ask himself what might be the nature of a society free from alienation. What might be a society free of the division of labour which expresses the alien power of society over individuals? In a famous passage he comments that as long as "man remains in a naturally evolved society" he is bound by the division of labour:

> He is a hunter, a fisherman, a shepherd or a critical critic, and must remain so if he does not want to lose his means of livelihood; whereas in communist society, where nobody has one exclusive sphere of activity but each can become accomplished in any branch he wishes, society regulates the general production and thus makes it possible for me to do one thing today and another tomorrow, to hunt in the morning, fish in the afternoon, rear cattle in the evening, criticise after dinner, just as I have a mind, without ever becoming hunter, fisherman, shepherd or critic.
>
> This fixation of social activity, this consolidation of what we ourselves produce into a material power above us, growing out of our control, thwarting our expectations, bringing to naught our calculations, is one of the chief factors in historical development til now.[45]

How is it possible for labour not to be "forced" by an alien power of physical necessity translated into social terms? How can one do as one has a mind in the duration of labour, or its degree of specialization? Marx realizes intuitively (and we can prove in an appendix to this chapter) that such a state is equivalent to a condition of complete satiation of consumer wants in an extraordinarily high production economy. Under such a situation which economists call a "bliss point" goods would cease to be scarce, and therefore free. As Marx says, the power of the relation of supply and demand is dissolved into nothing.

Marx realises that a non-alienated society under communism is not simply the revolutionary political act abolishing private property institutions. Abolition of alienation has as prerequisite abolition of scarcity itself. Marx sees the unification of men into a social cooperative as the ultimate outcome of productive forces that will change mankind as much as it changes society:

> This "estrangement" (to use a term which will be comprehensible to the philosophers) can, of course, only be abolished given two *practical* premises. In order to become an "unendurable" power, i.e., a power against which men make a revolution, it must necessarily have rendered the great mass of humanity "propertyless", and moreover in contradiction to an existing world of wealth and culture; both these premises presuppose a great increase in productive power, a high degree of its development.
>
> And, on the other hand, this development of productive forces (which at the same time implies the actual empirical existence of men in their *world-historical*, instead of local, being) is an absolutely necessary practical premise, because without it privation, *want* is merely made general, and with *want* the struggle for necessities would begin again, and all the old filthy business would necessarily be restored; and furthermore, because only with this universal development of productive forces is a *universal* intercourse between men established, which on the one side produces in *all* nations simultaneously the phenomenon of the "propertyless" mass (universal competition), making each nation dependent on the revolutions of the others, and finally puts *world-historical*, empirically universal individuals in place of local ones. Without this, 1) communism could only exist as a local phenomenon; 2) the *forces* of intercourse themselves could not have developed as *universal*, hence unendurable powers: they would have remained homebred "conditions" surrounded by superstition; and 3) each extension of intercourse would abolish local communism. Empirically, communism is only possible as the act of the dominant peoples "all at once: and simultaneously, which presupposes the universal development of productive forces

and the world intercourse bound up with them.[46]

Marx no longer sees men as species beings latent with all the Sunday-school virtues, waiting to identify themselves with the public interest at the stroke of the revolutionary act. On the contrary, in the presence of scarce products, communism will not be able to compete with egoistic self-interest. Individuals will behave precisely as Bentham said they would: they will maximize their satisfactions by working up to the point at which the dissatisfaction with an additional increment of labour will just match the satisfaction which they might obtain from an additional amount of scarce goods. Man will revert to the bourgeois, hedonistic, egoistic, "Jewish" calculation. Moreover, they will do so not only in terms of the currently produced and consumed goods but also in terms of production and saving of accumulated wealth to ensure their advantageous position in the future.

Now Marx knows what has to occur before he can think of the end of alienation. Unless a point of satiated wants is achieved the "whole filthy business will start again". Men will be concerned with their self-interest to the exclusion of others unless productivity reaches such a pitch that they see no point in property. Then men will change on the basis of a "real movement which abolishes the present state of things" not an "ideal to which reality will have to adjust itself". Once having seen that man must be changed, it is clearly nonsense to speak of his essential nature which is alienated from itself by the institution of private property. The inherent conservatism of the concept of a human essence makes itself felt in avoiding the issue of the need to change man as a social product.

The key utopian element in the mature formulation we have outlined is the belief that human wants are in fact satiable at some finite level of output, so that the physical constraints on possible production become irrelevant and goods and labour become free. There is no evidence for the existence of such a "bliss point", though it is of course conceivable. Thus, even though Marx is not free from such utopian speculation, he now sees very clearly that society must achieve a high level of output for such satiation to even be conceivable. Communism is not the abstemious world of those who sneer at the mundane pleasures of consumption, but the ultimate satisfaction of consumer desire which would follow from the escape of the forces of production from the "fetters" placed on them by capitalist economic institutions. Classless society would then be able to confront Nature, not itself, as the alien power and conquer it.

Marx always hankered after freedom in the unbounded sense of Hegel. But he had come to see that freedom from external constraints could be achieved only if scarcity could be made irrelevant relative to desire. If Man were able to wring all his pleasures from Nature with so little labour as to make work indistinguishable from play, then he would not only be free from natural constraint, but the social "filthy business" of human inhumanity to Man. Even though it would be nonsense for him to speak of absolute freedom from the laws and limitations of Nature, it is conceivable that its constraint would not be effective compared to the point of satiation. The transition to this state of freedom is the whole human evolution up to the highest stage of communism.

The historical transition itself, for Marx, remains within the realm of necessity. For him, necessity means more than the economists' understanding that scarcity implies the social necessity of meting out goods and requiring services by some means such as—but not limited too—the working of supply and demand to establish a market price. For the dialectical philosopher necessity encompasses the history of production, class struggles and advance of society through its stages. These, as Marx says in the "Preface" to the *Critique of Political Economy* constitute the "prehistory of mankind"; they are the days of historical time which will come to an end fulfilling the eschatological promise. In the meantime for Marx, as for his prophetic scriptural predecessors, the necessity is for the chosen to struggle and to obey the Law within the compelling constraints imposed by a Power which they cannot control, and which they must strive to comprehend.

Having put the motivating Hegelian conception of freedom in historical perspective, Marx is now able to review the Young Hegelian ideology in terms of class division.[47] He tells us that "the ideas of the ruling class are in every epoch the ruling ideas". Intellectual production reflects the material dominance of the ruling class. Like every other sort of production it is subject to the division of labour, in this case "mental and material labor". Inside the ruling class "one part appears as the thinkers of the class (its active conceptive ideologists, who make formation of the illusions of the class about itself their chief source of liveli-hood)".

As a result of this division of labour, it is all too easy, Marx con-tinues, "in considering the course of history" to "detach the ideas of the ruling class from the ruling class itself, and attribute to them an independent existence". This gives rise to the belief that the development of ideology brings about historical change "without bothering ourselves about the conditions of production and the producers of ideas... For instance ... during the time the aristocracy was dominant, the concepts of honor, loyalty, etc., were dominant, during the dominance of the bourgeoisie the concepts of freedom, equality, etc.". More than this, "the ruling class itself on the whole imagines this to be so [that] ever more abstract ideas hold sway, i.e. ideas which increasingly take on the form of universality. For each new class which puts itself in the place of the one ruling before is compelled, merely to carry through its aim, to present its interest as the common interest of all members of society, that is expressed in ideal form ... and present them as the only rational, universally valid ones".

In the *Manuscripts* this reification was taken to be an alienation of Man. But now Marx concludes that the notion of Man is itself such a self-deception:

> Once the ruling ideas have been separated from the ruling individuals and, above all, from the relations which result from a given stage of the mode of production, and in this way the conclusion has been reached that history is always under the sway of ideas, it is very easy to abstract from these various ideas "the Idea", the thought, etc., as the dominant force in history, and thus to consider all these separate ideas and con-cepts as "forms of self-determination" of the Concept develop-ing in history. It follows then naturally, too, that all the relations of men can be derived from the concept of man, man as conceived, the essence of man. Man. This has been done by speculative philosophy.[48]

The point for Marx at this stage is not that the estrangement of reality in thought constructs is the loss of reality in Man. The issue is the material reality of class exploitation by the ruling class in production. Estrangement, reification, the "fetishism of commodities" in *Capital* have as their significance the hiding of the material reality even from its participants. The intellectual crime is obfuscation. The material crime is the exploitation of labour.

The German ideologists, like all the others, imagine that their truth is the eternal one, when in fact they represent a specific class and historical stage in a given nation. They are, Marx says, the "hucksters of ideas" who imagine that their ideas have made history, when the real order of causation is precisely the reverse:

> The purely national character ... is shown by the fact that these theorists believe in all seriousness that chimeras like "the God–Man", "Man", etc., have presided over individual epochs of history... They forget all other nations, all real events... These pompous and arrogant hucksters of ideas, who imagine themselves infinitely exalted above all national prejudices, are thus in practice far more national than the beer-swilling philistines who dream of a united Germany.[49]

"German philosophy", Marx says in another passage, "is a consequence of German petty-bourgeois conditions."[50] The whole development from Kant to the Young Hegelians, he says, is a projection of the incomplete German industrial revolution, as contrasted with its canonical English development. The German petty-bourgeois emphasis on trade and huckstering instils in its intellectuals the ideology of the capitalist class, but owing to the inhibited economic basis does so on an unrealistic philosophical basis. To Marx, commerce, trade and huckstering are all the same filthy business he excoriated in his earlier work, but now he identifies them with the lesser petty-bourgeois enemy, an unworthy opponent of the proletariat.

Every vicious word Marx had for the Jews in the past may still represent his inner feeling, but petty trade, huckstering, dealing within the imperfections of the market failures, are the features of the petty bourgeois. It is not nationality that gives rise to wretched behaviour, but the petty-bourgeois economic relationship that gives rise to national traits. Marx is beginning to make the distinction so crucial for his later economic work between profits generated from competitive industry—the essential exploitation of labour—and profits based on swindling and imperfection of competition:

Let our bonhomme discover a textbook on political economy
where even theoreticians assert that in competition it is a
matter of "good performance" or "of doing a thing as well as
possible" and not of making "it as profitable as possible." Inci-
dentally, in any such book he will find it stated that under the
system of private property highly developed competition, for
example in England, certainly causes a "thing" to be "done as
well as possible." Small-scale commercial and industrial
swindling flourishes only in conditions of restricted competition, among the Chinese, Germans and Jews, and in general
among hawkers and small shopkeepers.[51]

Marx's venom is now directed at the petty bourgeois and petty
bureaucratic German service official. True they are not the main
enemy, but he despises them. They are beneath contempt. It does
not take too much imagination to realize that with the atrophy of
anti-semitism as a functional feature of Marx's ideology, self-
hatred is displaced into another feature of his father's life. The
displacement of self-hatred to the German petty bourgeois is not
inconsistent with continued anti-semitic expression. Marx continues to speak of a Jewish huckster[52] and to make disparaging
remarks about "lovers of unleavened bread, in common parlance
matzos".[53] But this nasty turn of phrase no longer identifies Jews
as the enemy of humanity.

As Marx's economics advances, he realizes that money and the
exchange process which he had identified with Jews is peripheral
to the class division which defines capitalism in terms of material
relations. Money measures the exploitation of labour in capitalist
society, and represents a facet of its technological advance by
facilitating the division of labour, but it does not directly cause
the degradation of the proletariat. Marx vents his contempt for
Max Stirner who believed:

all the evil of the existing social relations is reduced to the fact
that "burghers and workers believe in the 'truth' of money".
Jacques le bonhomme imagines that it is in the power of the
"burghers" and "workers", who are scattered among all civi-
lised states of the world, suddenly, one fine day, to put on
record their "disbelief" in the "truth of money"; he even believes that if this nonsense were possible, something would be
achieved by it. He believes that any Berlin writer could abolish

the "truth of money" with the same ease as he abolishes in his mind the "truth" of God or of Hegelian philosophy. That money is a necessary product of definite relations of production and intercourse and remains a "truth" so long as these relations exist.[54]

As Marx's fixation with Judaism wanes into mere nastiness,[55] he is able to take a more comprehensive and critical view of Christianity. Unlike his earlier contention that Christianity claims the expression of universal human ideals, Marx now finds fault with the Christian conception of man. Christianity denies and denigrates the natural—even egoistic—drives that arise from human earthly, material nature. Christianity wants us to pretend to be creatures of abstract spirit related to God through faith, and hence incapable of changing the material world through practice. Christianity and all its transmutations— Hegel's translation into the philosophy of the Idea, and the Young Hegelian retranslation into the essence of Man—all share the same idealistic and impotent characteristic. To put words into Marx's mouth: the trouble with Christians is that they are not Jews:

> The only reason why Christianity wanted to free us from the domination of the flesh and "desires as a driving force" was because it regarded our flesh, our desires as something foreign to us; it wanted to free us from determination by nature only because it regarded our own nature as not belonging to us. For if I myself am not nature, if my natural desires, my whole natural character, do not belong to myself—and this is the doctrine of Christianity—then all determination by nature— whether due to my own natural character or to what is known as external nature—seems to me a determination by something foreign, a fetter, compulsion used against me, *heteronomy as opposed to autonomy of the spirit* ... Christianity has indeed never succeeded in freeing us from the domination of desires ... it does not go beyond mere moral injunctions, which remain ineffective in real life.[56]

The doctrine of freedom which Hegel has espoused entailed a spiritualism which would free the individual from the constraints of his physical being. Marx derived his own conception of freedom through production and social revolution; he pointed to the Christian content of this notion of unbounded freedom as a denial of the real material nature of human beings and their desires. Translating him into economist's jargon, Christianity would place the "bliss-point" of satiation at some low level within the boundary of our present production constraints. Such freedom as his former colleagues propound is available only to a saint, Marx says, not to men:

> Whether a desire becomes fixed or not, i.e., whether it obtains exclusive [power over us]—which, however, does [not] exclude [further progress]—depends on whether material circumstances, "bad" mundane conditions permit the normal satisfaction of this desire and, on the other hand, the development of a totality of desires. This latter depends, in turn, on whether we live in circumstances that allow all-round activity and thereby the full development of all our potentialities ... in Stirner the domination of desires is a mere phrase, the imprint of an absolute saint.[57]

Freedom in the sense of purposive, voluntary change in the social order to meet a preconceived norm, is a chimera, Marx concludes. All the preaching in the world, all the philosophizing and praying over the essence of Man or the freedom of the Spirit will not change the world one whit. But when the time is ripe, social revolution will come about, and from it ultimately freedom.

Appendix

We shall make common sense difficult in showing that regardless of social institutions, labour is not a free expression of human activity unless there is a state of satiation in the consumption of commodities. That is to say, as long as commodities show a condition of scarcity (and hence show a positive implicit price) labour will exhibit a scarcity price. We show the contrapositive that free labour implies bliss in commodities by means of two non-linear programming exercises.

Exercise I. Where U is utility and Q is the quantity of a single good let the utility function be $U = U(Q)$. Let $Q = Q(L)$ where L is labour, and $Q(L)$ the production function with one variable input. Let dQ/dL, the marginal productivity of labour be positive, and L non-negative. Then we form the utility maximization problem as:

$$\text{Max } U = U(Q(L)); \text{ s.t. } L \leqslant T, \ L \geqslant 0$$

where T is the maximum amount of labour endurable before death from overwork. Then the Lagrangian is:

$$V(L) = U(Q(L)) + M(T - L),$$

and M is the Lagrange multiplier. The Kuhn–Tucker conditions for a maximum are:

(i) $\dfrac{dU}{dQ} \dfrac{dQ}{dL} - M \leqslant 0$

(ii) $L \dfrac{dU}{dQ} \dfrac{dQ}{dL} - M = 0$

(iii) $L \geqslant 0$

(iv) $T - L \geqslant 0$

(v) $M(T - L) = 0$

(vi) $M \geqslant 0$.

Then from (ii) either $L = 0$, which we can reject as trivial, or we have the "classical programming" solution.

$$\frac{\mathrm{d}U}{\mathrm{d}Q} \frac{\mathrm{d}Q}{\mathrm{d}L} = M.$$

M is zero or positive from (vi). If M is zero, then since $\mathrm{d}Q/\mathrm{d}L$ is positive, $\mathrm{d}U/\mathrm{d}Q = 0$. That is to say, the marginal utility of Q is zero, or the utility function satisfies the first order conditions an absolute unconstrained maximum. Alternatively, since

$$\frac{\mathrm{d}U}{\mathrm{d}Q} \frac{\mathrm{d}Q}{\mathrm{d}L} = \frac{\mathrm{d}U}{\mathrm{d}L}$$

a zero value of M implies that the marginal utility gained from an extra unit of work is zero.

If, on the other hand, M is positive, then $\mathrm{d}U/\mathrm{d}L > 0$; then the satisfaction of the worker from goods continues to increase as he produces more of them. The worker then attempts to maximize his satisfaction by producing, according to (v), at the point where $T = L$, the limit of human endurance. M can be interpreted as the implicit price for labour. If M is positive and labour is "free" (the constraint on labour effort is somewhat artificially written as the total effort possible T), the worker tends to continue to work, accumulating the satisfactions from the goods he produces until he literally can go no further. We conclude that "free" labour implies either bliss, or overwork to the point of exhaustion. The latter is hardly what Marx had in mind for communism.

Exercise II. The preceding is artificial as a result of the supposition that there is a fixed amount of labour, T, that can be expended, and that is entirely used. We can relax the artificiality in an instructive way by rewriting the labour constraint as $g(L) \leqslant T$. Take it that T is positive. Since $g(L)$ is the disutility of labour, then $-g(L)$ is the utility of labour. If $g(L)$ is taken as positive and *ex hypothesi* $g(L)$ is less than or equal to T, then also $-g(L) \leqslant T$. We form a new programme:

Max $U = U(Q)$; s.t. $g(L) \leqslant T, \ L \geqslant 0, \ Q = Q(L)L$

such that $\mathrm{d}Q/\mathrm{d}L > 0$ and the Lagrangian expression is:

$$V(L) = U(Q(L)) + M(T - g(L)).$$

The Kuhn–Tucker conditions for a maximum are:

(i) $\dfrac{\mathrm{d}U}{\mathrm{d}Q}\dfrac{\mathrm{d}Q}{\mathrm{d}L} - M\dfrac{\mathrm{d}g}{\mathrm{d}L} \leqslant 0$ 　　　　(iv) $T - g(L) \geqslant 0$

(ii) $L\dfrac{\mathrm{d}U}{\mathrm{d}Q}\dfrac{\mathrm{d}Q}{\mathrm{d}L} - M\dfrac{\mathrm{d}g}{\mathrm{d}L} = 0$ 　　　(v) $M(T - g(L)) = 0$

(iii) $L \geqslant 0$ 　　　　　　　　　　　(vi) $M \geqslant 0$

If $L = 0$, then

$$\frac{\mathrm{d}U}{\mathrm{d}L} = \frac{\mathrm{d}U}{\mathrm{d}Q}\frac{\mathrm{d}Q}{\mathrm{d}L} = \frac{M}{\mathrm{d}L}\,\mathrm{d}g$$

from (ii). If M is zero then $\mathrm{d}U/\mathrm{d}L = 0$, or the conditions for bliss as previously. A zero value of M means that in (v) and (iv) the labour constraint may be met with inequality, and the constraint is therefore not effective. The marginal utility gained from additional work is zero. Alternatively, if M is positive, then the constraint in (iv) must be met with equality, that is the constraint is binding. Then from (ii) it follows that $\mathrm{d}U/\mathrm{d}L = M(\mathrm{d}g/\mathrm{d}L)$ and hence $\mathrm{d}U/\mathrm{d}g = M > 0$. Then labour is not free, but has a positive shadow price, the utility achieved by an incremental relaxation of the labour constraint is positive. In terms of differentials $\mathrm{d}u = M\mathrm{d}g$, so if the increment in utility is positive as a result of an increase in output, so must be $\mathrm{d}g$ the increment in disutility of labour. Labour is forced, suffering and all that.

Notes

CHAPTER 1

1. McLellan, David, *Karl Marx; His Life and Thought* (London: Macmillan, 1973) p. 1.
2. Ibid., p. 3.
3. Ibid., p. 3.
4. Ibid., p. 5.
5. Cohen, Gerson D., "The Talmudic Age", in L. Schwarz (ed.), *Great Ideas and Ages of the Jewish People*, (New York: Modern Library, 1956), pp. 143–214.
6. A scholarly expression of these ideas is presented in terms of the origins of the Jewish people both in their ethnic and religious sense is to be found in Yehezkel Kaufmann, "The Biblical Age", ibid., pp. 3–94.
7. Poliakov, Léon, *The History of Anti-Semitism*, 3 vols (Paris: Calmann–Levy: 1968) Vol. III. Trans. Miriam Kochan (New York: Vanguard Press, 1975).
8. Sterling, Eleanore, "Jewish Reaction to Jew-Hatred in the First Half of the Nineteenth Century", in *Yearbook III, Leo Baeck Institute of Jews from Germany* (London: East and West Library, 1958), pp. 103–21.
9. Poliakov, op. cit., p. 53.
10. Arendt, Hannah, *The Origins of Totalitarianism* (New York: Harcourt Brace and World, 1966); Eugene Kamenka, "The Baptism of Karl Marx", *The Hibbert Journal*, Nov. 56 (1958) 340–51; Edmund Silberner, "Was Karl Marx an Anti-Semite?", *Historia Judaica*, xi (1949) 9–12.
11. Carsten, F. L., "The Court Jews, a Prelude to Emancipation", *Yearbook III, Leo Baeck Institute of Jews from Germany* (London: East and West Library, 1958) pp. 140–56.
12. Poliakov, op.cit., pp. 25–26
13. Ibid.
14. In the cover to his petition (*Eingabe*) sent to the Governor-General von Sack for approval and commentary, Heinrich Marx wrote: "*Ich bin weit entfernt zu behaupten, es seinen gar keine Massregeln nötig, um meine Glaubensgenossen ganz des Glückes werth zu machen, Bürger zu sein*". Reprinted in Kober, A., "Karl Marx' Vater und das napoleonische Ausnahmegesetz gegen die Juden 1808", in *Jahrbuch des Kölnischen Geschichtsvereins EV*, vol. 14, (Cologne: Verlag der Löwe 1932), p. 119.
15. Poliakov, op. cit., pp. 190–1.

16. The primary source for this argument is Kober's article cited above. His interpretation has been repeated by McLellan in opposition to Franz Mehring's view that Heinrich Marx was a dedicated bourgeois democrat and acted out of conviction. Mehring's orthodox Marxist biography, *Karl Marx*, is blotted by anti-semitic overtones. He gives Heinrich Marx credit for saving Karl the necessity for fighting through the escape from Judaism that Heine and others had to do for themselves. Mehring, a convinced atheist, does not seem to feel that Christian Marxists also had something to escape from.

17. Dohm, Christian Wilhelm, *Über die bürgerliche Verbesserung der Juden"* (1781) (On the civil betterment of the Jews); Reinhard Rürup, "Jewish Emancipation and Bourgeois Society", *Leo Baeck Institute*, xiv (1969), 71–3; Selma Stern-Täubler, "The Jew in the Transition from Ghetto to Emancipation", *Historia Judaica*, xi (1940), 111–12; W. Gurian, "Antisemitism in Modern Germany", in K. J. Pinson (ed.), *Essays on Antisemitism*. Conference on Jewish Relations, New York (1946); see also, K. Philipp, and M. Wolfson, "Marx as a Jew", paper, History of Economic Association Meeting, Chicago, August 1978.

18. *Es gibt nämlich Fälle, wo Strenge, Inconsequenzen, ja selbst augenblickliche Ungerechtigkeiten durch die Löblichkeit des sicher(e)n Endzwecks gerechtfertigt werden können. War das nun hi(e)r der Fall? Hatte man nämlich die Verbess(e)rung der Juden zum Zweck, und waren die ergriff(e)nen Massregeln zweckmässig? Der Sonderbarkeit wegen wollten wir einen Augenblick reine Absichten annehmen. Konnten dieselben auf diese Art erreicht werden? Auf das reifere Alter konnte man nicht wirken wollen. Familienväter konnten sich nicht mehr den Künsten, Wissenschaften und Handwerken widmen. Die Jugend also musste man zum Vorwurfe haben. Aber, um die Jugend zu gewinnen, fing man damit an, die Väter ihres Vermögens zu berauben; das hies(s), in der Kinder Herzen den Geist der Rache entflammen. Indem man zu diesem Ende noch vollends die Grundsetze des Staates verletzte und dazu sich nicht einmal der gewöhnlichen Formalitäten bedienen zu müssen glaubte, musste die Jugend natürlicherweise misstrauisch werden auf ihre staatsbürgerlichen Rechte und nur im alten Schlendrian Sicherheit für ihre Existenz zu finden wähnen, weil man in einer herabgewürdigten Lage wenigstens Mitleiden erregt. Indem man endlich die ganze Sekte der Verachtung preisgab, musste jeder Keim von Ehrgefühl, von Streben zum Guten ersterben. Und nur allzusehr bewährte sich diese nothwendige Folge. Die besten Köpfe wurden scheu und verliessen ihre Laufbahn; und die Wenigen, die standhaft genug waren, darauf fortzuwandeln, — liessen endlich in einem reifern Alter die Hände verzweifelt sinken, weil sie zu spät einsahen, dass sie allein nicht stark genug seyen, dem herrschenden Zeitgeiste zu tro(t)zen"*. Heinrich Marx, op.cit.

19. "In union with Christ, therefore, we turn above all our loving eyes to God, feel the most ardent thankfulness towards Him, sink joyfully on our knees before Him.

Then, when by union with Christ a more beautiful sun has risen for us, when we feel all our iniquity but at the same time rejoice over our redemption, we can for the first time love God, who previously appeared to us as an offended ruler but now appears as a forgiving father, as a kindly teacher.

But if it could feel, the branch would not only look upwards to the husbandman, it would fondly snuggle up to vine, it would feel itself most closely linked with it and with the branches which have sprung from it; it would love the other branches if only because the husbandman tends them and the vine gives them strength.

Thus, union with Christ consists in the most intimate, most vital communion with Him, in having Him before our eyes and in our hearts, and being so imbued with the highest love for Him, at the same time we turn our hearts to our brothers whom He has closely bound to us, and for whom also He sacrificed Himself.

But this love for Christ is not barren, it not only fills us with the purest reverence and respect for Him, it also causes us to keep His commandments by sacrificing ourselves for one another, by being virtuous, but virtuous solely out of love for Him (John 15: 9, 10, 12, 13, 14).

This is the great abyss which separates Christian virtue from any other and raises it above any other: this is one of the greatest effects that union with Christ has on man.

Virtue is no longer a dark distorted image, as it was depicted by the philosophy of the Stoics; it is not the offspring of a harsh theory of duty, as we find it among all heathen peoples, but what it achieves is accomplished through love for Christ, through love for a divine Being, and when it springs from this pure source it is seen to be free from all that is earthly and to be truly divine. All repulsive aspects disappear, all that is earthly is suppressed, all coarseness is removed, and virtue is more brilliant by having become at once milder and more human".

Karl Marx, "The Union of Believers with Christ according to John 15: 1–14—Showing its Basis and Essence, its Absolute Necessity, and its Effects", *Collected Works*, vol. I (New York: International Publishers, 1975) pp. 638–9. In passing we note the identification of Christianity and love as "human" characteristics. This theme will reappear later in the discussion of the *Paris Manuscripts*.

20. Pollack, Herman, *Jewish Folkways in Germanic Lands (1648–1806)* (Cambridge, Mass.; MIT Press, 1971), pp. 25–7.
21. "Letter", Karl Marx to Arnold Ruge, July 1842, *Collected Works*, vol. I, p. 389.
22. "Reflections of a Young Man on the Choice of a Profession", *Collected Works*, vol. I, pp. 3–10.
23. Ibid. p. 8.
24. Compare Marx's adolescent behaviour with Poliakov's comment:

The Jews' proverbial 'restlessness' or 'rootlessness' also partly originated in the mystical idea of the Exile, leading, through fascinating historical vicissitudes, to a very particular relationship between the scattered people and their 'natural environment', heavy with psychological and social consequences. But wherever such phenomena first originated, the link between the Jews' particular history and the vast gamut of their characteristic features cannot be seriously doubted. The Jews' nonviolence is an example of this, a non-aggressiveness, and which in its extreme form tended toward a characteristic "masochism". (Poliakov, op. cit., vol. III, pp. 52–3)

25. Marx, *Collected Works*, vol. I, p. 7. The reference to physical weakness makes

it clear that he really is speaking of himself despite his high-flown prose, since his parents were concerned for his health and he was exempt from military service for "spitting up blood" and other health problems.
26. Künzli, Arnold, *Karl Marx, Eine Psychographie* (Vienna: Europa Verlag, 1966).
27. Marx, *Collected Works*, vol. I, p. 26.

CHAPTER 2

1. "Philosophical Manifesto of the Historical School of Law", *Collected Works*, vol. I, p. 206.
2. Marx and Engels, "The Holy Family", *Collected Works*, vol. IV, pp. 124–34. This portion was written by Marx.
3. Engels, F., *Ludwig Feuerbach and the Outcome of Classical German Philosophy* (New York: International Publishers, 1888), pp. 32–3.
4. The classic statement of this position is in John Stuart Mill, *A System of Logic* (London: Longmans, 1970), pp. 578–95, where the "geometrical method" is rejected in favour of the "physical".
5. *Collected Works*, vol. I, p. 15. "Letter", Berlin, 10–11 November 1837.
6. The classic modern statement which has had an extraordinary influence on social science research is Karl R. Popper, *The Logic of Scientific Discovery* (New York: Science Editions, 1961).
7. *Collected Works*, vol. I, p. 18.
8. Ibid. p. 12. See also Hegel's discussion of Epicurus' empiricism, discussed in later chapters.
9. "Letter", Heinrich Marx to Karl Marx in Berlin, 9 December 1837; *Collected Works*, vol. I, pp. 685–91.
10. One should see in this the precursor of Marx's use of practice to justify his materialist epistemology. K. Marx, "Theses on Feuerbach", Thesis 2, *Collected Works*, vol. V, p. 3.
11. "Letter", Heinrich Marx to Karl Marx, 17 November 1835, *Collected Works*, vol. I, pp. 647–8.
12. Ibid.
13. Künzli, op. cit., p. 114.
14. The engagement was kept secret from Baron Westphalen for almost two years even though both Heinrich Marx and Sophie assisted in the liaison. Finally he gave permission for the engagement in 1837. Hypersensitive to the possibility that anti-semitism might have affected him, Marx wrote to his daughter, Jenny Longuet, in 1881 that the suggestion by her husband Charles Longuet, that Marx's marriage might have met objections owing to Marx's "Israelite" origins was "a simple invention". Some have taken this remark at face value, but one would be more justified in doing so if Marx had ever been able to admit to his origins, and to the ever-present anti-semitism aimed at him. In the same paragraph of this letter is a passage where Marx rages at Longuet for crediting Lassalle as well as Marx for writing on aspects of limiting the work day in the factory acts in an issue of *Justice*. Provoked as Marx always was by Lassalle's Jewishness as well as his success, he concludes: "Longuet would greatly oblige me in never mention-

ing my name in *his* writings" [Cf *Marx Engels Werke*, vol. XXXV, pp. 241–2 (Berlin: Dietz Verlag, 1961–8)].
15. "Letter", Heinrich Marx to Karl Marx in Berlin, 9 December 1837, loc.cit. pp. 685–91, *passim*.
16. "Letter", Heinrich Marx to Karl Marx in Berlin, 10 February 1838, *Collected Works*, vol. I, pp. 692–4.
17. "Letter", Henrietta Marx to Karl Marx in Berlin, 15–16 February 1838, *Collected Works*, vol. I, p. 694.

CHAPTER 3

1. E.g. Marx, K., "Introduction" to *Critique of Hegel's 'Philosophy of Right'*, *Collected Works*, vol. III, pp. 175–87, and Marx and Engels, *The German Ideology*, *Collected Works*, vol. V, p. 24 and *passim*.
2. Cf. Barzun, J., *Darwin, Marx, Wagner*, 2nd ed. (New York: Anchor Books, 1958), Section III, pp. 231–362. See also K. Popper, *The Open Society and its Enemies*, (New York: Harper and Row, 1963).
3. Hegel, G.W.F., *The Phenomenology of Mind*, trans. J.B. Baillie, 2nd ed. (London: Macmillan, 1931), pp. 180–213. See also W.T. Stace, *The Philosophy of Hegel* (New York: Dover Books, 1955), and J. Findlay, *The Philosophy of Hegel, An Introduction and Re-Examination* (New York: Macmillan, 1966. A concise statement of Hegel's general position is to be found in his "Preface" to *The Philosophy of Right*, trans. T.M. Knox (London: Oxford University Press, 1952), pp. 1–13, and also "Introduction", pp. 14–16.
4. Hegel, *Phenomenology*, pp. 151–60.
5. Marx and Engels, *The German Ideology*, *Collected Works*, vol. V, pp. 23–4 and p. 24n.
6. Hegel, G.W.F., *Science of Logic*, 2 vols., trans. N.H. Johnston and L.G. Shuthers, (London: George Allen and Unwin, 1929).
7. Quoted in *Encyclopedia of Philosophy* (New York: Macmillan, 1967), III–IV, p. 437.
8. "Letter", Karl Marx to Heinrich Marx, 10 November 1837, *Collected Works*, vol. I, p. 12.
9. Ibid., pp. 17–19.
19. Ibid., p. 17.
11. Ibid., p. 17.
12. Ibid., p. 15.
13. Hegel, G.W.F., *Lectures on the History of Philosophy*, trans. E.S. Haldane and F.H. Simson (London: Routledge and Kegan Paul, 1955) vol. II, pp. 394–6 *passim*.
14. Marx, *Collected Works*, vol. I, p. 22.

CHAPTER 4

1. Marx, *Collected Works*, vol. I, pp. 25–106.
2. Ibid., p. 29.
3. Ibid., p. 30. It is suggestive to realize that *apikoros* is a common term for "atheist" among Jews; it must have come up in Trier between Karl's father and his rabbi uncle, Samuel.

4. Ibid., p. 39.
5. Ibid., p. 40, cf. pp. 42–5.
6. Ibid., p. 40.
7. Hegel, G. W. F., *History of Philosophy* II, p. 227. Marx, op.cit., pp. 39–40, cf. p. 79, n. 13. The statement is quite right, if it means that singular statements are non-testable, cf. Karl Popper, *Logic of Scientific Discovery* on falsification of propositions rather than singular, existential statements.
8. Hegel, *History of Philosophy*, II, pp. 291–6.
9. An excellent elementary introduction to these matters is to be found in J. G. Kemeny, J. L. Snell and G. L. Thompson, *Introduction to Finite Mathematics*, 2nd ed. (New Jersey: Prentice-Hall, 1966), pp. 194–8.
10. Hegel, *History of Philosophy*, II, p. 290.
11. Ibid., p. 291.
12. Ibid. p. 299
13. Ibid. p. 307.
14. Marx, *Collected Works*, vol. I, pp. 43–4.
15. Ibid. p. 50.
16. Ibid. p. 61.
17. Hegel, *History of Philosophy*, II, pp. 300–4.
18. Marx's religious radicalism extends to an atheistic attack on all concepts of God, not only the polytheism of finite gods. In the "Foreword" to his dissertation Marx hints at this view in his appeal to the authority of Hume in permitting scholars to examine sceptical views of religion. Marx's discretion is easily understood—after all he did want to get his degree from Jena.
19. Marx, op. cit., p. 45. *passim*.
20. "Letter", Georg Jung to Arnold Ruge, cited in M. Rubel and M. Manale, *Marx without Myth* (New York: Harper and Row, 1975), pp. 21–2.
21. Kamenka, E., *The Philosophy of Ludwig Feuerbach*, (New York: Praeger, 1970), p. 27.
22. McLellan, D., *Karl Marx; His Life and Thought*, p. 42.
23. "Letter", Marx in Cologne to Ruge in Dresden, 13 March 1843, *Collected Works*, vol. I, p. 400.
24. K. Marx, and F. Engels, *The German Ideology*, *Collected Works*, vol. V.
25. Marx, "The Philosophical Manifesto of the Historical School of Law", *Collected Works*, vol. I, pp. 203–10.
    In some places Marx also advances a utilitarian defence of freedom of expression and criticism of the law of tradition. This is a secondary theme, but it is not surprising to find it appearing, in the light of the previous observations we have made about Bentham, himself a legal critic.
26. Marx, "Debates on the Law of Thefts of Wood", *Collected Works*, vol. I, p. 231.
27. Ibid., p. 227.
28. Ibid., p. 233.
29. Marx, *Collected Works*, vol. I. pp. 109–31.
30. Marx, *Collected Works*, vol. I, pp. 132–82.
31. Marx, "Comments on the Latest Prussian Censorship Instruction", *Collected Works*, vol. I, pp. 119–21, *passim*.
32. An explicit criticism of the dialectic from the points of view of its inability to generate testable predictions is given in K. Popper, *The Open Society and its*

Enemies, and the *Poverty of Historicism* (New York: Harper Books, 1964; see also Wolfson, M., *A Reappraisal of Marxian Economics*, Ch. I (New York: Columbia University Press, 1965).

33. Marx, *Collected Works*, vol. III, pp. 3–129.
34. Marx, *Collected Works*, vol. III, pp. 175–87.
35. See Joseph O'Malley, "Introduction" to his translation of the *Critique* (London: Cambridge University Press, 1970).
36. See "Letter", Marx to Arnold Ruge, March 1843, *Collected Works*, vol. I, pp. 389–400.
37. Althusser, L., *Pour Marx* (For Marx) (Paris: F. Maspero, 1965, and New York: Pantheon Books, 1969).
38. Kamenka's gloss of Feuerbach's critique of Hegel from the empiricist standpoint is worth quoting *in extenso* (Kamenka, E., op. cit., pp. 74–6):

Hegel claimed that his philosophy was without presuppositions. He therefore began his Logic with Pure Being. Nothing, according to Hegel, could be less tendentious than this—a pure category which begs no question and implies no suspect content. But Hegel's deductions from this point on are purely formal, on paper; they do not represent the real movement of his thought. For in reality, Hegel does not begin with Pure Being, but with the Absolute Idea, in which the totality and connection which he wants to establish are already assumed (*Sämtliche Werke*, vol. II pp. 181–2) While it is one of Hegel's merits that he brings distinction, variety, into his totality, it is never in Hegel real empirical variety, it is always the thought of empirical variety. Hegel's philosophy is able to triumph over sensory experience only because it never deals with it; when Hegel writes of the "other-than-thought" he is not dealing with it, but with a mental conception, with the "thought of the other-than-thought" (*Sämtliche Werke*, vol. II, p. 187). The contradictions that Hegel overcomes are never "real contradictions", the being that he dissolves into the Idea is not real, empirical being, but the philosophical category "being", the thought of being. "The Hegelian philosophy is thus the culminating point of speculatively systematic philosophy" (*Sämtliche Werke*, vol. II, p. 175); everything "demonstrates" itself, i.e., is "posited" and connected in thought; nothing is concretely demonstrated from what actually happens, in the world. "The Hegelian system is the *absolute self-alienation* of reason"; the logical demonstration which should be a means, becomes an end in itself; the theatrical representation is mistaken for the reality and substituted for it. When Hegel, in the famous first chapter of the *Phenomenology*, wants to show the inadequacy of sensory perception by showing that there are no individuals, that there is no singular "this, here, now", what does he do? He does not deal with what we experience, with "this", but with the concept of "thisness" and tries to show that we never experience particulars, but only universals. Characteristically, Hegel is not concerned with the tree that man experiences, leans against, falls over, comes up against as a fact limiting man's movements, but with the "tree" which man fixes in his consciousness. Are we to conclude, from any discussion of the latter, that the former does not exist? If there were no trees, Feuerbach wants to suggest, there would be nothing for us to talk about or analyse in our consciousness. Speech, logic, philosophy are all ways of identifying and organizing an empirical reality coming to us through our senses; without this reality, there would be nothing to talk about. The "concept" of a tree can neither establish nor disprove the existence of actual as opposed to conceptual trees. Idealist philosophy, on the one hand needs actual trees in order to give content to its concepts; on the other hand, it needs to deny actual trees in order to "posit" as the ultimate reality the mind or spirit which has these concepts.

The philosophy which derives the finite from the infinite, the determinate from the indeterminate, *can never truly establish the finite and the determinate*. The finite is derived from the infinite—in other words, the infinite, the indeterminate, is made determinate, *is negated*. It is admitted that the infinite is nothing *without being determinate*, i.e., *that it is nothing unless it is finite*. The *reality* of the infinite is therefore posited as *finite*. But the negative non-Being of the Absolute continues to underlie the whole position; the finitude that has been posited therefore has to be dissolved again [*wieder aufgehoben*]. The *finite* is the *negation* of the *infinite* and again the *infinite* is the *negation* of the *finite*. The Philosophy of the Absolute is a *contradiction*. E. Kamenka, op. cit. pp. 74–6.

39. Kamenka continues:
Feuerbach wrote in the *Preliminary Theses for the Reform of Philosophy* (*Sämtliche Werke*, vol. II, p. 229):

The beginning of philosophy is not God, not the Absolute, not Being as a predicate of the Absolute or of the Idea—the beginning of philosophy is the finite, the determinate, the *actual* (*wirklich*). The infinite cannot even be thought *without* the finite. Can you think of a quality, define it, without thinking of a definite quality? Therefore not the indefinite, the indeterminate, but the definite, the determinate comes first. For the *definite* quality is nothing but the actual quality; the quality that is thought of is preceded by the actual ... The infinite is the *true essence* of the finite, the *true* finite. True speculation of philosophy is nothing but *true and universal empiricism*. (*Sämtliche Werke*, vol. II, pp. 230–1)

40. Marx, *Critique of Hegel's "Philosophy of Right"*, trans. A. Jolin and J. O'Malley (London: Cambridge University Press, 1970), pp. 17–18.
41. Hegel, G. W. F., *Philosophy of Right*, trans. T. M. Knox (Oxford: Oxford University Press 1952), pp. 10–11.
42. Cited by Marx, *Critique*, p. 15.
43. Marx, ibid., p. 6.
44. Marx, ibid., p. 16.
45. Wolfson, M., *Reappraisal of Marxian Economics*, Ch. I (New York: Columbia University Press, 1966).
46. Marx, *Critique*, p. 89.
47. Mill, John Stuart, *A System of Logic*, 8th ed. (London: Longman, reprinted 1970).
48. Marx, *Critique*, p. 12.
49. Ibid., p. 14.
50. Mill, John Stuart, "On Liberty" p. 209–10, *The Philosophy of John Stuart*

Mill, ed. Marshall Cohen (New York, Modern Library 1961). See also John M. Robson, *The Improvement of Mankind: The Social and Political Thought of John Stuart Mill* (Toronto: University of Toronto Press, 1968).

51. Marx, *Critique*, p. 39.
52. Marx, ibid., p. 40.
53. For opposing views see the preface to the *Critique* by the translator, Joseph O'Malley, (pp. lvi–lviii), and E. K. Hunt, "The Invention of New Marxes to Debunk: A Comment on Professor Wolfson's 'Three Stages in Marx's Thought'", *History of Political Economy*, Winter 1979, and M. Wolfson, "Mr Hunt and Mr Marx", in the same issue.
54. Marx, *Critique*, p. 98.
55. Ibid., p. 102. See also "The Industrialists of Hanover and Protective Tariffs" in the *Rheinische Zeitung* (1842) where Marx makes the standard free trade argument. Protective tariffs

> come into prominence in a system which is no longer a system of our time, however much it might have corresponded to medieval conditions based on division and not a unity, which in the absence of general protection, a rational state and a rational system of individual states had to provide *special* protection for each *particular* sphere. Trade and industry ought to be *protected*, but the debatable point is precisely whether *protective tariffs* do in reality protect *trade* and *industry* ... But in any case an *individual* country, however much it may recognize the principle of free trade, is dependent on the state of the world in general, and therefore the question can be decided only by a congress of nations, and not by an individual government. (*Collected Works*, vol. I p. 286.)

This piece should be compared with Marx's diatribes in *Capital* against the classical economists as "apostles of free trade".

56. E.g. E. K. Hunt, op. cit.
57. Marx, *Critique of Hegel's Philosophy of Right*, *Collected Works*, vol. III, p. 109.
58. Ibid., p. 119.
59. "Letter", Marx to Ruge, 13 March 1843, *Collected Works*, vol. I p. 339.
60. Ibid.

CHAPTER 5

1. Marx wrote to Ruge in March that he had just read through Feuerbach's *Preliminary Theses*. Jenny's love letter to Karl, also reveals the intensity with which he was reading Feuerbach that spring. Jenny writes, affecting the self-demeaning style of the "woman's role" which she adopted in her relations with Karl:

> This morning, when I was putting things in order, returning the draughtsmen to their proper place, collecting the cigar butts, sweeping up the ash, ... I came across the enclosed page. You have dismembered our friend Ludwig and left a crucial page here. If you are already past it

in your reading, there is no hurry; but for the worthy bookbinder, in case it is to be bound, it is urgently needed. The whole work would be spoilt. You have certainly scattered some more pages. It would be a nuisance and a pity. Do look after the pages. ("Letter", Jenny von Westphalen to Karl Marx, March 1843, *Collected Works*, vol. I, p. 728)

2. A hint as to Jenny's own preconceptions about her Jewish mother in law is her surprise at the affection of her mother in law. McLellan says, she could only attribute the change of heart "to the impression made by their new prosperity with the 1000 thalers sent by Jung". Jenny wrote to Karl from Trier that Sophie and Henrietta Marx embraced her:

> Your mother called me "thou"... She has been terribly ravaged by illness, looks like C x C, and is hardly likely to get well again.... Next morning your mother came already at 9 o'clock to see the baby... Can you imagine such a change? I am very glad about it... but how has it come about so suddenly? What a difference success makes, or in our case rather the *appearance* of success, which by the subtlest tactics I know how to maintain. ("Letter", Jenny Marx to Karl Marx, June 21, 1844 *Collected Works*, vol. III, p. 579)

This was the same letter in which Jenny confessed her concern for her own economic welfare in light of the prospects of her husband's literary career. She advised him to moderate his "rancour and irritation" as well as rigid literary style. She likens Marx's words to troops in the field. Bidding him farewell she says: "Good luck to the general, my dusky master!....my heart is sad because you are absent; it yearns for you, and it hopes for you and your black messengers". (Ibid.)

3. McLellan, David, *Marx before Marxism* (London: Macmillan, 1970), p. 32.
4. Mehring, F., *Karl Marx* (Leipzig: Soziologische Verlaganstelt, 1933), p. 549. *Er war auch in der Tat sehr kräftig, seine Grösse ging über das Mittelmass, die Schultern waren breit, die Brust gut entwickelt, die Glieder wohl proportioniert, obgleich die Wirbelsäule im Vergleich zu den Beinen etwas zu lang war, wie es bei der jüdischen Rasse häufig zu finden ist.*
5. Westphalen (Marx), Jenny, "Letter" March 1843, p. 730.
6. Quoted in Rubel, M., and Manale, M., *Marx without Myth*, (New York: Harper and Row, 1975), p. 43.
7. Cited in Poliakov, op. cit., p. 425. Cf. A. Kunzli, *Karl Marx, Eine Psychographie* (Vienna: Europa Verlag, 1966), p. 209.
8. Engels, F., *Ludwig Feuerbach and the Outcome of Classical German Philosophy* (1888) (New York: International Publishers, n.d.) p. 28, The first edition of the *Essence of Christianity* is dated 1841. The second edition (1843) is the most widely cited.
9. Marx, *Economic and Philosophic Manuscripts of 1844*, *Collected Works*, vol. III, p. 328.
10. Marx came as close to adulation of Feuerbach as his personality permitted. Marx addressed letters to him in obsequious language in the fall of 1843 and in 1844 (*Collected Works*, vol. III, pp. 349–51, 354–7). The change in Marx's viewpoint in 1845 is mirrored in the sardonic critique of Feuerbach in the *German Ideology* (*Collected Works*, vol. IV, pp. 21–93.)

11. Feuerbach, L., *Werke*, vol. VI, p. 57, cited in E. Kamenka, *op. cit.*, pp. 48–9.
12. Kamenka, ibid., p. 46. Feuerbach, *Werke*, vol. II, p. 246.
13. Feuerbach, L., *The Essence of Christianity*, 2nd ed., trans. Marian Evans, (London: Kegan Paul, 1893), p. 298.
14. Ibid., p. 119.
15. Ibid., p. 118.
16. Ibid., pp. 112–19.
17. One should note that this is precisely the view of the contradiction between Man and Nature that characterized mature Marxism.
18. Feuerbach, *The Essence of Christianity*, p. 114.
19. Poliakov, op. cit., vol. III, p. 164.
20. Ibid., vol. III, pp. 413–14.
21. Ibid.
22. Feuerbach, *The Essence of Christianity*, p. 299.
23. Marx, *On the Jewish Question, Collected Works*, vol. III, p. 146–7, *passim*.
24. Ibid., p. 152.
25. Ibid., p. 153–4.
26. Ibid., p. 153.
27. Ibid., p. 156.
28. Ibid., p. 168.
29. Ibid., pp. 169–70.
30. Ibid., p. 170.
31. Loc. cit.
32. Ibid., p. 171.
33. Marx, *Theses on Feuerbach, Collected Works*, vol. V, p. 3. At this later stage, when anti-semitic language persists, but is no longer functional in Marx's system of thought, Feuerbach is criticized for seeing "practice" only as if it were a "dirty Jewish" activity.
34. *On the Jewish Question*, p. 172.
35. Ibid., p. 173.
36. Ibid., p. 174.
37. Ibid.
38. Marx, "Introduction" to contribution to *A Critique of Hegel's "Philosophy of Law"* (Right), *Collected Works*, vol. III, pp. 175–87.
39. Ibid., p. 175.
40. Ibid., p. 176.
41. Ibid., p. 182.
42. Ibid., p. 177.
43. Ibid., pp. 177–9 *passim*. In denouncing the Savigny "historical school of law" as protective of the old regime, Marx displays his anti-semitism once more. He suggests a parallel between Savigny and the despised image of the Jew as Shylock.

A school which legitimizes the baseness of today by the baseness of yesterday, a school that declares rebellious every cry of the serf against the knout once the knout is a time-honored, ancestral, historical one. A school to which history only shows its *posterior* as the God of Israel did to his servant Moses—the *historical school* of law— would hence have invented German history had it not been an invention of German history. For

every pound of flesh cut from the heart of the people, the historical school
of law—Shylock, but Shylock the bondsman—swears on its bond, its historical bond, its Christian–Germanic bond. (*Collected Works*, vol. III, p.
177. "Introduction" to *Critique of Hegel's "Philosophy of Law"*)

44. Ibid., p. 182.
45. Ibid., p. 186.
46. Ibid., pp. 184–5
47. Ibid., p. 180.
48. Ibid., pp. 186–7.
49. Ibid., p. 187.
50. Ibid.
51. Ibid., p. 182.
52. Ibid., p. 187.
53. Marx, *Capital*, vol. I, Modern Library (Chicago: Charles H. Kerr, 1906), "Preface", p. 13.
54. Marx, Letter to Vera Sassoulitch, February 1881, in D. McLellan (ed.), *Karl Marx, Selected Writings* (Oxford: Oxford University Press, 1977), pp. 576–7.
55. Marx, *Collected Works*, vol. III, p. 189ff.
56. Ibid., p. 192.
57. Ibid., pp. 199.
58. Ibid., p. 198.
59. Ibid., pp. 195–6.
60. Ibid., p. 203.

CHAPTER 6

1. Marx and Engels, *The German Ideology* (1845), *Collected Works*, vol. V, pp. 23–4.
2. Feuerbach, L., *Preliminary Theses for the Reform of Philosophy* cited in E. Kamenka, *The Philosophy of Ludwig Feuerbach* (New York: Praeger, 1970).
3. Engels, F., "Outlines of a Critique of Political Economy" (*Umrisse*), *Collected Works*, vol. III, pp. 418–43.
4. Marx, *A Contribution to the Critique of Political Economy* (1859), trans. (from the 2nd German ed.) M. Stone, (Chicago: C. H. Kerr, 1913), p. 10.
5. Ibid., pp. 11–12.
6. Marx and Engels, *The Holy Family*, *Collected Works*, vol. IV, pp. 78–143.
7. Engels, *Umrisse*, p. 426.
8. Ibid., p. 426.
9. Ibid, p. 427. The *Umrisse* has more than developmental interest as a step in Marx's evolving ideology. It shows that he was familiar with at least the bare outlines of utility theory, and in his mature economic works chose to reject it on materialist philosophical grounds. He was not, as is sometimes said, simply repeating the orthodox theory of value.
10. Mill, James, *Elements of Political Economy* (1821), 3rd ed., (New York: Augustus M. Kelley, 1963).
11. Mill, Op. cit., p. 2.

12. Marx, *Critique of Political Economy*, pp. 123–4, 250ff.
13. Marx, *Theories of Surplus Value*, trans. Jack Cohen (London: Lawrence and Wishart, 1972), vol. III pp. 84–106.
14. Koopmans, T. C., "Concepts of Optimality and their Uses", *American Economic Review*, LXVII, 3 (June 1977), 261–74.
15. Cf. Blaug, M., *Economic Theory in Retrospect*, 2nd ed., (Homewood, Ill.: 1978 Irwin), p. 96; P. Sraffa, *Collected Works of David Ricardo* (Cambridge: Cambridge University Press, 1951–73) I, xxx–xxxiii; P. A. Samuelson, "The Canonical Classical Model of Political Economy", *Journal of Economic Literature*, December 1978, xvi, 4 (December 1978), 1415–34; G. Stigler, "Ricardo and the 93% Labor Theory of Value", *American Economic Review*, XLVIII, 3, 357–67.
16. For a sophisticated treatment of Ricardo's theory, see Samuelson's argument that it was more a land theory of value than a labour theory. Other articles cited here discuss the "Ricardo Effect" as it reappears as Marx's "Transformation Problem".
    Samuelson, Paul A., "Wages and Interest: A Modern Dissection of Marxian Economic Models", *Amer. Econ. Rev.*, 47 (December 1957), pp. 884–912; reprinted in Joseph E. Stiglitz (ed.), *The Collected Scientific Papers of Paul A. Samuelson*, vol. 1, (Cambridge, Mass.: MIT Press, 1965), pp. 341–69.
    Samuelson, Paul A., "A Modern Treatment of the Ricardian Economy: I. The Pricing of Goods and of Labor and Land Services", *Quart. J. Econ.*, 13 (February 1959), 1–35; reprinted in Joseph E. Stiglitz (ed.), *The Collected Scientific Papers of Paul A. Samuelson*, vol. 1, (Cambridge, Mass.: MIT Press, 1965), pp. 373–407.
    Samuelson, Paul A., "A Modern Treatment of Ricardian Economy: II. Capital and Interest Aspects of the Pricing Process", *Quart. J. Econ.*, 73 (May 1959), 217–31; reprinted in Joseph E. Stiglitz (ed.), *The Collected Scientific Papers of Paul A. Samuelson*, vol. 1, (Cambridge, Mass: MIT Press, 1965), pp. 408–22.
    Samuelson, Paul A., "Understanding the Marxian notion of Exploitation: A Summary of the So-Called Transformation Problem between Marxian Values and Competitive Prices", *J. Econ. Lit.*, 9(2) (June 1971), 399–431; reprinted in Robert C. Merton (ed.), *The Collected Scientific Papers of Paul A. Samuelson*, vol. 3, (Cambridge, Mass.: MIT Press, 1972), pp. 276–308.
    Samuelson, Paul A., "Marx as Mathematical Economist: Steady-State and Exponential Growth Equilibrium", in George Horwich and Paul Samuelson (eds.), *Trade, stability, and macroeconomics: Essays in honor of Lloyd A. Metzler* (New York: Academic Press, 1974), pp. 269–307; reprinted in Hiroaki Nagatini and Kate Crowley (eds.), *The Collected Scientific Papers of Paul A. Samuelson*, vol. 4, (Cambridge, Mass.: MIT Press, 1977), pp. 231–69.
    Morishima, Michio, *Marx's economics: A dual theory of value and growth* (New York and London: Cambridge University Press, 1973).
    Wolfson, M., "The Empirical Content of the Labor Theory of Value: The Transformation Problem once again, *Keio Economic Studies*, 14 (2) (1978), 67–84.
17. Mill, op. cit., p. 4.

18. Ibid., p. 6.
19. Ibid., p. 99.
20. Ibid., p. 95.
21. Ibid., p. 98.
22. Loc. cit.
23. Marx, K., "Comments on James Mill", *Collected Works*, vol. III, p. 210.
24. Ibid., p. 212.
25. Marx. *Capital, A Critique of Political Economy*, trans. S. Moore, and E. Aveling. (New York: Modern Library), vol. I, pp. 81–95. Reprinted from C. H. Kerr & Co., Chicago (1906).
26. At every point of fact or positive analysis, Marx concedes that Mill is correct. Their significance must be inverted, however, because Marx claims that Mill has presumed the institutions of private property. In "Comments on James Mill", he concedes the gains from trade, and yet insists it is an alienation of man:

> Political economy—like the real process—starts out from the *relation of man to man* as that of *property owner to property owner*. If man is presupposed as property owner, i.e., therefore as an exclusive owner, who proves his personality and both distinguishes himself from, and enters into relations with, other men through this exclusive ownership—private property is his personal, *distinctive*, and therefore essential mode of existence—then the *loss or surrender* of private property is an *alienation of man*, as it is of *private property* itself. Here we shall only be concerned with the latter definition. If I give up my private property to someone else, it ceases to be *mine*, it becomes something independent of me, lying *outside* my sphere, a thing *external* to me. Hence I *alienate* my private property. With regard to me, therefore, I turn it into *alienated* private property. But I only turn it into an *alienated* thing in general, I abolish only my personal relation to it, I give it back to the *elementary* powers of nature if I alienate it only with regard to myself. It becomes alienated *private property* only if, while ceasing to be *my* private property, it on that account does not cease to be *private property* as such, that is to say, if it enters into the same relation to *another* man, *apart* from me, as that which it had to myself; in short, if it becomes the *private property* of *another* man. The case of *violence* excepted—what causes me to alienate *my* private property to another man? Political economy replies correctly: *necessity, need*. The other man is also a property owner, but he is the owner of *another* thing, which I lack and cannot and will not do without, which seems to me a *necessity* for the completion of my existence and the realisation of my nature.
>
> The bond which connects the two property owners with each other is the *specific kind of object* that constitutes the substance of their private property. The desire for these two objects, i.e., the need for them, shows each of the property owners, and makes him conscious of it, that he has yet another *essential* relation to objects besides that of private ownership, that he is not the particular being that he considers himself to be, but a *total* being whose needs stand in the relationship of *inner* ownership to all products, including those of another's labour. For the need of a thing is the most evident, irrefutable proof that the thing belongs to my essence,

that its being is for me, that its *property* is the property, the peculiarity, of my essence. Thus both property owners are impelled to give up their private property, but to do so in such a way that at the same time they confirm private ownership, or to give up the private property, within the relationship of private ownership. Each therefore alienates a part of his private property to the other ...

Exchange or *barter* is therefore the social act, the species-act, the community, the social intercourse and integration of men within *private ownership*, and therefore the external, *alienated* species-act. It is just for this reason that it appears as *barter*. For this reason, likewise, it is the opposite of the *social* relationship.

Through the reciprocal alienation or estrangement of private property, *private property* itself falls into the category of *alienated* private property. For, in the first place, it has ceased to be the product of the labour of its owner, his exclusive, distinctive personality. For he has alienated it, it has moved away from the owner whose product it was and has acquired a personal significance for someone whose product it is *not*. It has lost its personal significance for the owner. Secondly, it has been brought into relation with another private property, and placed on a par with the latter. Its place has been taken by a private property of a *different* kind, just as it itself takes the place of a private property of a *different* kind. On both sides, therefore, private property appears as the representative of a different kind of private property, as the *equivalent* of a *different* natural product and both sides are related to each other in such a way that each represents the mode of existence of the *other*, and both relate to each other as *substitutes* for themselves and the other. Hence the mode of existence of private property as such had become that of a *substitute*, of an *equivalent*. Instead of its immediate unity with itself, it exists now only as a relation to *something else*. Its mode of existence as an *equivalent* is no longer its specific mode of existence. It has thus become a *value*, and immediately an *exchange-value*. Its mode of existence as *value* is an *alienated* designation *of itself*, different from its immediate existence, external to its specific nature, a merely *relative* mode of existence of this.

How this *value* is more precisely determined must be described elsewhere, as also how it becomes *price*. (Marx, "*Comments on Mill*", pp. 217–19).

27. Ibid., p. 213.
28. Ibid., p. 214.
29. Mill, op. cit., p. 147.
30. Marx, *Capital*, p. 220.
31. In his maturity, Marx would come to regard the division of labour as part of the development of productive forces, and see in it a part of the advance that would lead to its own elimination under a high productivity communist regime when each would receive "according to his needs". At this later stage Marx differed with Smith for the identification of the origin of division of labour in exchange, pointing instead to its earlier origins in the history of man. He writes:

To all the different varieties of values in use there correspond as many different kinds of useful labor, classified according to the order, genus, species, and variety to which they belong in the social division of labor. This division of labor is a necessary condition for the product of commodities, but it does not follow conversely, that the production of commodities is a necessary condition for the division of labor. In the primitive Indian community there is a social division of labor, without the production of commodities. Or, to take an example nearer home, in every factory the labor is divided according to a system, but this division is not brought about by the operatives mutually exchanging their individual products. Only such products can become commodities with regard to each other, as result from different kinds of labor, each kind being carried on independently and for the account of private individuals. (*Capital*, vol. I, p. 49)

32. Marx, "On Mill", p. 220.
33. Ibid., pp. 227–8.
34. Ibid., p. 227.
35. Ibid.
36. Marx, *Capital*, vol. I, p. 91.
37. Ibid.
38. Ibid., p. 92.
39. Marx, *Economic and Philosophic Manuscripts of 1844, Collected Works*, vol. III, p. 235.
40. Ibid., p. 236.
41. Ibid., pp. 237–8.
42. Ibid., p. 238.
43. Ibid., p. 239.
44. Ibid., p. 241.
45. Ibid., p. 246.
46. Ibid., p. 263.
47. Ibid., p. 263.
48. Ibid., pp. 266–7. It is interesting that, having moved himself to a more romantic view, despite himself Marx would feel the pull toward the medieval past that characterized German romantic nationalism. His comments against the nobility have a curious ambivalent overtone of regret:

In the first place, feudal landed property is already by its very nature huckstered land—the earth which is estranged from man and hence confronts him in the shape of a few great lords.

The domination of the land as an alien power over men is already inherent in feudal landed property. The serf is the adjunct of the land. Likewise, the lord of an entailed estate, the first-born son, belongs to the land. It inherits him. Indeed the domination of private property begins with property in land—that is its basis. But in feudal property the lord at least *appears* as the king of the estate. Similarly, there still exists the semblance of a more intimate connection between the proprietor and the land than that of mere *material* wealth. The estate is individualized with its lord: it has his rank, is baronial or ducal with him, has his privileges, his jurisdiction, his political position, etc. It appears as the inorganic body of its lord. Hence the proverb *nulle terre sans maitre*, which expresses the fusion of nobility and landed property. Similarly the rule of landed property does not appear directly as the rule of mere capital. For those belonging to it, the estate is more like their fatherland. It is a constricted sort of nationality.

In the same way, feudal landed property gives its name to its lord, as does a kingdom to its king. His family history, the history of his house, etc.—all this individualizes the estate for him and makes it literally his house, personifies it. Similarly those working on the estate have not the position of *day-laborers*; but they are in part themselves his property, as are serfs; and in part they are bound to him by ties of respect, allegiance and duty. His relation to them is therefore directly political, and has likewise a human, *intimate* side. Customs, character, etc., vary from one estate to another and seem to be one with the land to which they belong; whereas later, it is only his purse and not his character, his individuality, which connects a man with an estate. Finally the feudal lord does not try to extract the utmost advantage from his land. Rather, he consumes what is there and calmly leaves the worry of producing to the serfs and the tenants. Such is *nobility*'s relationship to landed property which casts a romantic glory on its lords.

It is necessary that this appearance be abolished—that landed property, the root of private property be dragged completely into the movement of private property and that it become a commodity.

49. Ibid., p. 270.
50. Ibid., p. 275.
51. Ibid., p. 272.
52. Loc. cit.
53. Loc. cit.
54. Ibid., p. 276.

CHAPTER 7

1. Feuerbach, L., *The Essence of Christianity*, 2nd ed. (1842), trans. Marian Evans (London: Kegan, Paul, Trench, Trübner, 1893) p. viii.
2. Ibid., p. 113.
3. Marx, K., "Letter" to Arnold Ruge, 13 March 1843, *Collected Works*, vol. I, p. 400.
4. Marx, K., *Economic and Philosophic Manuscripts of 1844, Collected Works*, vol. III, pp. 326–46.
5. Ibid., p. 328.
6. Ibid., p. 329.
7. "Despite the thoroughly negative and critical appearance and despite the genuine criticism contained in it, which often anticipates far later development, there is already latent in the *Phenomenology* as a germ, a potentiality, a secret uncritical positivism and the equally uncritical idealism of Hegel's later works—that philosophic dissolution and restoration of the existing empirical world" (ibid., p. 332–3).
8. Ibid., p. 329.
9. Ibid., p. 336.

10. "The *estrangement*, which therefore forms the real interest of this alienation and of the transcendence of this alienation is the opposition of *in itself* and *for itself* [*an sich* and *für sich*, categories of the Hegelian system M. W.] of *consciousness and self-consciousness, object and subject*—that is to say it is the opposition between abstract thinking and sensuous reality or real sensuousness within thought itself" (ibid., p. 333).
11. Ibid., p. 331.
12. "[In Hegel] it is not the fact that the human being *objectifies himself inhumanly*, in opposition to himself, but that he *objectifies himself in distinction* from and *in opposition* to abstract thinking, that constitutes the posited essence of the estrangement and the thing to be superseded" (ibid., p. 333).
13. Ibid., p. 332.
14. "But *nature* too, taken abstractly, for itself—nature fixed in isolation from man—is *nothing* for man. It goes without saying that the abstract thinker who has committed himself to intuiting, intuits nature abstractly. Just as nature lay enclosed in the thinker in the form of the absolute idea, in the form of a thought-entity—in a shape which was obscure and enigmatic even to him—so by letting it emerge from himself he has really let emerge only this *abstract nature*, only nature as a *thought-entity*—but now with the significance that it is the other-being of thought, that it is real, intuited nature—nature distinguished from abstract thought. Or to talk in human language, the abstract thinker learns in his intuition of nature that the entities which he thought to create from nothing, from pure abstraction—the entities he believed he was producing in the divine dialectic as pure products of the labour of thought, for ever shuttling back and forth in itself and never looking outward into reality—are nothing else but *abstractions* from *characteristics of nature*. To him, therefore, the whole of nature merely repeats the logical abstractions in a sensuous, external form. He once more *resolves* nature into these abstractions. Thus his intuition of nature is only the act of confirming his abstraction from the intuition of nature—is only the conscious repetition by him of the process of creating his abstraction. Thus, for example, time equals negativity referred to itself. To the superseded becoming as being there corresponds, in natural form, superseded movement as matter" (ibid., p. 345).
15. Ibid., p. 332.
16. Ibid., p. 333.
17. Hegel having posited man as equivalent to self-consciousness, the estranged object—the estranged essential reality of man—is nothing but *consciousness*, the thought of estrangement merely—estrangement's *abstract* and therefore empty and unreal expression, *negation*. The supersession of the alienation is therefore likewise nothing but an abstract, empty supersession of that empty abstraction—*the negation of the negation*. The rich, living, sensuous, concrete activity of self-objectification is therefore reduced to its mere abstraction, *absolute negativity*—an abstraction which is again fixed as such and considered as an independent activity—as sheer activity. Because this so-called negativity is nothing but the *abstract, empty* form of that real living act, its content can in consequence be merely a *formal* content produced by abstraction from all content. As a result therefore one gets general, abstract *forms of abstraction* pertaining to every content and on

that account indifferent to, and consequently, valid for, all content—the thought-forms or logical categories torn from *real* mind and from *real* nature. (We shall unfold the *logical* content of absolute negativity further on.)

Hegel's positive achievement here, in his speculative logic, is that the *definite concepts*, the universal *fixed thought-forms* in their independence *vis-à-vis* nature and mind are a necessary result of the general estrangement of the human being and therefore also of human thought, and that Hegel has therefore brought these together and presented them as moments of the abstraction-process. For example, superseded being is essence, superseded essence is concept, the concept superseded is—absolute idea. But what, then, is the absolute idea? It supersedes its own self again, if it does not want to perform once more from the beginning the whole act of abstraction, and to satisfy itself with being a totality of abstractions or the self-comprehending abstraction. But abstraction comprehending itself as abstraction knows itself to be nothing: it must abandon itself—abandon abstraction—and so it arrives at an entity which is its exact opposite—at *nature*. Thus, the entire logic is the demonstration that abstract thought is nothing in itself; that the absolute idea is nothing for itself; that only *nature* is something (ibid., p. 343).

18. Ibid., p. 336.
19. Ibid., pp. 341–2.
20. Ibid., pp. 272–3
21. Ibid., p. 276–7.
22. Engels, F., *Ludwig Feuerbach and the Outcome of Classical German Philosophy* (New York: International Publishers, n.d), pp. 46–7.
23. Marx, *Manuscripts*, p. 278.
24. Ibid., 279.
25. Loc. cit.
26. Ibid., p. 280.
27. Ibid., p. 270.
28. Ibid., p. 271.
29. Ibid., pp. 290–1.
30. Ibid., p. 317.
31. Loc. cit.
32. Ibid., p. 321.
33. Ibid., p. 325.
34. Ibid., p. 346.
35. Ibid., p. 297.
36. Loc. cit.
37. When Marx broke with the humanist doctrine finally in *The German Ideology*, he exposed its German petty-bourgeois roots. See below, Chapter 10.
38. Cf. Schoenbaum, D., *Hitler's Social Revolution* (New York: Doubleday Anchor Books, 1966). See especially Chapter 2, "The Third Reich and its Social Ideology". Also see Ralf Dahrendorf, *Society and Democracy in Germany* (New York: Doubleday, 1967).
39. Ibid., p. 320.
40. Ibid., p. 301.
41. Ibid., pp. 301–2.

42. Ibid., p. 303–4.
43. Ibid., p. 300.
44. Loc. cit.

CHAPTER 8

1. Marx, K., and Engels, F., *The Holy Family*, or *Critique of Critical Criticism. Against Bruno Bauer and Company, Collected Works*, vol. VI, pp. 5–211 (written September–November 1844 and published 1845).
2. Engels, F., "Feuerbach", *Collected Works*, vol. V, p. 11.
3. *The Holy Family*, p. 7.
4. Loc. cit.
5. Ibid., p. 21.
6. Loc. cit.
7. Ibid., p. 22.
8. Ibid., pp. 21–2.
9. Ibid., p. 22.
10. Proudhon, Pierre-Joseph, *System of Economical Contradictions: or The Philosophy of Misery*, trans. B. R. Tucker (Boston: B. R. Tucker, 1888). *Misère* is, of course, usually translated as "poverty" rather than "misery".
11. Ibid., p. 21.
12. Ibid., pp. 21–2.
13. Ibid., pp. 23–4.
14. Ibid., p. 24.
15. "The French Enlightenment of the eighteenth century, and in particular *French materialism*, was not only a struggle against the existing political institutions and the existing religion and theology; it was just as much an *open, clearly expressed* struggle against the *metaphysics of the seventeenth century*, and against *all metaphysics*, in particular that of *Descartes, Malebranche, Spinoza* and *Leibniz*. *Philosophy* was counterposed to *metaphysics*, just as *Feuerbach*, in his first resolute attack on *Hegel*, counterposed *sober philosophy* to *wild speculation*. Seventeenth century *metaphysics*, driven from the field by the French Enlightenment, notably, by *French materialism* of the eighteenth century, experienced a *victorious and substantial restoration* in *German philosophy*, particularly in the *speculative German philosophy* of the nineteenth century. After *Hegel* linked it in a masterly fashion with all subsequent metaphysics, and with German idealism and founded a metaphysical universal kingdom, the attack on theology again corresponded as in the eighteenth century, to an attack on *speculative metaphysics* and *metaphysics in general*. It will be defeated for ever by *materialism*, which has now been perfected by the work of *speculation* itself and coincides with *humanism*. But just as *Feuerbach* is the representative of *materialism* coinciding with *humanism* in the *theoretical* domain, French and English *socialism* and *communism* represent *materialism* coinciding with *humanism* in the *practical* domain" *(The Holy Family*, pp. 124–5).
16. Ibid., p. 125.
17. Ibid., p. 127.
18. Ibid., p. 129.
19. Loc. cit.

20. Ibid., p. 127.
21. Ibid., p. 130.
22. Ibid., pp. 132–4.
23. Ibid., p. 134.
24. Ibid., p. 131.
25. Proudhon, P. J., *What is Property? An Inquiry into the Principle of Right and of Government*, trans. B. R. Tucker (London: William Reeves, n.d.).
26. *The Holy Family*, p. 39.
27. Ibid., p. 31–2.
28. "When ... the economists become conscious of these contradictions, *they themselves* attack *private property* in one or other *particular* form as the falsifier of what is in itself (i.e., in their imagination) rational wages, in itself rational value, in itself rational trade. Adam Smith, for instance, occasionally polemicises against the capitalists, Destutt de Tracy against the money-changers, Simonde de Sismondi against the factory system, Ricardo against landed property, and nearly all modern economists against the *non-industrial* capitalists, among whom property appears as a mere *consumer*.

  Thus, as an exception—when they attack some special abuse—the economists occasionally stress the semblance of humanity in economic relations, but sometimes, as a rule, they take these relations precisely in their clearly pronounced *difference* from the human, in their strictly economic sense. They stagger about within this contradiction completely unaware of it.

  Now *Proudhon* has put an end to this unconsciousness once and for all. He takes the *human semblance* of the economic relations seriously and sharply opposes it to their *inhuman reality*. He forces them to be in reality what they imagine themselves to be, or rather to give up their own idea of themselves and confess their real inhumanity. He therefore consistently depicts as the falsifier of economic relations not this or that particular kind of private property, as other economists do, but private property as such and in its entirety. He has done all that criticism of political economy from the standpoint of political economy can do" (ibid., p. 33).
29. *What is property?*, pp. 159–218.
30. *The Holy Family*, p. 32; cf. *What is Property?*, p. 143ff.
31. Marx, *Capital*, vol. II, trans. E. Untermann (Chicago: Charles Kerr & Co. 1933), pp. 475–6. Cf. M. Wolfson, *A Reappraisal of Marxian Economics* (New York: Columbia University Press, 1966), pp. 133–43.
32. *The Holy Family*, pp. 32–3.
33. *What is Property?*, pp. 139–40.
34. Proudhon expressed himself with unusual clarity on this score (*What is Property?*, pp. 141–2)

> Every transaction ending in an exchange of products or services may be designated as a commercial operation.
>
> Whoever says commerce, says exchange of equal values; for, if values are not equal, and the injured party perceives it, he will not consent to the exchange and there will be no commerce.
>
> Commerce exists only among free men. Transactions may be effected between other people by violence or fraud, but there is no commerce.
>
> A free man is one who enjoys the use of his reason and his faculties;

who is neither blinded by passion, nor hindered or driven by oppression, nor deceived by erroneous opinions.

So, in every exchange, there is a moral obligation that neither of the contracting parties shall gain at the expense of the other; that is, that, to be legitimate and true, commerce must be exempt from all inequality. This is the first condition of commerce. Its second condition is, that it be voluntary; that is, that the parties act freely and openly.

I define, then commerce or exchange as an act of society.

Proudhon then goes on to enumerate transactions which are not free:

The negro who sells his wife for a knife, his children for some bits of glass, and finally himself for a bottle of brandy, is not free . . .

The civilized labourer who bakes a loaf that he may eat a slice of bread . . . who produces everything that he may dispense with everything is not free. His employer, not becoming his associate in the exchange of salaries or services which takes place between them is his enemy . . .

The soldier who serves his country through fear instead of through love is not free . . .

The peasant who hires land, the manufacturer who borrows capital, the tax-payer who pays tolls, duties, patent and licence fees, personal and property taxes, etc., and the deputy who votes for them,—all act neither intelligently nor freely. Their enemies are the proprietors, the capitalists, the government.

He concludes:

Give men liberty, enlighten their minds that they may know the meaning of their contracts, and you will see the most perfect equality in exchanges without regard to superiority of talent and knowledge.

35. *The Holy Family*, p. 41.
36. Ibid., p. 43. The judgment that Proudhon remained within the concepts of private property was made in much more vitriolic terms in Marx's *Poverty of Philosophy* (1847). This is also the judgment of other commentators on Proudhon. Stewart Edwards says in his Introduction to Proudhon's essay: "It is nevertheless his defense of the small-property owner that provides the logic to Proudhon's writings . . . Proudhon's early notoriety as the author who had shown that "property is theft is misleading" (Edwards, S., *Selected Writings of Pierre-Joseph Proudhon*, London: Macmillan, 1969), p. 33.
37. *The Holy Family*, p. 114.
38. Ibid., p. 115.
39. "Just as *industrial activity* is not abolished when the *privileges of the trades*, guilds and corporations are abolished, but, on the contrary, real industry begins only after the abolition of these privileges; just as *ownership of the land*, is not abolished when *privileged* land ownership is abolished, but, on the contrary, begins its universal movement only with the abolition and with the free division and free sale of land; just as *trade* is not abolished by the abolition of *trade privileges*, but finds its true realisation in free trade; so re-

ligion develops in its practical universality only where there is no privileged religion (cf. the North American States)" (ibid., pp. 115–16).
40. Ibid., p. 116.
41. Ibid., p. 117.
42. Marx refers Bauer to Hegel's *History of Philosophy* which "presents French materialism as the *realization* of the substance of Spinoza (ibid., p. 131) and then goes on to carefully piece together the following excerpts from three pages of Hegel's *Phenomenology of Mind*:

> Regarding that Absolute Being, *Enlightenment* in self falls out with itself ... and is divided between the view of *two parties* ... the one ... calls *Absolute Being* that predicateless Absolute ... the other calls it *matter* ... Both are entirely the *same* notion—the distinction lies not in the objective fact, but purely in the diversity of the starting point adopted by the two developments. (Ibid., p. 132. Cf. Hegel, *Phenomenology*, pp. 591–3)

43. Poliakov reads Marx's shift of mood the same way (op. cit., p. 427).
44. *The Holy Family*, pp. 109–10.
45. Ibid., p. 113.
46. Riesser, G., *Die Judenfrage Gegen Bruno Bauer von Dr. Gabriel Riesser in Hamburg, Konstitutionelle Jahrbücher*, hg. von Dr. Karl Weill, Bd. 2–3, (Stuttgart, 1843).
47. *The Holy Family*, pp. 94–7.
48. Ibid., pp. 88–9.
49. Ibid., p. 96.
50. Ibid., p. 96.

CHAPTER 9

1. "Letter", Karl Marx to Leopold I, King of Belgium, Brussels, 7 February 1845, *Collected Works*, vol. IV, p. 676; "Marx's Undertaking Not to Publish Anything in Belgium on Current Politics", 22 March 1845, ibid., p. 677.
2. Marx, *Theses on Feuerbach*, *Collected Works*, vol. V, pp. 3–5. These were published some years later by Engels in amended form. In this chapter we will refer to the original formulation.
3. Marx and Engels, *The German Ideology. Critique of Modern German Philosophy according to its Representatives Feuerbach, B. Bauer and Stirner, and of German Socialism according to its Various Prophets, Collected Works*, vol. pp. 15–539.
4. *Thesis 3.*
5. *Thesis 6.*
6. *Thesis 7.*
7. *Thesis 6.*
8. *Thesis 7.*
9. *Thesis 3.*
10. Loc. cit.
11. *Thesis 1.*
12. *Thesis 2.*
13. Loc. cit.
14. *Thesis 1.*

15. Popper, K., *The Poverty of Historicism* (New York: Harper and Row, 1977).
16. *Thesis 8.*
17. *Thesis 9.*
18. *Thesis 10.*
19. *Thesis 11.*
20. *Thesis 3.*
21. *Collected Works*, vol. V, pp. 4–7. Cf. *Karl Marx Friedrich Engels Werke*, (*Institut für Marxismus–Leninismus*, (Berlin: Dietz Verlag, 1962), vol. III, pp. 6, 534. See also H. C. Sasse, and J. Jorne, *Cassell's New Compact German–English Dictionary*, 20th ed. (London: Cassell, 1964), p. 237.
22. The literature on prophecy and eschatology is, of course, immense. The modern reader interested in a sympathetic account from Jewish sources might consult Samuel Sandmel, *The Hebrew Scriptures, an Introduction to their Literature and Religious Ideas* (New York: Knopf, 1963), or more briefly the excellent article, "Prophets and Prophecy", in *Encyclopedia Judaica* (Jerusalem: Keter, 1971), vol. XIII, pp. 1150–71.
23. Consider the famous passage from the Second Book of Isaiah, in which Jehovah addresses Israel:

> I knew that thou wouldest deal very treacherously, and wast called a transgressor from the womb. For my name's sake will I defer mine anger, and for my praise will I refrain for thee, that I cut thee not off. Behold, I have refined thee but not with silver; I have chosen thee in the furnace of affliction. For mine own sake, even for mine own sake, will I do it: for how should my name be polluted? and I will not give my glory unto another. Hearken unto me, O Jacob and Israel, my called: I am he: I am the first, I also am the last. Mine hand also hath laid the foundation of the earth, and my right hand spanned the heaven ... Isaiah, 48: 8–13.

CHAPTER 10

1. Marx and Engels, *The German Ideology, Critique of Modern German Philosophy according to its Representatives Feuerbach, B. Bauer and Stirner, and of German Socialism according to its Various Prophets, Collected Works*, vol. V, pp. 23–4.
2. Ibid., p. 30.
3. Loc cit.
4. Ibid. p. 58.
5. Loc. cit. Marx reads this as counsel to the workers to accept their lot. He proposes active revolution to reconcile "being" and "essence". The inverted commas are Marx's, used to emphasize his rejection of Feuerbachian terminology. Marx means much more than his earlier reproach that Feuerbach was insufficiently political.
6. Ibid., p. 250.
7. Loc. cit.
8. Ibid. pp. 55–7.
9. Ibid., pp. 40–1.
10. Ibid., p. 39.
11. Ibid., p. 231.

12. Ibid., p. 31.
13. Loc. cit.
14. Ibid., pp. 31–2; cf. pp. 230–1.
15. Ibid., pp. 35–6.
16. Ibid., p. 36.
17. Loc. cit.
18. Ibid., pp. 36–7.
19. Ibid., p. 38.
20. "The lower middle class, the small manufacturer, the shopkeeper, the artisan, the peasant, all these fight against the bourgeoisie, to save from extinction their existence as fractions of the middle class. They are therefore not revolutionary, but conservative. Nay more, they are reactionary, for they try to roll back the wheel of history" (*Communist Manifesto, Collected Works*, vol. VI, p. 494).
21. *The German Ideology*, p. 52.
22. Loc. cit.
23. Ibid., p. 59.
24. Ibid., p. 32. Marx's repetition of the classical orthodoxy of Adam Smith which identifies advances in the force of production with the division of labour leads him to difficulties when he contemplates the ultimate state of communism. On one hand he makes clear that high levels of productivity are a prerequisite for this ultimate solution, and at the same time regards one of its prime virtues to be the abolition of the division of labour. Later, Marx defined the advance in the productive forces in terms of the accumulation of capital as well as its specialization. His critique of Proudhon written in 1847 took his erstwhile colleague to task for following Smith as Marx and Engels had done in 1845. Smith had matters "upside-down", he said:

> The accumulation and concentration of instruments and workers preceded the development of the division of labor inside the workshop. Manufacture consisted much more in the bringing together of many workers and many crafts in one place, in one room, under the command of one capital, than in the analysis of labor and the adaptation of a special worker to a very simple task. The utility of a workshop consisted much less in the division of labor as such than in the circumstance that work was done on a much larger scale. (Marx, K., *The Poverty of Philosophy, Collected Works*, vol. IV, p. 186)

Of course there were feedback effects "as the concentration of the instruments develops, the division of labor develops also, and *vice versa*. This is why every big mechanical invention is followed by a greater division of labor, and each increase in the division of labor gives rise in turn to new mechanical inventions" (ibid. p. 187). Nevertheless, there is now doubt that it is the progress of capital accumulation and the growth of the proletarian workforce that is the key to the capitalist division of labour:

> Labor is organized, is divided differently according to the instruments it has at its disposal. The hand mill presupposes a different division of labor

from the steam mill. Thus it is slapping history in the face to want to begin with the division of labor in general, in order to arrive subsequently at a specific instrument of production, machinery. (Ibid., p. 183).

On this basis it is possible for Marx to imagine a state of communist bliss which would achieve its satiation through the accumulation and improvement of automatic machinery, rather than requiring an ever finer division of labour. The continuation of the debilitating effects of the division of labour is seen as the consequence of the fetters capitalism places on production and its chronic tendency to undervalue the social cost of living human labour as compared to dead capital in the form of machinery. It is machines and automatic controls that produce the state of satiation and free labour. Far from being inhuman, this is the route to human freedom.

25. *The German Ideology*, p. 32.
26. Ibid., pp. 32–5, *passim*.
27. Ibid., p. 36. The iterated word "definite" is translated from the German *bestimmte*, which has various connotations of determinateness. Perhaps a more felicitous translation might be that *"given* individuals who are productively active in a *certain* way enter into these *determined* [definite] social and political relations" (cf. *Marx–Engels Werke*, vol. III, p. 25).
28. *The German Ideology*, pp. 64–74, *passim*.
29. "With intercourse vested in a particular class, with the extension of trade through the merchants beyond the immediate surroundings of the town, there immediately appears a reciprocal action between production and intercourse. The towns enter into relations *with one another*, new tools are brought from one town into the other, and the separation between production and intercourse soon calls forth a division of production between the individual towns ... The immediate consequence of the division of labour between the various towns was the rise of manufactures, branches of production which had outgrown the guild system" (Ibid., p. 67, *passim*).
30. Ibid., p. 72.
31. Ibid., pp. 73–4.
32. Ibid., pp. 47–8.
33. Ibid., p. 49 and note.
34. Ibid., p. 335.
35. Marx, "Letter to Mikhailovsky" (1877) in D. McLellan, *Karl Marx, Selected Writings* (London: Oxford University Press, 1977), pp. 571–2; cf. "Letter to Vera Sassoulitch" (1881), ibid., pp. 576–80.
36. *The German Ideology*, p. 37.
37. Ibid., p. 37.
38. *Capital*, vol. I (Preface) (New York: Modern Library, n.d.) (Reprinted from Chicago: C. H. Kerr, 1906).)
39. E.g. Prinz, Arthur, "New Perspectives on Marx as a Jew", *Yearbook of the Leo Baeck Institute*, xv (1970), 107–24. Prinz notes the amelioration of Marx's attitude toward Jewishness as he aged. He attributes the shift to the growth of anti-semitism in Germany and the observation that "when Catholics are dying they turn to their religion; when Jews are dying they turn to their race" (p. 124). In the course of this very interesting article, Prinz makes clear the degree to which Marx was bombarded by anti-

semitism all his life. It turns out that Eugen Dühring whom Engels attacked so forcefully in *Anti-Dühring (Herr Eugen Dühring's Revolution in Science)* was a vicious anti-semite, directing his attacks at "the Jew Marx". As we have seen, Marx was unable to defend himself against such abuse since childhood, so that it was left to Engels to mount the counter-attack. Noteworthy is the fact that neither Marx nor Engels (nor such anti-semitic biographers of Marx such as Franz Mehring) ever mentioned the Jewish dimensions of the difference between the men. One may speculate that a similar issue was involved in the personal animosity associated with Marx's break with Proudhon, who is identified as a vicious anti-semite by the authoritative *Encyclopedia Judaica.*

Prinz's article goes on to point out that Marx's increasing affinity toward the Judaic, even while expressing his own version of the anti-semitic stereotype, is to be evidenced by his friendship for the Jewish scholar, Heinrich Graetz, and the circle of Jewish visitors Marx met during his stay at the Karlsbad spa.

The Prinz article also suggests that Marx was well tutored in the Hebrew prophetic writings. In particular he studied *Isaiah* with Bruno Bauer in the University of Berlin. Further when pressed by his family—his daughter Eleanor in particular—for spiritual outlets, Marx is reported to have said, according to Eleanor, "He told mother that if she wanted edification or satisfaction of her metaphysical needs she would find them in the Jewish prophets rather than in Mr Bradlaugh's [Sunday services м. w.] shallow reasonings" op. cit., p. 123). Eleanor's comments identifying herself with Jews and Jewish socialist movements are documented further in the Prinz article.

Documentation of Marx's own anti-semitism is given in the classic article by Edmund Silberner, "Was Marx an Anti-Semite?", *Historica Judaica*, XI (1949). His continuing relationship with his Dutch Jewish relatives is given in W. Blumenberg, *"Ein Unbekanntes Kapitel aus Marx' Leben, Briefe an die Holländischen Verwandten"*, *International Review of Social History*, I (1956), 54–111.

40. Ezekiel, 37.
41. *The German Ideology*, pp. 408–14.
42. Ibid., p. 415, *passim.*
43. Ibid., p. 47.
44. Ibid., p. 48; cf. ibid., pp. 86–9.
45. Ibid., pp. 47–8.
46. Ibid., pp. 48–9.
47. Ibid., pp. 59–61, *passim.*
48. Ibid., p. 61.
49. Ibid., pp. 56–7.
50. Ibid., p. 447.
51. Ibid., pp. 368–9; cf. ibid. pp. 370–1.
52. Ibid., p. 407.
53. Ibid., p. 445.
54. Ibid., p. 203. Engels strikes a similar note in *German Socialism in Verse and Prose* in 1847 with respect to the "true socialist" Karl Beck's poems about the Rothschild bankers. At the same time as he identifies Jews with "selfish-

ness, cunning and the practice of usury" (*Collected Works*, vol. VI, p. 239), he disparages the poetry which complains about the lack of emancipation of the Jews as "that kind of blathering about the Jews which is typical of the liberal Young Germans" (ibid., p. 243). Engels's point is that the preoccupation with Jews is misplaced, in any case. The real issue is the proletariat versus the bourgeoisie.

55. For instance, Marx writes the following vignette describing his table companion at a dinner given by Ferdinand Lasalle:

> I was seated at table between the countess and Fräulein Ludmilla Assing, the niece of Varnhagen von Ense, and the editor of Varnhagen's correspondence with Humboldt. This Fräulein, who really swamped me with her benevolence, is the most ugly creature I ever saw in my life, a nastily Jewish physiognomy, a sharply protruding thin nose, eternally smiling and grinning, always speaking poetical prose, constantly trying to say something extraordinary, playing at false enthusiasm, and spitting at her auditory during the trances of her ecstasies. I shall to-day be forced to pay a visit to that little monster which I treated with the utmost reserve and coldness. ("Letter to Nannette Philips", 24 March 1861, in Blumenberg, op. cit., p. 83.)

56. Ibid., p. 254.
57. Ibid., p. 255.

Index